KEITH UNDERDAHL

GW01003731

50 FAST WINDOWS® XP TECHNIQUES

WILEY

Wiley Publishing, Inc.

50 Fast Windows® XP Techniques

Published by
Wiley Publishing, Inc.
111 River Street
Hoboken, NJ 07030-5774

www.wiley.com

Copyright © 2004 by Wiley Publishing, Inc., Indianapolis, Indiana

ISBN: 0-7645-5823-4

Manufactured in the United States of America

10 9 8 7 6 5 4 3 2 1

1V/ST/QT/QU/IN

Published by Wiley Publishing, Inc., Indianapolis, Indiana
Published simultaneously in Canada

For general information on our other products and services or to obtain technical support, please contact our Customer Care Department within the U.S. at 800-762-2974, outside the U.S. at 317-572-3993 or fax 317-572-4002.

Wiley also publishes its books in a variety of electronic formats. Some content that appears in print may not be available in electronic books.

Library of Congress Controle Number: 2004102361

WILEY

50 Fast Windows® XP Techniques

PREFACE

When computers were invented, the hope was that they would make things easier by giving us more control over the information that shapes our lives. But in recent years, as computers have advanced, it's easy to feel that rather than giving us more control, computers have actually *taken* control of our lives. If you use computers on a daily basis you've probably felt frustrated – if not downright helpless – at some point when your computer did something you didn't expect, you were unable to solve a problem, or you just couldn't get your PC to work quite the way you wanted it to.

If you use Windows XP, *50 Fast Windows XP Techniques* helps you regain the power over your PC. Although Windows XP is Microsoft's most advanced operating system ever, the really important aspects of Windows sometimes seem secret or so complex that only an expert can command them. Fortunately, Windows XP is actually very easy to use and control if you know the right steps. I've been using and supporting various versions of Windows for more than a decade, and I've been working with Windows XP since it was unreleased beta software, so I've had some time to learn the ins and outs of Microsoft's premiere operating system. This book provides you with 50 techniques that I've developed over the years and use to fine-tune the way Windows XP works, fix problems, or add features that truly make my computing life easier. I think you'll find these techniques equally valuable as you work and live with your computer.

HOW THIS BOOK IS DIFFERENT

Peruse the bookshelves of your local bookstore and you see literally dozens – if not hundreds – of books covering Windows XP. Many Windows XP books detail all the clicks and menus of basic computer use. Others are meant to serve as reference material for power users and developers. *50 Fast Windows XP Techniques* assumes that you already know the basics. I show you techniques that help you complete specific tasks that aren't always covered in the big Windows XP books, and I show you how to complete those tasks fast. I don't show you how to use the Start menu or save files, nor do I show you how to write advanced code for Windows programming languages, but I do show you how to encrypt your wireless network, make your laptop's battery last longer, recover from a serious system crash, create home movies, crush annoying pop-up windows, and much more. These are tasks that virtually all Windows XP users perform, but *50 Fast Windows XP Techniques* is the only book that puts them all together in one friendly place.

As the name of this book implies, I don't just show you how to do 50 useful tasks in Windows XP, I show you how to do them *fast*. If you're like me, you are a very busy person, and you probably don't read computer books for fun. The techniques in this book show you how to get started, finish the task, and get on with your work in minimal time. As you page through the text you'll notice that most techniques are only a couple of pages long, and there are lots of illustrative pictures so you know exactly what you're supposed to see as you follow the simple, step-by-step instructions. The text is as brief as possible, giving you just the information you need to be successful.

WHO THIS BOOK IS FOR

In this book I assume that you have been using Windows for a little while and you know the basics, but you certainly don't have to be a power user, either. Although the text is usually brief, the instructions are complete and easy to follow. Even if you're relatively new to Windows XP you'll be able to follow along as I show you how to safeguard your Internet connection with a firewall or change the programs that are used to open certain kinds of files.

If you're an advanced Windows user with years of experience, I still think you'll find that this book is a valuable resource, because it skips most of the basic stuff that you probably already know. Even the most advanced user can't remember everything, and you'll appreciate having this handy reference available so that you don't have to spend hours trying to figure out how to disable startup items or manage system services.

50 Fast Windows XP Techniques includes techniques that help you make better use of your Windows XP computer whether that computer is your home digital media server, the PC your kids use to access the Internet and do homework, a workstation on your company's network, or even the server on a small business network. If your computer runs Windows XP and you want more control over it, *50 Fast Windows XP Techniques* is for you.

WHAT YOU NEED TO USE THIS BOOK

All you really need to benefit from this book is a computer running Windows XP. Most techniques in *50 Fast Windows XP Techniques* apply to all Windows XP computers whether they run Windows XP Home Edition, Professional Edition, or Media Center Edition. A couple of techniques cover features that are only available in Professional Edition and Media Center Edition, and I clearly state such requirements at the beginning of each technique.

Some techniques help you work with special hardware configurations, and in those cases you need the hardware noted in the technique. For example, Technique 16, "Seeing

Double with Dual Monitors," in Chapter 3, requires that you have two or more monitors and special video cards. And, of course, Technique 25, "Networking with a Macintosh," in Chapter 5, assumes that you also own an Apple Macintosh computer. Again, if a technique requires special hardware or other items, I tell you up front. Most techniques in this book can be done using tools that are already on your computer or that can be downloaded free from Microsoft.

HOW TO USE THIS BOOK

Each technique in *50 Fast Windows XP Techniques* can be used individually, and you can follow the techniques in any order. Of course, some techniques complement each other. For example, if you want to share your Internet connection with your network as described in Technique 24, "Sharing Your Internet Connection," you first need a properly configured network as described in Technique 23, "Configuring Your Network." And while you're at it, you should safeguard your shared Internet connection with a firewall as described in Technique 35, "Protecting Your Internet Connection with Firewalls." Throughout the book I provide handy cross-references where appropriate.

Some techniques may not be immediately useful to you right now. For example, if you don't have a digital camcorder yet you probably don't need to read through Technique 43, "Creating Home Movies." But some techniques guide you through preventive maintenance and Windows configuration tasks that improve the way Windows XP works right now. I recommend that you start with the techniques in Chapter 1, which put you in charge of Windows and your PC. The techniques in Chapters 3 and 4 improve the overall performance and efficiency of Windows XP. And if you're setting up a new network, go straight to Chapter 5.

CONVENTIONS USED IN THIS BOOK

I know you don't want to learn a bunch of technical jargon and geek-speech, so I try to use plain-language instructions for most tasks in *50 Fast Windows XP Techniques*. But some of the language forms in this book are peculiar to any computer-related text. For example, HTML and other text that you must type exactly as I show in the book use a monospace font that looks like this:

```
<TITLE>My Home Page</TITLE>
```

Many steps in this book require you to click on specific buttons, menu commands, and other options. If I want you to click on a button named "Save" I say something like, "Click the **Save** button." If I want you to open the File menu and choose a command named "Save" from that menu, I say, "Click **File ➤ Save**." I also often refer to special keyboard buttons such as Alt, Ctrl, and Tab. If I want you to hold down the Ctrl key while you press the C key, I say, "Press **Ctrl+C**."

ACKNOWLEDGMENTS

My name appears on the cover of *50 Fast Windows XP Techniques*, but this book is the result of the tireless efforts of many dedicated people. The folks at Wiley Publishing have done a superb job of transforming my late-night scribblings into a book that I think is useful, accurate, attractively designed, and well-organized. I would like to thank acquisitions editor Tom Heine, project editor Sarah Hellert, technical editor Lee Musick, copy editor Kim Heusel, production coordinator Maridee Ennis, and everyone else at Wiley who helped with this project.

I also received quite a bit of help from industry people, including Anna-Marie Claassen, Mischa Dunton, Andy Marken, Brian Underdahl, and a sales manager at the local Circuit City store.

Finally, and most of all, I thank my family for their continuing and unwavering support. Christa, Soren, and Cole serve as my pit crew, photo models, technical assistants, and counselors, and I absolutely would not have been able to write this book without their support.

CONTENTS AT A GLANCE

CONTENTS

CHAPTER 1: TAKING COMMAND OF WINDOWS XP   1

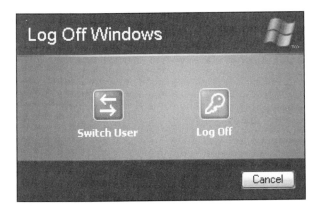

TECHNIQUE 1
MANAGING USER ACCOUNTS   3

TECHNIQUE 2
CONTROLLING STARTUP ITEMS   7

TECHNIQUE 3
CHANGING THE WAY FILES OPEN   11

TECHNIQUE 4
TRACKING ERRORS AND EVENTS   15

TECHNIQUE 5
MANAGING MEMORY   19

CHAPTER 2: CUSTOMIZING WINDOWS XP'S INTERFACE 25

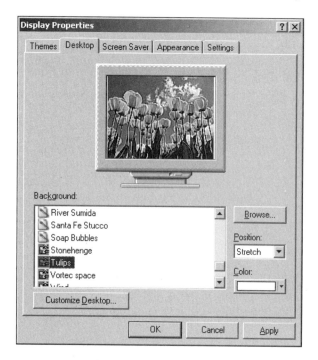

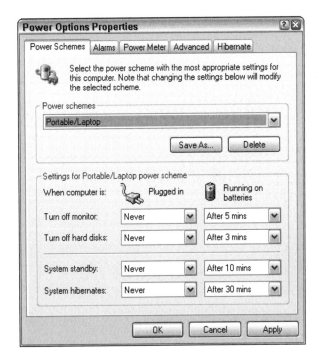

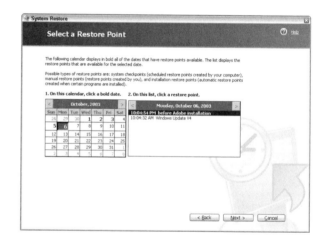

Chapter 5: Managing Your Network   119

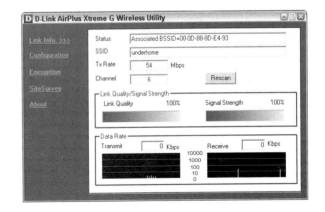

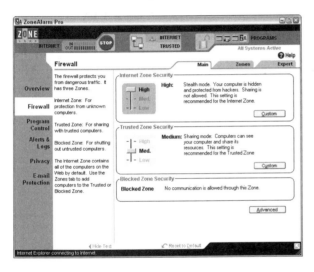

CHAPTER 8: USING WINDOWS XP ADD-ONS   243

CHAPTER 1

TAKING COMMAND OF WINDOWS XP

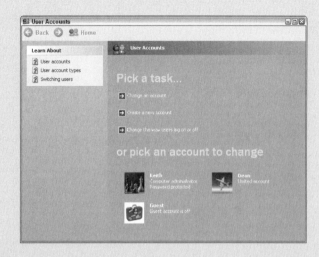

C onsider this story line: Man creates technology; technology gains power; technology controls Man. This story line is a popular theme in science fiction, but when we consider the important roles that computers play in modern society the theme feels more like reality than fiction.

Fortunately, humans haven't entirely given up control to the machines just yet, not even those machines that run Windows XP. You can control virtually every aspect of the way Windows XP looks and behaves, whether you're running XP on your personal laptop or your company's network server.

This chapter shows you how to take command of Windows XP's behavior. You can take charge of the way Windows starts up, as well as control if and how others use your computer. You can specify which program is used to open files of a certain type. Techniques in this chapter also show you how to track errors and system events, and how to take charge of the way Windows XP handles system memory.

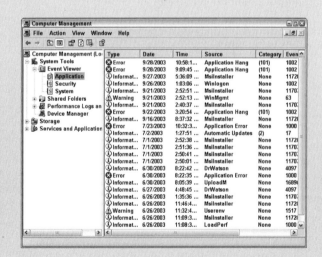

MANAGING USER ACCOUNTS

Managing Memory

Tracking Errors

Folder Options

MANAGING USER ACCOUNTS

1.1

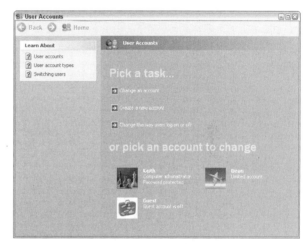

1.2

A little more than a decade ago home computers weren't very common. But today many households have two or more computers, and modern offices often have more computers on hand than people. But even with so many computers on hand, many computers are still used by more than one person. At home you may use your computer to shop online and file taxes, while your children use the same PC to do their homework.

If you share your computer with others, you may find it handy — or even necessary — to control who can use the computer and what features they can access. Windows XP helps you do this with user accounts. The computer shown in **Figure 1.1** has two user accounts, named **Keith** and **Dean**. Each authorized user can have his or her own account on the computer. As an *administrator*, you control who gets an account and what they are allowed to do when they log on. Creating separate accounts for each user has several benefits:

- Your personal files, e-mail, and documents remain private.
- You can prevent others from modifying important system settings.
- Each user can use his own unique display and appearance settings for Windows.
- Restricted users may not install new programs.
- Favorite Web sites and other Internet files are unique to each user.

STEP 1: CREATE AN ACCOUNT

At a minimum, your computer already has an administrator account. As the name implies, the administrator account is for the person in charge of the computer, probably you. Before you can create a user account, you must log in to Windows as an administrator or with an account that has administrator rights. The steps below show you how to specify whether or not an account has administrator rights. To create a new user account:

- Open the Windows XP Control Panel by choosing **Start ➢ Control Panel**.
- Click the **User Accounts** icon. The User Accounts control panel appears as shown in **Figure 1.2**.
- Click **Create a new account**. Type a name for the account when prompted to do so, and then click **Next**.

NOTE

Even if you don't share your computer with anyone, it's a good idea to set up a user account for yourself. This helps ensure that unauthorized persons can't use the computer.

- On the **Pick an account type** screen shown in **Figure 1.3**, choose an account type. If you choose **Computer administrator**, the user will have full access to the computer. An administrator can install software, create or delete user accounts, and access all files on the computer. If you want to limit access to the computer, choose the **Limited** account type. A limited user cannot create, modify, or delete accounts, nor can a limited user install new software. Limited users can only access files they create, as well as any files located in the **Shared Documents** folder.
- Click **Create Account** to complete the process.

TIP

Account types can be changed easily. Simply open the User Accounts control panel, click the name of an account that you want to change, and click **Change the account type** in the list of options that appears.

1.3

STEP 2: SET LOG ON/OFF OPTIONS

An important aspect of managing user accounts in Windows XP is controlling how users log on and off Windows.

■ Open the User Accounts control panel if it isn't already open, and then click **Change the way users log on or off** from the list of tasks.

■ Choose whether or not you want to use the Windows XP Welcome screen like the one shown in **Figure 1.4**. The Welcome screen is faster and easier to use if some or all of your user accounts don't use passwords. If you choose not to use the Welcome screen, users instead use a classic login dialog box like that used by older versions of Windows.

■ Choose whether you want to use Fast User Switching. Like the name implies, Fast User Switching lets you switch between users faster. To use Fast User Switching you must also use the Welcome screen. With Fast User Switching enabled, you can change user accounts without closing programs. To use Fast User Switching, click **Start** and then **Log Off**. As shown in **Figure 1.5**, the Log Off Windows dialog box has a button

named **Switch User**. Click this button to open the Welcome screen and switch to a new user account.

■ Click **Apply Options** when you are done adjusting log-on and log-off options.

> **NOTE**
>
> Passwords in Windows XP are case-sensitive. If your password includes a combination of upper- and lowercase letters, such as **APRILfools**, you must type your password exactly the same when you log in to Windows.

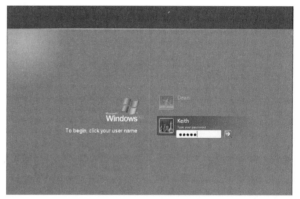

1.4

1.5

> **TIP**
>
> If your screen saver activates and you use the Windows XP Welcome screen, you'll have to go through the Welcome screen every time you turn off the screen saver and try to get back to work. This can be annoying if your account happens to be password protected, because it means you must retype your password every time the screen saver starts. To avoid this, uncheck the **Use the Welcome screen** option in the User Accounts control panel.

STEP 3: CREATE PASSWORDS (OPTIONAL)

Passwords aren't absolutely mandatory for all user accounts in Windows XP, but it's usually a good idea to at least create a password for all administrator accounts. For more on advanced password management techniques, see "Managing Passwords" in Chapter 6.

■ Open the User Accounts control panel if it isn't already open, and then click the name of an account for which you want to create a password.
■ Follow the instructions on-screen to type and retype a password for your account. You should also type a word or phrase in the **password hint** field, but keep in mind that this hint is visible to anyone who uses your computer. For example, if your password is the name of your dog, and the hint is, "What is the dog's name?" other family members can probably figure out the password.
■ Click the **Create Password** button to create the password.

STEP 4: DELETE ACCOUNTS (OPTIONAL)

It's always a good idea to get rid of old user accounts that are no longer needed. To delete an account, open the User Accounts control panel, click the name of the account you want to delete, and click **Delete the account**. Keep in mind that when you delete an account, you usually delete all of the files and documents associated with that account, including:

■ E-mail messages
■ Internet files and favorites
■ Display settings
■ Desktop items
■ The **My Documents** folder and all of its contents

You can preserve items from the account's desktop and **My Documents** folder. To do so, click **Keep Files**. If you click **Delete Files**, all of the above listed items are deleted along with the account.

2

CONTROLLING STARTUP ITEMS

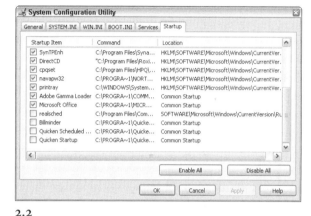

2.1

2.2

When you launch Windows, various other programs launch as well. Some of these programs — such as antivirus programs — are important, but others simply waste system resources. You can control which programs start up when you launch Windows XP.

Take a look at the Windows XP system tray, which is the area in the lower-right corner of the screen next to the clock. Your system tray probably shows a collection of icons similar to the system tray shown in **Figure 2.1**. Some of these icons provide a visual indication of system status. If you're using a laptop, for example, you should see a small power cord icon in the system tray if you are plugged in to AC wall power, and you should see a battery icon if you are currently running on battery power. Other system tray icons — like the speaker — provide links to basic Windows features.

Many system tray icons represent third-party programs that launched when Windows XP started up and are currently running in the background. These programs are often called *memory resident* programs, because they've taken up residence in your computer's memory and have no plans for moving out. Among the most annoying types of memory resident programs are spyware or adware, programs that I describe in Technique 40, "Finding and Destroying Spyware" in Chapter 6.

Some memory resident programs, such as antivirus programs and firewalls, are desirable. But others may be just wasting system resources. This technique helps you identify and disable startup items on your system using tools such as the System Configuration Utility, shown in **Figure 2.2**. Disabling startup programs simply turns them off; it does not delete the program, so this is a change that can be safely undone if you don't like it or if it causes problems.

STEP 1: REVIEW STARTUP ITEMS IN THE SYSTEM CONFIGURATION UTILITY

One of Windows XP's most useful yet little-known tools is the System Configuration Utility. This utility is little known because you won't find it in the Windows Control Panel or the **Start** menu. To launch the System Configuration Utility, choose **Start ➢ Run**. In the Run dialog box, type **msconfig** as shown in **Figure 2.3**, and then click **OK**. The System Configuration Utility opens.

In the System Configuration Utility, click the **Startup** tab to bring it to the front. A list of items similar to **Figure 2.4** appears. Each item in the list

represents an application that launches with Windows and runs in the background. To disable a startup item, simply remove the check mark next to it in the list. Consider each item carefully. Some items are easy to identify based on their name. In **Figure 2.4**, the last two items have "Quicken" in the name, which identifies them as part of a personal finance software installed on this computer. I can safely disable those items because they don't serve a function that is crucial to system function. The third-to-last item, "Billminder," has a less descriptive name, but the Command column shows that it resides in the same "Quicken" folder as the other two items. I can safely disable "Billminder" as well.

Click **OK** to close the System Configuration Utility. Windows prompts you to restart your computer to put your changes into effect.

CAUTION

When in doubt, keep it. Some startup items may serve important system functions such as antivirus protection or laptop touch pad controls. Only disable items that you can clearly identify as noncrucial.

TIP

It's a good idea to create a system restore point before you make any system changes such as the ones described here. See Chapter 4 for more on using system restore points.

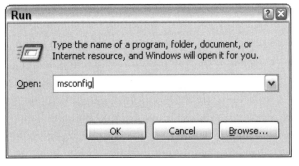

2.3

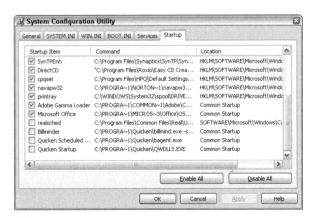

2.4

STEP 2: CLEAN OUT THE STARTUP FOLDER

Some startup items are stored in a Windows Start menu folder aptly titled **Startup**. To view the contents of this folder choose **Start ➢ All Programs ➢ Startup**. You can easily remove an item from the **Startup** folder. Just right-click the item and choose **Delete** from the menu that appears. Deleting items from the **Startup** folder is usually safe because the programs themselves are not deleted. The only thing you delete here is a shortcut to the program.

Although this technique is about removing startup items, you can add items to the **Startup** folder as easily as you remove them. Simply click and drag items to the **Startup** folder. For example, if you want your e-mail program to open when you start Windows, click and drag the shortcut for the e-mail program to the **Startup** folder.

STEP 3: EDIT THE REGISTRY

The Windows registry controls some Windows startup items. The registry is a fundamental component of the Windows XP operating system, and it should be modified with great care. If you accidentally delete the wrong thing in the registry your computer may stop working, and your only solution may be to reinstall Windows. Still, sometimes the only way to completely disable a startup item is to edit the registry.

To review and disable startup items in the registry:

■ Choose **Start ➢ Run** to open the Run dialog box.
■ Type **regedit** in the Run dialog box and click **OK**. The Registry Editor opens as shown in **Figure 2.5**. Registry keys are listed on the left side of the screen in a folder-tree manner. Click a plus sign next to a key to expand the list.
■ Open the key **HKEY_LOCAL_MACHINE\ SOFTWARE\Microsoft\Windows\CurrentVersion\ Run**. A list of values appears on the right. Your list

may look similar to **Figure 2.5**. To remove an item, select it in the list on the right and choose **Edit ➢ Delete**. Remember, deletions are permanent; the Registry Editor does not have an undo feature. Don't delete any value unless you can positively identify it as a noncritical item. For example, if you see a key that is obviously related to a program that you uninstalled, you can safely delete it.
■ Open the key **HKEY_CURRENT_USER\ Software\Microsoft\Windows\CurrentVersion\ Run**. As before, review and delete values as needed.

CAUTION

The Windows Registry Editor does not have an undo feature, and changes take effect immediately. Because of this, trial and error is not a good methodology to use when editing the registry. Be very careful and absolutely certain before making any registry changes. Also, set a system restore point before editing the registry. See Chapter 4 for more about using system restore points. It's also a good idea to back up the registry. Chapter 4 also shows you how to back up the registry and other system components.

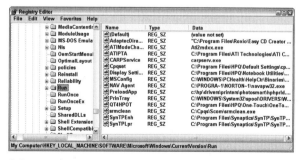

2.5

CHANGING THE WAY FILES OPEN

3.1

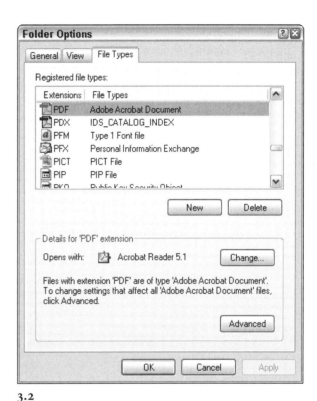

3.2

I f you've been using PCs since the days of DOS, you're probably familiar with filename extensions. Extensions are typically two-, three-, or four-character suffixes appended to a file's name, and they identify the file's format. For example, a Microsoft Word document has the extension **.doc**, and a JPEG image usually has the extension **.jpg** or **.jpeg**. Extensions are still used by Windows XP, although the extensions are usually hidden when you view a list of files in Windows Explorer or My Computer. By default, Windows XP hides extensions that are understood, so that only unknown file extensions are displayed.

When you double-click a file, Windows XP looks at the filename extension to determine the file's format. This information is used to determine which program should be used to open the file. Of course, some files can be

11

opened by more than one program. A text file (**.txt**) can be opened by Notepad, WordPad, or any word processor. A JPEG image can be opened by Internet Explorer, Windows Picture and Fax Viewer, Microsoft Paint, or any graphics program.

You may or may not be happy with the default programs used to open certain types of files. Fortunately, Windows lets you change program file associations. You may need to do this after installing a new media player program. When you install a new program like RealOne or QuickTime, the new program probably takes over file associations for common media formats such as MPEG video and MP3 audio. But if you want to continue using your old media player — such as Windows Media Player — for those file types, you need to manually adjust file association settings. In **Figure 3.1** you can see that some of the video file formats are associated with Windows Media Player, while others are associated with RealOne Player. Other programs in the list — non-video files — are associated with programs such as Adobe Acrobat and Microsoft Word. Windows XP lets you easily control which programs are used to open certain types of programs. In **Figure 3.2** I'm checking the file association for Adobe Acrobat documents.

TIP

If you get an error message stating that Windows cannot find a program to open a given file, the file association setting for that program may simply be broken. If you know that a program is installed that can handle the file type, follow the steps here to fix the file association setting.

STEP 1: LAUNCH FOLDER OPTIONS

You can change file associations using the Folder Options dialog box. To open the Folder Options dialog box, open Windows Explorer or My Computer and then choose **Tools ➢ Folder Options**. The Folder Options dialog box appears. Click the **View** tab to bring it to the front as shown in **Figure 3.3**.

As mentioned earlier, Windows XP normally hides filename extensions. If you want to view extensions all the time, scroll down the list of Advanced Settings, and remove the check mark next to **Hide extensions for known file types**. When you're done reviewing options on the **View** tab, click the **File Types** tab.

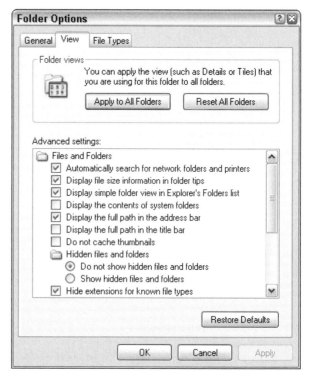

3.3

STEP 2: CHANGE A FILE ASSOCIATION

The **File Types** tab of the Folder Options dialog box provides a list of all file types known to the computer. The list on your computer is probably long. Formats are listed in alphabetical order by extension, and you may need to scroll down before you find the extension that you want to change. To change a file association:

■ Locate the file extension that you want to change. Click it once to view details about the extension in the bottom half of the **File Types** tab as shown in **Figure 3.4**.
■ Click **Change**. The Open With dialog box appears as shown in **Figure 3.5**. Choose a program from the list, preferably one from the Recommended Programs list. If the program you

want to use isn't listed at all, click **Browse** and browse to the executable program file for the program you want to use.

■ Click **OK** to close the Open With dialog box.

> **NOTE**
>
> Some file formats are identified by several different filename extensions. For example, an MPEG movie file can have the extension .MPG, .MPEG, .MPE, or one of several other alternate extensions. Carefully review the list of file extensions in the Folder Options dialog box; you may need to change the file association for several different filename extensions.

3.4

3.5

STEP 3: CREATE A NEW FILE TYPE (OPTIONAL)

It is possible — though unlikely — that a file extension you need to use isn't associated with any program. In that case, you can create a file extension from scratch and associate it with a program.

■ On the **File Types** tab of the Folder Options dialog box, click **New**. The Create New Extension dialog box appears.
■ Click the **Advanced** button to expand the dialog box as shown in **Figure 3.6**.
■ Type an extension in the **File Extension** field.
■ Choose an **Associated File Type** from the menu. In **Figure 3.6** I am associating the extension **PHP** with the **Text Document** file type so that I

can easily edit PHP files in a text editor. This step is optional; if you don't choose an Associated File Type or if nothing in the list seems to match, you can specify a program to open the file later. Follow the instructions under step 2 to associate the extension with a program.

■ Click **OK** when you're done.

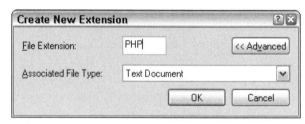

3.6

TRACKING ERRORS AND EVENTS

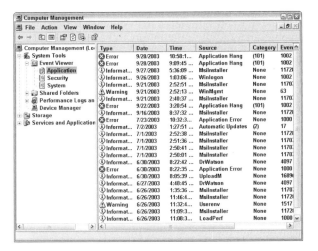

4.1

Event Properties

Event

Date: 9/28/2003 Source: Application Hang
Time: 9:09:45 AM Category: (101)
Type: Error Event ID: 1002
User: N/A
Computer: COMPAQ2170

Description:

Hanging application IEXPLORE.EXE, version 6.0.2800.1106, hang module hungapp, version 0.0.0.0, hang address 0x00000000.

For more information, see Help and Support Center at http://go.microsoft.com/fwlink/events.asp.

Data: ⦿ Bytes ○ Words

```
0000: 41 70 70 6c 69 63 61 74    Applicat
0008: 69 6f 6e 20 48 61 6e 67    ion Hang
0010: 20 20 49 45 58 50 4c 4f    IEXPLO
```

OK   Cancel   Apply

4.2

ABOUT THE FEATURE

Windows XP keeps track of all errors, security events, network events, software installations, and other important actions. Logs of these events and errors can prove invaluable as you troubleshoot problems.

Have you ever experienced an error with a program, but when you tried to explain the problem later — say, to technical support staff — you couldn't remember some important details? Helpfully, Windows XP logs all system errors, as well as security and network events. A tool called the Event Viewer, shown in **Figure 4.1**, allows you to review these logs, providing information that will prove useful whether you troubleshoot the problem yourself or consult outside help. The Event Viewer gives you more control over your computer by keeping you informed about things that are happening.

STEP 1: OPEN THE EVENT VIEWER

The Event Viewer is part of the Computer Management control panel. To open it:

- Choose **Start ➢ Control Panel** to open the Windows XP Control Panel. If your Control Panel is set up in Category view, click the **Performance and Maintenance** category.
- Double-click the **Administrative Tools** icon in the Control Panel. A list of administrative tools appears.
- Double-click the **Computer Management** icon. The Computer Management window opens. Click the plus sign next to **Event Viewer** under **System Tools** on the left side of the window, and click one of the event categories to view it.

In **Figure 4.1** I am viewing Application events, which usually consist of application errors and crashes, installations, and other program events. Security events include security-related events, including policy changes. Every time a user logs in to Windows a security event is logged, so the list of Security events can get quite long. System events are operating system events, such as hardware drivers and Windows components. As with Security events, the list of System events can get lengthy because drivers and components are loaded every time you start Windows.

STEP 2: REVIEW EVENTS

To review details of an event, simply double-click it in the Event Viewer. An Event Properties dialog box appears, the contents of which vary depending on the type of event. **Figure 4.2** shows an error event that was logged when the application IEXPLORER.EXE hung, which is how Windows XP describes a program that freezes or crashes. Additional information may prove useful when contacting technical support or researching solutions.

Figure 4.3 shows another type of event. This event is a little more mundane; Microsoft Office 2000 was installed on this computer.

STEP 3: FILTER RESULTS

The Event Viewer logs can grow pretty long, with many of the entries pertaining to mundane events such as logging on to Windows. You can filter events in the Event Viewer so that only events of a certain type — errors or warnings, for example — are displayed. To filter events:

- In the Computer Management window, choose **View ➢ Filter**. The **Filter** tab of the properties dialog box appears as shown in **Figure 4.4**.
- Remove check marks next to event types that you don't want to view.

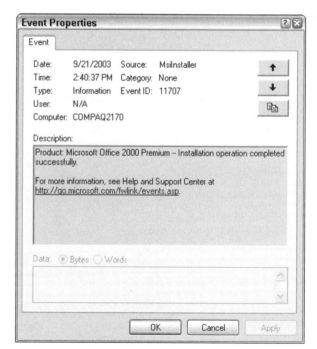

4.3

- If you know that you want to view events only from one specific source, choose an option in the **Event source** menu. If you choose a specific **Event source**, you can further filter the results by choosing a **Category**.
- Enter information in the **Event ID**, **User**, and **Computer** fields if you want to filter results by those criteria.
- Use the drop-down menus at the bottom of the **Filter** tab to view results from a specific date range.
- Click **OK** when you have set up all of your filter rules.

STEP 4: EXPORT A LOG

Event logs can be exported to a text file. This allows the log to be easily shared with others. To export a log:

- Choose **Action ➤ Export List** in the Computer Management window. An Export List dialog box appears.
- Choose a location in which to save the file, provide a filename, and click **Save**. The file is saved as a tab delimited text file. You can open the file in any text editor, as shown in **Figure 4.5**. Tab delimited files can also be easily imported into a spreadsheet program.

STEP 5: CLEAR EVENTS (OPTIONAL)

Your Event Viewer will start to get full after a while. If you have resolved all outstanding issues, you can clean up the logs by clearing out old events. To do so, simply choose **Action ➤ Clear All Events**. Before doing so, I recommend you first export your logs as described in the previous step. If a problem occurs in the near future, you can use information in the exported log files for troubleshooting.

4.4

4.5

5

MANAGING MEMORY

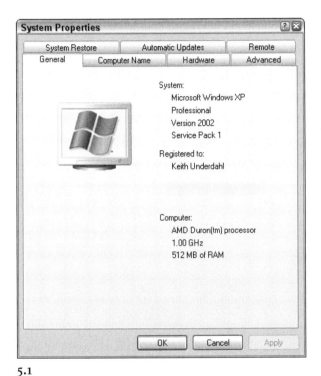

5.1

5.2

One of the most important hardware components of your computer is the *random access memory*, or *RAM*. If your hard drive can be thought of as a filing cabinet, RAM is the top of the desk where the computer actually does its work. If you have a bigger desk, your work is more efficient and you're less likely to lose something important. Likewise, if your computer has more RAM it performs faster, more efficiently, and more reliably.

Because RAM is so important, it's usually one of the first things listed on the spec sheet for a new computer. But no matter how much RAM is installed, some programs need more. To accommodate this, the operating system uses some hard drive space to supplement system RAM. Windows

XP calls this space *virtual memory*, and it is similar to the swap space used by other operating systems such as Linux.

Windows XP manages the size and location of virtual memory behind the scenes so effectively that most computer users are never even aware of it. But even though virtual memory seems to be working fine in the background, it may not be set up for greatest efficiency on your computer. This technique shows you how to review the way Windows XP manages memory usage on your system, as shown in **Figure 5.2**, and adjust virtual memory settings for best efficiency.

STEP 1: DETERMINE HOW MUCH RAM IS INSTALLED

Before you start changing memory settings, you need to know how much RAM is installed on your system. Although you may remember the computer's specs from when you bought it or upgraded RAM, a more reliable way to measure available RAM is to check the Windows XP System Properties control panel:

- Choose **Start ➢ Control Panel** to open the Windows XP Control Panel. If you see the **Performance and Maintenance** category, click that category to open it.
- Double-click the **System** icon to open the System Properties control panel as shown in **Figure 5.3**.
- On the **General** tab, note how much RAM is listed under the processor information. The system shown in **Figure 5.1** has 512 MB of RAM installed, while the system in **Figure 5.3** has only 192 MB of RAM.

Checking the amount of RAM shown in the System Properties control panel is important, because in some cases the amount of RAM listed here isn't what you expect. For example, the computer in **Figure 5.3** shows only 192 MB of RAM, even though the specs for this computer listed 256 MB of RAM when I bought it. The reason for this discrepancy is that the computer's built-in display adapter uses 64 MB of the computer's RAM. Such sharing of system RAM is common, and any memory that is used by the computer's display adapter isn't available for running Windows XP or other programs. As far as Windows is concerned those 64 MB of RAM don't exist.

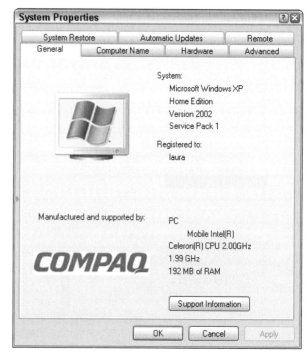

5.3

STEP 2: ADJUST VISUAL EFFECTS SETTINGS

When you know how much RAM is available on your computer, you're ready to start taking control of memory management.

■ In the System Properties control panel, click the **Advanced** tab to bring it to the front.
■ Click the **Settings** button under **Performance**. The Performance Options dialog box appears as shown in **Figure 5.4**.

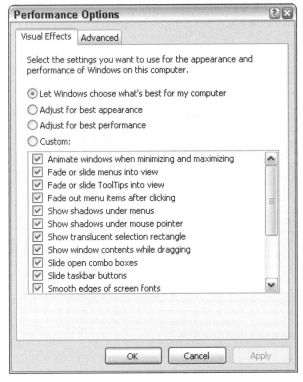

5.4

■ Windows XP includes some new visual effects that make the interface more attractive. These effects include menus that fade gradually in and out, drop shadows behind desktop icons, sliding taskbar buttons, and more. These visual effects are cool, but they can negatively affect performance. This is especially true if your computer has a processor that is slower than 1.0 GHz or less than 256MB of RAM. You can control whether or not these visual effects are enabled on the **Visual Effects** tab of the Performance Options dialog box. It's usually safe to just let Windows decide what's best for your computer, but if you feel that the visual effects are just a pointless waste of system RAM and processor power, choose **Adjust for best performance**.
■ If you want to activate some visual effects but not others, choose **Custom** and remove the check marks next to effects that you don't want to use.

STEP 3: REVIEW PROCESSOR AND MEMORY USAGE

Click the **Advanced** tab in the Performance Options dialog box. This **Advanced** tab contains three categories of options:

■ **Processor scheduling:** This setting determines whether priority for processor power is given to whatever program you are currently using or things that are running in the background. If you have a compiler, printing service, or other memory-intensive tool running in the background, you may want to choose **Background services** to give those background items priority with the processor. Otherwise, keep the default **Programs** setting.

- **Memory usage:** If your computer is used primarily as a server, choose **System cache**. This gives priority for memory usage to server operations. Otherwise, if your computer is a workstation or a stand-alone unit, choose **Programs**.
- **Virtual Memory:** Here is where you manage virtual memory settings. Click **Change** to open the Virtual Memory dialog box as shown in **Figure 5.5**.

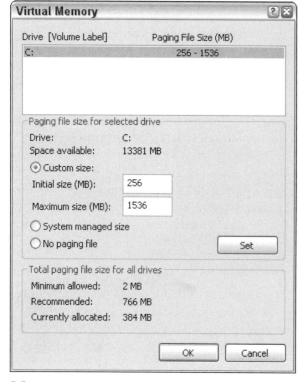

5·5

STEP 4: CHOOSE A LOCATION FOR VIRTUAL MEMORY

Because virtual memory resides on a hard drive, it works better if the hard drive is faster. Chances are your computer only has one hard drive, but if you have more than one hard drive and you know one of them is faster — say, one is a 5,400 rpm drive and the other is a 7,200 rpm drive — you should choose the faster drive. Check the documentation for your computer or hard drive if you're not sure how fast it is. Virtual memory also works best on a drive with lots of free space.

If your computer has more than one hard drive, each is listed under **Drive** in the Virtual Memory dialog box. Click the drive you want to use to select it.

STEP 5: SET VIRTUAL MEMORY SIZE

When Windows XP is installed it analyzes the amount of RAM installed on the computer and sets the size of virtual memory based on what it finds. By default, the initial size of virtual memory is 1.5 times the size of RAM, and the maximum size is three times the size of RAM. For example, if your computer has 192 MB of RAM, the default initial size is:

$$192 \text{ MB} \times 1.5 = 288 \text{ MB}$$

The default maximum size is:

$$192 \text{ MB} \times 3 = 576 \text{ MB}$$

This means that no matter what, 288 MB of hard drive space is always used for virtual memory, and the most that will ever be used by virtual memory is

576 MB. On a computer with only 192 MB of RAM, these are good settings to stick with. However, the more RAM that is installed on your computer, the less virtual memory is needed. Consider the default initial and maximum virtual memory sizes on a computer with 512 MB of RAM:

```
512 MB × 1.5 = 768 MB
512 MB × 3 = 1536 MB
```

On a computer with 512 MB of RAM, 768 MB is excessive. If your computer has 512 MB or more RAM installed, you can safely reduce the minimum virtual memory size to one-half the size of installed RAM. So on a computer with 512 MB of RAM, 256 MB

> **TIP**
>
> If you upgrade the RAM in your computer, review the virtual memory settings and adjust using the guidelines described here. Virtual memory settings do not automatically update when RAM is removed from or added to the computer.

is an acceptable minimum virtual memory size. No matter how much RAM is installed, it's safe to keep the maximum virtual memory size at three times the size of RAM. It is unlikely that virtual memory will ever actually consume that much space anyway.

When you're done making changes, click **Set** to set your changes. You must restart the computer to put your changes into effect.

STEP 6: DIVIDE VIRTUAL MEMORY UP OVER MULTIPLE DRIVES (OPTIONAL)

If you have two or more hard drives, you may specify space on each drive for virtual memory if you want. If both drives are equally fast, using both of them for virtual memory provides the maximum possible performance.

To add virtual memory to a second hard drive, choose the drive in the list of drives in the Virtual Memory dialog box, and specify virtual memory settings as described in step 5. Divide virtual memory up evenly over each drive. If you have 512 MB of RAM and you want to divide virtual memory up over two drives, specify minimum sizes of 128 MB on each drive and maximums of 768 MB on each drive.

CHAPTER 2

CUSTOMIZING WINDOWS XP'S INTERFACE

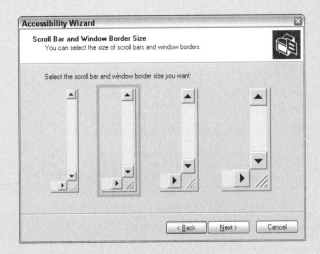

When Windows XP was introduced in 2002, it featured the most radical appearance change to Microsoft's operating system since Windows 95 was introduced seven years earlier. Naturally, while some people love the look and feel of the new XP interface, others prefer the old way. Fortunately, the Windows interface is fully customizable so that everyone can be happy.

Not only does Windows XP accommodate people who prefer the old Windows interface, it also accommodates users of many languages and users with disabilities. The techniques in this chapter show you how to customize Windows XP to look and work exactly the way you like or need it.

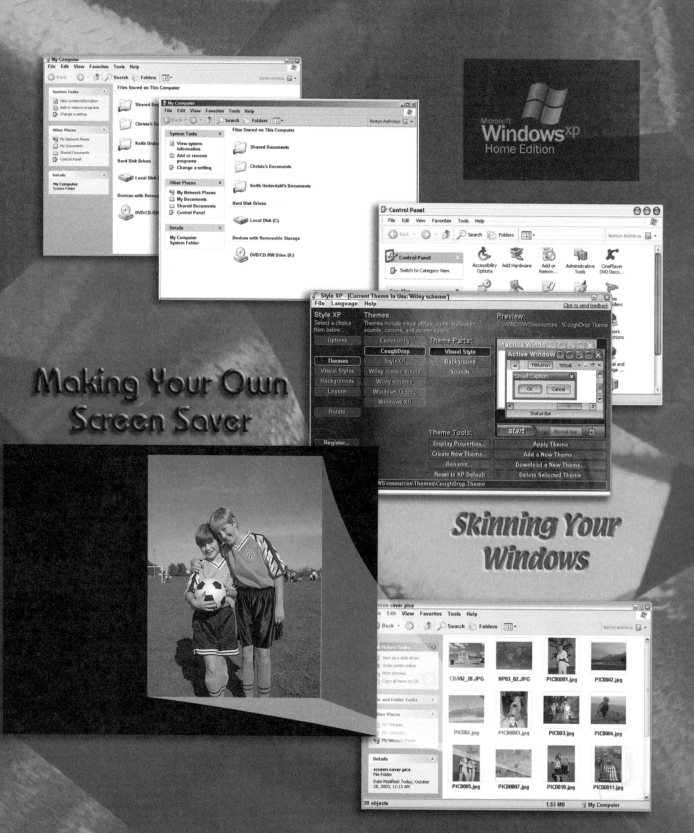

6

SWITCHING BETWEEN NEW INTERFACE AND CLASSIC

6.1

6.2

ABOUT THE FEATURE

If you like the look and feel of earlier versions of Windows, Windows XP allows you to quickly and easily change from the new Windows XP interface shown in Figure 6.1 back to the classic interface shown in Figure 6.2.

Since its introduction by Xerox more than two decades ago, the graphical user interface — GUI — has revolutionized the way we use computers. Rather than type strings of cryptic command line instructions, you control your computer by pointing and clicking with the mouse. Microsoft has revamped its own version of the GUI a few times over the years.

The interface changes introduced in Windows XP (**Figure 6.1**) are less radical compared to the changes brought by Windows 95, but they are significant nonetheless. For some people, the changes are too significant. If you're not entirely satisfied with the Windows XP interface, and you want to have the look of your old Windows 2000 or Windows 98 computer back, you're in luck. With just a few mouse clicks you can change back to the Windows Classic interface (**Figure 6.2**) while retaining the behind-the-scenes performance enhancements of Windows XP.

The appearance of Windows XP can be changed very quickly thanks to appearance *themes*. **Windows Classic** is just one theme you can use with

Windows. For more on customizing the appearance of Windows XP using themes, see Technique 11, "Skinning Your Windows."

STEP 1: OPEN THE DISPLAY CONTROL PANEL

Most interface changes are made using the **Display** control panel. Of course, you can open it from the **Windows Control Panel**, but an even easier way to open the **Display** control panel is to right-click a blank area of the Windows desktop and click **Properties** in the context menu that appears, as shown in **Figure 6.3**. The **Display** control panel appears.

STEP 2: CHOOSE A THEME

When you first open the **Display** control panel, the **Themes** tab is in the front as shown in **Figure 6.4**. To change back to the classic interface, choose **Windows Classic** from the **Theme** menu. The preview area in the bottom of the window shows the basic appearance of the theme. If this is what you want, click **Apply**. The appearance of your interface changes to the **Windows Classic** theme.

STEP 3: FINE-TUNE SCREEN ELEMENTS

If you're completely happy with the Windows Classic theme, you can click **OK** to close the Display Properties dialog box. However, you may want to fine-tune the display a bit. You may want to change the basic color scheme, place an image on the desktop, or simply change the fonts used in menus and program windows. To fine-tune screen elements:

- Click the **Desktop** tab to bring it to the front as shown in **Figure 6.5**.
- Scroll down the list of **Background** images, and click one to preview it. In **Figure 6.5**, I have chosen a picture of some tulips. This image is included with Windows XP. If you don't like any of the images that come with Windows, you can browse for an image of your own. Click **Browse**, and browse to a folder on your hard drive that contains pictures. Windows XP can use bitmap, GIF, JPEG, DIB, or PNG images as desktop background images. You can even use HTML files for the desktop.

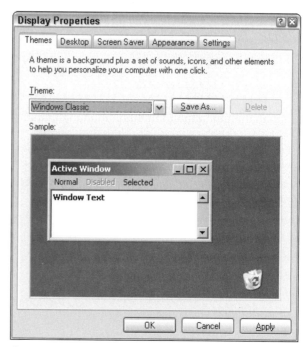

6.4

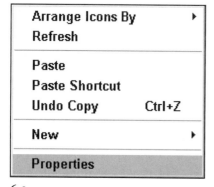

6.3

■ If you don't want an image on the background, choose **None** at the top of the **Background** menu.

■ Click **Apply** to apply you changes.

■ Click the **Appearance** tab to bring it to the front.

■ On the **Appearance** tab, choose a different color scheme in the **Color scheme** menu. Many different color schemes are available, and a preview of each is shown when you choose it from the menu.

■ When you find the color scheme you want to use, click **Apply**.

■ If you often find yourself squinting at tiny menu and button labels on your computer, choose **Large** or **Extra Large** from the **Font size** menu. This increases the size of fonts used in menus, buttons, program title bars, desktop icons, and other on-screen elements.

■ To further fine-tune the desktop appearance, click **Advanced**. The Advanced Appearance dialog box appears. Here you can specify exact colors and sizes for various screen elements. Choose an element from the **Item** menu, and change its attributes. A preview appears above. In **Figure 6.6** I have applied the **Old English Text MT** font to text in title bars, menus, and message boxes. When you're done, click **OK** to close the Advanced Appearance dialog box. Click **Apply** and then **OK** in the Display Properties dialog box.

STEP 4: CUSTOMIZE DESKTOP ITEMS

The Windows XP desktop contains shortcuts to your programs as well as standard elements of Windows. These standard elements include the **Recycle Bin**, **My Computer**, and others. You can customize which Windows elements are part of the desktop. This is nice if you want your desktop to have a **My Documents** shortcut, or if you feel that the **My Computer** icon is

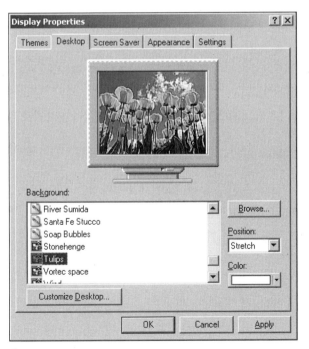

6.5

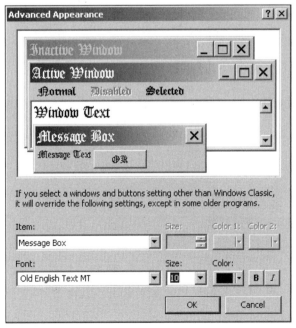

6.6

just a waste of screen space. To change which elements are displayed:

■ In the Display Properties window, click the **Desktop** tab to bring it to the front, and then click **Customize Desktop**. The Desktop Items dialog box appears, as shown in **Figure 6.7**.

■ Place check marks next to the items that you want to appear on the desktop. Choices include **My Documents**, **My Computer**, **My Network**

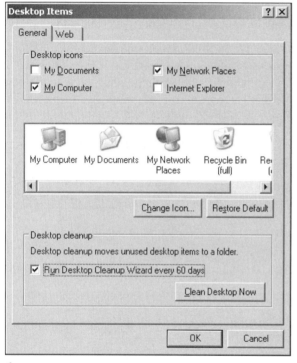

6.7

Places, and **Internet Explorer**. Enabling or disabling an item does not change its location on your computer. For example, if you add a check mark next to **My Documents**, the **My Documents** folder will not be moved to the Windows desktop. This simply adds a shortcut to **My Documents** to the desktop.

■ Click the **Web** tab to bring it to the front. If you want a Web page to appear on the desktop, choose it here.

■ Click **OK** to close the Desktop Items dialog box and apply your changes.

STEP 5: ADJUST EFFECTS SETTINGS

Windows XP includes some special appearance effects that improve the general appearance but also affect system performance slightly. To adjust these effects, click the **Appearance** tab in the **Display Properties** window, and then click **Effects**. The Effects dialog box appears. Options here include:

■ **Fade and Scroll effects:** These effects enhance the appearance and function of menus, but if you feel they are superfluous simply uncheck the menu containing these two effects.

■ **Font smoothing:** The second menu provides several methods of font smoothing. As the name implies, font smoothing smoothes the appearance of fonts on-screen. Usually this provides favorable results, but if fonts look blurry on your computer you may want to disable this option.

■ **Use large icons:** You can check this option if desktop icons and other icons seem too small.

■ **Show shadows under menus:** Shadows under menus look nice, but they detract slightly from system performance and can make menu edges look blurry on some monitors.

■ **Show window contents while dragging:** If your computer is powerful enough to run Windows XP, it's probably powerful enough to use this setting. If you disable it, only an outline of a window will be shown when you click and drag. This was a popular Windows display feature to disable back when 100MHz Pentiums were still considered high-tech, but it shouldn't cause too many problems on your computer now.

■ **Hide underlined letters for keyboard navigation:** Most menus and commands in Windows programs can be manipulated without using the mouse. For example, press **Alt+F** to open the **File** menu in virtually any Windows program. When you press the Alt key, small underlines appear under the letters that activate each menu or command. These are sometimes called *hotkeys*. Windows XP hides hotkeys most of the time, but if you want them to be always visible, disable this option.

Click **OK** to close the Effects dialog box, and then click **Apply** in the Display Properties window to apply your changes.

STEP 6: SAVE A CUSTOM THEME

If you've made a lot of changes to Windows XP's appearance, it's a good idea to save those changes in a new theme of your own. This allows you to quickly restore your settings if they ever get changed for some reason. You can also copy themes to other computers and apply them there as well. To save a theme:

■ In the Display Properties dialog box, click the **Themes** tab to bring it to the front. The **Theme** menu should show **Modified Theme**.

■ Click **Save As**.

■ Name your theme and click **Save**.

The theme file is saved in the folder you specify. This file can be copied to any other computer. To use the theme on another Windows XP computer, open the Display Properties window, choose **Browse** from the **Theme** menu, and browse to the copied theme file.

7

ENHANCING THE TASKBAR

7.1

7.2

The taskbar (Figure 7.1) controls the most basic functions of Windows XP. Like other parts of the Windows interface, the taskbar can be customized to better suit the way you use your computer. You can make the taskbar larger and add elements to it as shown in Figure 7.2.

When Windows 95 was introduced, one of the most important new features of the interface was the taskbar, located across the bottom of the screen. The taskbar continues in Windows XP and serves many important functions:

- Access programs and Windows components through the **Start** menu
- Switch between open programs
- Quickly launch your favorite programs from the Quick Launch toolbar
- Review and change the status of antivirus programs and other memory-resident programs
- See what time it is

Of course, you are probably quite familiar with the taskbar and some of its features. But is the taskbar on your computer ideally configured for the way you work? Are you wondering what happened to the Quick Launch toolbar, a popular feature in Windows 98 and Windows Me? Fortunately the taskbar is easy to customize.

STEP 1: ADD TOOLBARS TO THE TASKBAR

Among the best-kept secrets of the taskbar are the various toolbars you can add to it. To add a toolbar to the Windows taskbar, right-click the taskbar and choose **Toolbars** from the menu that appears, as shown in **Figure 7.3**. A submenu lists available toolbars. The taskbar toolbars are:

- **Address:** This toolbar places an Internet Explorer Address bar on the taskbar. Type a Web address in the Address bar and press **Enter** to quickly visit a Web site using Internet Explorer.
- **Links:** The Internet Explorer Links bar is added to the taskbar. If you frequently use the Links bar to open favorite Web sites in Internet Explorer, you may find this toolbar handy.
- **Desktop:** This toolbar contains all of the items on your Windows desktop, including **My Documents**, **My Computer**, the **Recycle Bin**, and anything else on your desktop.
- **Quick Launch:** This toolbar contains links to popular programs. By default the Quick Launch toolbar includes links to Internet Explorer and Windows Media Player. It also has a **Desktop** button. When you click the **Desktop** button, all open

> ### TIP
>
> The Address toolbar takes up a lot of space on the taskbar. If you use the Address bar a lot, expand the height of the taskbar as described later in this technique.

program windows minimize to the taskbar so that only the Windows desktop is shown. Some programs place an icon on the Quick Launch toolbar when they are installed.

Click a toolbar in the submenu to select it and add it to the taskbar. When you add a new toolbar to the taskbar, the view of the new toolbar is collapsed by default. Click the right-pointing arrows on the right side of the collapsed toolbar to view links in the toolbar. In **Figure 7.4**, I am viewing items in the Desktop toolbar.

To remove a toolbar from the Windows taskbar, right-click the taskbar, choose **Toolbars**, and click the name of the toolbar you want to remove. Active toolbars have check marks next to their names.

STEP 2: CUSTOMIZE THE QUICK LAUNCH TOOLBAR

The Quick Launch toolbar, shown in **Figure 7.5**, first appeared with Windows 98. Beloved by some and reviled by others, the Quick Launch toolbar no longer

7.3

appears by default in the Windows XP interface, but it is still available if you want to use it.

Of course, the Quick Launch toolbar is most useful if it contains links to programs you actually use. No doubt it currently contains buttons for programs you seldom if ever use, and there are probably other programs that you want on the Quick Launch toolbar. To customize the Quick Launch toolbar, simply use the time-honored click and drag technique.

- To remove an item from the Quick Launch toolbar, click and drag it from the toolbar to the Windows **Recycle Bin**. Don't worry: Only the **Quick Launch** button associated with the program is deleted, not the program itself.
- To add an item to the Quick Launch toolbar, click and drag it to the toolbar. In **Figure 7.5**, I am dragging a link to Microsoft Word from the **Start** menu to the Quick Launch toolbar. The result, as shown in **Figure 7.6**, is a button for Microsoft Word on the Quick Launch toolbar.

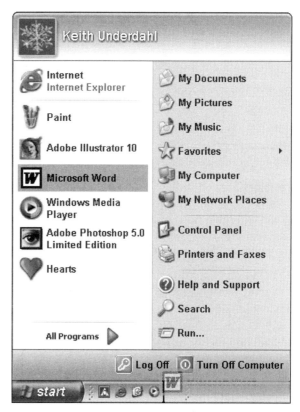

7.5

7.4

7.6

STEP 3: MODIFY THE SYSTEM TRAY

The Windows *system tray* — the area on the right side
of the taskbar that includes the clock — provides
visual indicators for various system tasks and programs. In previous versions of Windows the system
tray tended to fill up with countless icons, so Windows
XP includes a new feature that hides system tray icons
that are currently not being used. You can change this
behavior, as well as other aspects of the system tray:

- Right-click the taskbar and choose **Properties**
from the menu that appears. The Taskbar and
Start Menu Properties dialog box appears, as
shown in **Figure 7.7**.
- On the **Taskbar** tab of the Taskbar and Start
Menu Properties dialog box, review the settings in
the **Notification area** section. "Notification area"
is just another name for the system tray.
- If for some reason you don't want the clock to
display in the system tray, remove the check mark
next to **Show the clock**.
- If you want all system tray icons to remain
visible at all times, remove the check mark next
to **Hide inactive icons**.
- Click **Apply** to apply your changes, and click
OK to close the dialog box.

STEP 4: EXPAND THE TASKBAR

If you like using the taskbar and you have added toolbars to it — particularly the Address bar — you may
find that it doesn't have enough room. To devote

7.7

more real estate to the taskbar, simply drag the top edge of the taskbar up. It expands to provide more room for taskbar items, as shown in **Figure 7.8**.

STEP 5: HIDE THE TASKBAR

If you feel that rather than needing more space the taskbar is actually in the way most of the time, you can tell the taskbar to disappear when it isn't needed. Right-click the taskbar and choose **Properties**. In the Taskbar and Start Menu Properties dialog box shown in **Figure 7.7**, place a check mark next to **Auto-hide the taskbar** and click **OK**. The taskbar now slides down out of view when you aren't using it. To reveal the taskbar again, simply hover the mouse pointer at the bottom of the screen. The taskbar slides back into view.

Another option you can disable in the Taskbar and Start Menu Properties dialog box is **Keep the taskbar on top of other windows**. When you remove the check mark next to this option, other program windows can cover the taskbar. Normally, the taskbar is a permanent fixture at the bottom of the screen that cannot be covered.

> **NOTE**
>
> An added benefit of expanding the taskbar is that the clock provides additional information. As shown in Figure 7.8, the expanded taskbar makes room for the clock to show the date and the day of the week.

7.8

8

MAKING YOUR OWN SCREEN SAVER

8.1

8.2

Chances are you're already quite familiar with the concept of screen savers. Years ago, screen burn was a major problem on computer monitors. If a single, static image remained on a CRT screen for hours at a time, a ghost of the image could become burned into the phosphorous material on the inside surface of the picture tube. To prevent this, Windows and other operating systems provided screen savers. After a few minutes of inactivity the screen saver would activate, displaying a moving graphic image on the screen that prevented screen burn.

Modern computer monitors are far more resistant to screen burn, so screen savers aren't as critical as they used to be. Screen savers are still popular, however, because they can add a pleasant aesthetic element to your idle computer. And if you have a media center PC that is connected to a TV monitor, it may still be important to protect the TV with a screen saver. Windows XP comes with countless screen savers from which to choose, and chances are you've already explored some of them.

The only problem with the screen savers that come with Windows XP is that everyone has them. There isn't anything terribly creative or personal about using the 3D FlowerBox or Mystify screen savers because the same ones can be found on literally millions of other computers running Windows XP. To personalize your computer, you can make a custom screen saver consisting of your own digital images. Consider the screen savers in **Figure 8.1** and **Figure 8.2**. The screen saver in **Figure 8.1** is the same boring Windows XP screen saver that can be found on almost every computer running XP. But **Figure 8.2** shows the My Pictures Slideshow screen saver, which consists of a slideshow displaying my own pictures. This screen saver gives my computer a far more personalized feel.

STEP 1: GATHER YOUR IMAGES

One of the screen savers available in Windows XP is the **My Pictures Slideshow** screen saver. This screen saver basically takes all of the pictures in a given folder and displays those pictures in a slideshow format. The screen saver displays pictures in random order. By default, this screen saver takes pictures from your **My Pictures** folder, including all subfolders.

I recommend that you organize all of the pictures you want to use in your screen saver in a single subfolder in the **My Pictures** folder. Open the **My Pictures** folder, choose **File ➢ New ➢ Folder** to create a new folder, and give the folder a name. As you can see in **Figure 8.3**, I have created a subfolder within My Pictures called **screen saver pics**. The exact name of the folder isn't important, so long as it's something that you will remember. Copy the pictures you want to use into this folder.

STEP 2: ACTIVATE THE MY PICTURES SLIDESHOW SCREEN SAVER

After you have gathered your images, you're ready to configure the screen saver. Follow these steps:

- Right-click a blank area of the Windows desktop and choose **Properties** from the menu that appears. The Display Properties dialog box appears.
- Click the **Screen Saver** tab to bring it to the front.

8.3

- In the **Screen saver** menu, choose **My Pictures Slideshow** as shown in **Figure 8.4**.
- Adjust the **Wait** time for the screen saver if you want. This is the amount of time that your computer must be unused before the screen saver activates.
- Click **Apply**, but leave the Display Properties dialog box open for now.

STEP 3: ADJUST SCREEN SAVER SETTINGS

The My Pictures Slideshow screen saver can be customized. To adjust settings, follow these steps:

- On the **Screen Saver** tab of the Display Properties dialog box, click **Settings**. The My Pictures Screen Saver Options dialog box appears as shown in **Figure 8.5**.

8.4

8.5

- Adjust the **How often should pictures change** slider to change the amount of time that each picture is displayed.

- Move the **How big should pictures be** slider to change the maximum size of pictures. Pictures that are smaller than the size you specify will remain at their normal size unless you choose the **Stretch small pictures** option at the bottom of the dialog box. I don't recommend that you enable this option because the resolution of small pictures will distort.

- Click **Browse**. The Browse for Folder dialog box appears as shown in **Figure 8.6**.

- Choose the subfolder containing your screen saver images, and then click **OK**.

- Review the remaining options in the My Pictures Screen Saver Options dialog box. The four options at the bottom of the dialog box are self-explanatory. Click **OK** to close the dialog box and return to the Display Properties dialog box.

STEP 4: TEST THE SCREEN SAVER

Testing the screen saver is easy. Simply click **Preview** on the **Screen Saver** tab of the Display Properties dialog box. The screen saver activates, as shown in **Figure 8.7**. If you left the **Allow scrolling through pictures with the keyboard** option enabled in the My Pictures Screen Saver Options dialog box, you can scroll through the pictures using the arrow keys on your keyboard. If you press any other key or move the mouse, the screen saver preview ends and you return to the Display Properties dialog box. If you're happy with the screen saver, click **OK** to close the Display Properties dialog box.

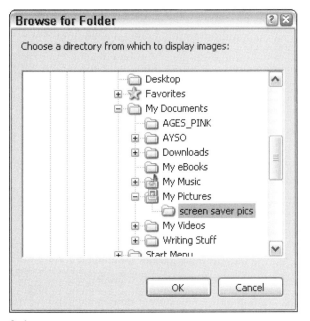

8.6

8.7

MAKING WINDOWS XP ACCESSIBLE

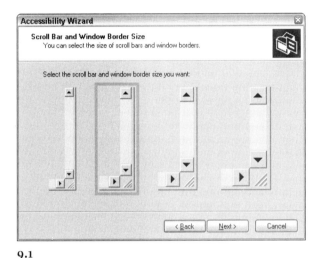

9.1

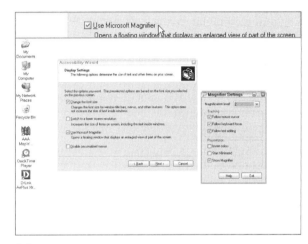

9.2

When Microsoft made Windows XP, an important design goal was that Windows be usable for the greatest number of people, including those with disabilities that might otherwise hinder their ability to use a computer. If you have a disability, you are by no means in a fringe group. According to the U.S. Census Bureau, nearly 20 percent of all Americans — that's about one in five people — have a disability of some kind.

Windows XP incorporates a variety of features to make your computer more usable no matter your needs. You can use Windows XP accessibility features to make screen items more visible as shown in **Figure 9.1** and **Figure 9.2**, you can add audio feedback, and you can make input devices like the keyboard and mouse better suit your needs.

STEP 1: RUN THE ACCESSIBILITY WIZARD

The easiest way to start configuring Windows XP accessibility options is to use the Accessibility Wizard. Follow these steps:

- Choose **Start** ➢ **All Programs** ➢ **Accessories** ➢ **Accessibility** ➢ **Accessibility Wizard**. The Accessibility Wizard begins.
- Click **Next**. The Text Size screen appears as shown in **Figure 9.3**. This screen shows three lines of text, each a different size. If you want the text in title bars and menus to be a little larger than they are now, click the middle line as shown in **Figure 9.3**. If you want even larger text, and you want to use the Microsoft Magnifier, click the bottom line.
- Click **Next**. The Display Settings screen appears. Some options may already be enabled based on the choices you made in the Text Size screen.
- The **Change the font size** option allows font sizes in menus, title bars, tool tips, and other

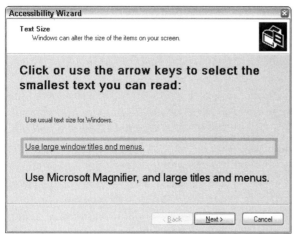

9.3

features to be increased. This option does not affect the size of text inside program windows, however.

- To make everything on-screen more visible, check **Switch to a lower screen resolution**. Lower screen resolutions like **800 × 600** or **640 × 480** make everything on-screen appear larger.
- To use the Microsoft Magnifier, place a check mark next to **Use Microsoft Magnifier**. The Microsoft Magnifier creates a bar across the top of the screen that provides a greatly magnified view of the current mouse position. **Figure 9.4** shows the Microsoft Magnifier view across the top of the screen.
- The **Start** menu and most other menus in Windows XP use a feature called personalization. Windows remembers which programs or menu choices you use most and hides the items that you use less often. To view the hidden items, click an arrow at the bottom of the menu to expand its view. You may find this feature handy, or you may find it irritating. If you fall into this latter group, choose **Disable personalized menus** in the Accessibility Wizard.
- Click **Next**. The Set Wizard Options screen appears. Choose the option or options that apply to you. For example, if you have a vision impairment, choose **I am blind or have difficulty seeing things on screen**.
- Click **Next**. Which screens you see next vary depending on the options you choose on the Set Wizard Options screen. Most of the screens are self-explanatory, such as the screen shown in **Figure 9.5**. This screen — which allows you to customize the size of scroll bars and window borders — appears if you choose **I am blind or have difficulty seeing things on screen**.

■ When you are done setting options in the Accessibility Wizard, a final screen shows you a summary of the changes you've made. Click **Finish** to complete the wizard.

STEP 2: OPEN THE ACCESSIBILITY OPTIONS

You can fine-tune the accessibility settings in Windows XP at any time. To do so, choose **Start** ➢ **Control Panel** to open the Windows Control Panel. If your Control Panel uses Category view, click the **Accessibility Options** category to open it. Open the **Accessibility Options** icon. The Accessibility Options

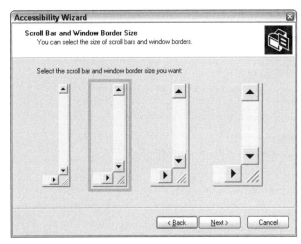

9.5

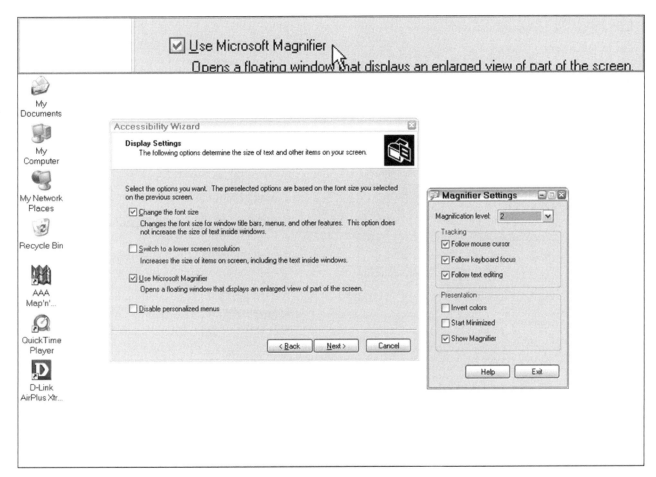

9.4

dialog box appears as shown in **Figure 9.6**. This dialog box provides control over most of Windows XP's accessibility settings.

STEP 3: ADJUST KEYBOARD AND MOUSE SETTINGS

Windows XP includes some special features that change the mouse and keyboard behavior to make

them more usable. To change the way the keyboard works, use the **Keyboard** tab of the Accessibility Options dialog box as shown in **Figure 9.6**. Keyboard options include:

- **StickyKeys.** This feature allows you to easily use the keyboard with one hand. With StickyKeys enabled, modifier buttons like the **Shift** and **Alt** keys are easier to use. When you press a modifier key, it behaves as if the key is stuck down even after you remove your finger from the key. This allows you to press key combinations like **Ctrl+S** with one finger.
- **FilterKeys.** Use this to filter repeated keystrokes, or to slow the repeat rate when you press and hold a key.
- **ToggleKeys.** Enable this option to hear audible signals whenever you press **Caps Lock**, **Num Lock**, or **Scroll Lock**.

Click **Settings** next to any of the categories to fine-tune keyboard options. Windows XP also allows you to control the mouse pointer using the keypad on your keyboard. With MouseKeys enabled, use the numbers on your keyboard's keypad to move the mouse pointer. Follow these steps:

- Click the **Mouse** tab in the Accessibility Options dialog box to bring it to the front.
- Place a check mark next to **Use MouseKeys**.
- Click **Settings** to adjust settings, and click **OK** to close the Settings for MouseKeys dialog box.
- Click **Apply** to activate MouseKeys.

If MouseKeys doesn't work, press the **Num Lock** key.

9.6

STEP 4: FINE-TUNE THE DISPLAY AND SOUNDS

The Windows XP interface provides both visual and audible feedback. You can modify this feedback to improve the appearance of the display or provide visual cues for sounds made by Windows and various other programs.

- In the Accessibility Options dialog box, click the **Sound** tab to bring it to the front.
- Place a check mark next to **Use SoundSentry**, and choose a visual warning from the menu below. This option causes Windows to show a significant visual warning when there is a system sound.
- Place a check mark next to **Use ShowSounds**. This option makes many programs show visual captions when program sounds occur.
- Click the **Display** tab to bring it to the front as shown in **Figure 9.7**.

TIP

SoundSentry and ShowSounds can come in handy even if you don't have a hearing disability. If your computer speakers don't work, or if you must work with the sound muted, you may appreciate visual indication of system and program sounds.

- If you want Windows to use a display color scheme with greater contrast, place a check mark next to **Use High Contrast**.
- Adjust the **Blink Rate** and **Width** sliders to change the appearance of the cursor on-screen. The cursor is more visible if it is wider and blinks faster.
- Click **OK** to apply your changes and close the Accessibility Options dialog box.

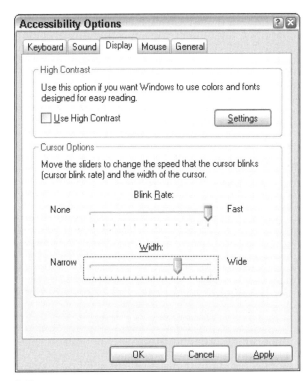

9.7

TWEAKING YOUR INTERFACE
WITH TWEAK UI

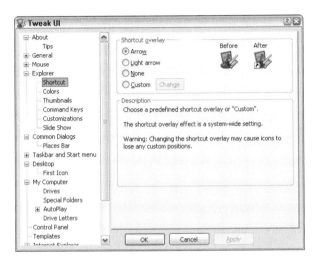

10.1

10.2

ABOUT THE FEATURE

Tweak UI gives you exten-
sive control over many of the
finer aspects of the Windows
XP interface.

Consider for a moment the layout of your office. Over the years you've developed a set of needs or preferences to make your office comfortable and organized in a way that complements your work. You want your chair to be a certain height, your monitor is set at a specific angle and brightness, and you have a special place for your coffee cup. But even with all your tireless tweaking and ergonomic adjustments, there are probably still some workspace details that bother you. Maybe you often bump your knee on a sharp corner or your chair's cushion packs down uncomfortably after a long day in the saddle. Some of these annoyances may be so subtle that you've trained yourself to ignore them, but they're still there.

Windows XP is another aspect of your office that you fine-tune to better suit the way you work. And like the rest of your office, Windows probably has some features or behaviors that get on your nerves but you don't know how to change them. The Control Panel and other tools can help you customize Windows XP, but some things can't be easily changed using the provided tools.

Hope isn't entirely lost, however, because Microsoft provides a tool called Tweak UI that provides an extensive set of controls to help you fine-tune many aspects of Windows XP that otherwise seem written in stone. Tweak UI, shown in **Figure 10.1**, has been a favorite tool among Windows experts for years, but you don't have to be an expert to use it. All you really need is a little frustration with the way Windows XP sometimes works.

This technique shows you how to find and install Tweak UI, and how to use some of the tools it offers. Unfortunately I can't show you every single detail or feature in Tweak UI, so I'll show you how to do a couple of my favorite Tweak UI tasks. Fortunately, Tweak UI is pretty easy to use, and it can be an excellent Windows XP learning tool. For example, in **Figure 10.2** I am viewing the Tweak UI **Tips** window, which provides advanced Windows XP user information that you won't find anywhere else.

STEP 1: DOWNLOAD AND INSTALL TWEAK UI

Tweak UI used to be included on Windows installation CD-ROMs, but it is not found on Windows XP discs. You must download Tweak UI from the Microsoft Web site. You can download it from www.microsoft.com/windowsxp/pro/downloads/powertoys.asp.

> **NOTE**
>
> Microsoft provides Tweak UI merely as a convenience and provides no support for the product. Although most Tweak UI features are pretty harmless, be careful not to activate or deactivate any feature in Tweak UI that you don't fully understand. If you damage your computer using Tweak UI or have questions, Microsoft's support resources won't be able to help.

This is the page for Microsoft's so-called "Power Toys" for Windows XP. You'll find a lot of interesting tools here, but for now we're just interested in Tweak UI. Find the link to download Tweak UI and click it. The download is less than 300KB so it doesn't take long, even on a dial-up connection.

After the Tweak UI installation file is downloaded, close your Web browser and other open programs. Use **My Computer** or Windows Explorer to locate the downloaded installer file, and double-click it. Follow the instructions on-screen to install Tweak UI.

STEP 2: LAUNCH TWEAK UI

When Tweak UI is installed, you can launch it directly from the **Start** menu. Choose **Start ➢ All Programs ➢ Powertoys for Windows XP ➢ Tweak UI**. Tweak UI opens to the **About** screen, as shown in **Figure 10.3**.

> **NOTE**
>
> To install and use Tweak UI you must be logged in to Windows XP with administrator rights.

10.3

Make sure it says "For Windows XP" in the **About** screen, as my Tweak UI window does in **Figure 10.3**. If your version of Tweak UI does not seem to correspond to your version of Windows, uninstall Tweak UI using the **Add or Remove Programs** icon in the Windows Control Panel. Return to the Microsoft Web site listed previously and make sure you download the correct version.

STEP 3: CONTROL THE FREQUENTLY USED PROGRAMS LIST

One of the handiest and, at the same time, most annoying new features of Windows XP is the list of frequently used programs found in the **Start** menu. Click the **Start** button, and a list of all the programs you've been using often immediately appears. Usually this is helpful, but sometimes programs sneak into the frequently used list that you know you're not going to be using as much. For example, if you open a system tool such as the Character Map it may become part of your frequently used programs list, even though it could be months before you use it again. Such programs waste screen space in a list that should only include the programs that actually *do* get used frequently.

Tweak UI allows you to bar some programs from ever appearing in the frequently used programs list. Follow these steps:

WARNING

Do not try to use a version of Tweak UI that is not specifically designed for Windows XP. The wrong version of Tweak UI could damage your system, and, as mentioned earlier, Microsoft does not support Tweak UI or any damage it may cause.

■ In Tweak UI, click the plus sign next to **Taskbar and Start** menu to expand the list, and click **Start Menu** to select it. A list of **Frequently Used Programs** options appears on the right. The list includes virtually every program in the **Start** menu, even programs like configuration utilities or product registration tools.

■ Scroll down the list of programs and remove the check mark next to each program that you want to bar from ever appearing in the frequently used programs list. As you can see in **Figure 10.4**, I've deselected many of the programs in my own list.

■ Click **Apply** to apply your changes.

STEP 4: HIDE CONTROL PANEL ICONS

The Windows XP Control Panel is a crucial part of the operating system, because it provides access to virtually all of the most important system settings. Unfortunately, there are so many icons in the Control Panel that it can seem like kind of a mess at times. It may come as a pleasant surprise, then, that you can hide Control Panel icons that you never use. For example, if you never use game controllers you can hide the Game Controllers icon if you want.

10.4

Hiding icons can also discourage other computer users from adjusting settings, but keep in mind that Control Panel items can only be hidden; they are not uninstalled or disabled. This means that a savvy user can open hidden Control Panel items if they are persistent and knowledgeable.

To hide Control Panel icons, click **Control Panel** on the left side of the Tweak UI window, and remove checkmarks next to Control Panel items on the right. Click **Apply** to put your changes into effect. To reveal hidden items, reactivate them by using the **Control Panel** window in Tweak UI.

STEP 5: ADJUST LOGON SETTINGS

Another useful feature of Tweak UI is the ability to fine-tune Windows XP logon settings. To review and adjust the way Windows logs on:

- Click **Logon** on the left side of the Tweak UI screen. A list of logon options appears on the right.
- Remove the checkmark next to accounts that you do not want to appear on the Welcome screen.

WARNING

Do not use automatic logon unless physical access to your computer is absolutely controlled.

This can be an effective way to temporarily disable a user account without deleting that account's files, settings, and other details.

- Click the plus sign next to **Logon** on the left side of the Tweak UI screen, and click **Autologon**. Automatic logon settings appear as shown in **Figure 10.5**.
- If you want Windows XP to automatically log on to an account when the computer starts, place a check mark next to **Log on automatically at system startup**. Type the user name for the account you want to use, and click **Set Password** to set the account's password.

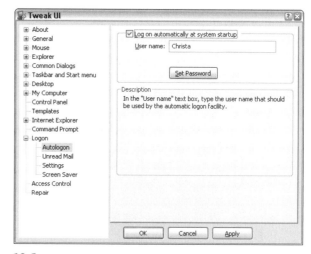

10.5

STEP 6: SET A SCREEN SAVER GRACE PERIOD

If you use the Windows XP Welcome screen, one thing you'll notice is that if the screen saver activates, the Welcome screen appears when you come back to the computer again. This means you have to enter your user account password again to regain access to Windows.

Repeating the logon process every time the screen saver kicks on can be a pain, especially if you are sitting nearby and simply haven't touched the computer for a few minutes because you are on the phone or in a meeting. Windows XP actually provides a grace period between the time when the screen saver starts and when the Welcome screen is called for. If you return to the computer within the grace period, you don't have to reenter your user password. This grace period is nice because if you notice that the screen saver comes on, you can quickly wiggle the mouse or press a key to stop the screen saver and avoid the Welcome screen.

As you can see in **Figure 10.6**, the default screen saver grace period is five seconds, but you can customize the grace period using Tweak UI. Under **Logon** on the left side of the Tweak UI screen, click Screen Saver. On the right side of the screen, adjust the grace period setting to a longer time if you want.

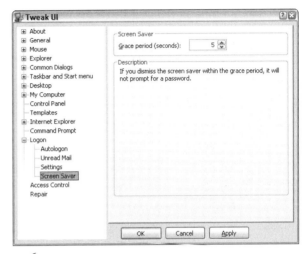

10.6

SKINNING YOUR WINDOWS

11.1

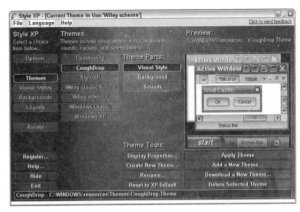

11.2

Not happy with the appearance of Windows XP? In Technique 6, "Switching Between New Interface and Classic," I show you how to change Windows XP so that it looks like previous versions of Windows. You've probably explored some of the other visual themes available in the Windows XP Display Properties dialog box. Alas, most of the built-in themes are simply colored variations on the same basic Windows XP design developed by Microsoft.

Looking for a more radical or artistic look to Windows? Skins make it easy to quickly give Windows XP a new look on your computer. When you consider how much time you spend looking at your computer, it makes sense to give Windows an appearance that you like. For example, in **Figure 11.1** I have installed a skin that makes Windows XP look like the Macintosh Aqua interface. If you're a longtime Macintosh fan who must begrudgingly use Windows XP, a skin like this probably appeals to you. The skin in **Figure 11.1** is managed by a skin program called Style XP, shown in **Figure 11.2**.

STEP 1: INSTALL A SKIN PROGRAM

Skins are developed by various third parties, and they can be downloaded from the Internet. To use a third-party skin, you'll need to install a skin program such as Style XP from TGT Soft. You can visit TGT Soft online at www.tgtsoft.com. TGT Soft provides a trial version of Style XP that you can install and use for free for 30 days. After the trial period you can register the software for about $20.

Skin programs such as Style XP usually include a control panel program to help you manage Windows skins, as shown in **Figure 11.3**. To open the Style XP control panel after the program is installed, choose **Start ➤ All Programs ➤ TGT Soft ➤ Style XP**. Style XP also installs an icon in the Windows system tray in the lower-right corner of the screen next to the clock. Right-click this icon and choose **Open** from the menu that appears. Tasks you can perform in the Style XP control panel include:

- Click a button on the left side of the control panel to view a category of settings.
- Click the **Options** button to view basic settings as shown in **Figure 11.3**. To use Style XP you must choose **Enable Style XP**. If you choose **Use no Resources**, Style XP will not place an icon in the system tray.

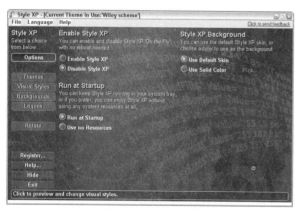

11.3

- Click **Themes** to manage themes. The Style XP control panel doesn't just manage skins designed to work with Style XP. It also manages other themes available on your computer. In **Figure 11.2**, the themes "Wiley Classic Theme," "Wiley Scheme," "Windows Classic," and "Windows XP" are themes installed on my computer.
- Click **Visual Styles** to customize the visual style of the theme you choose. For example, you can change the basic colors used in the themes included with Style XP.
- Click **Backgrounds** to choose and manage background images for the Windows desktop.
- Some skins include custom Windows XP welcome screens. Click **Logons** to manage custom welcome screens.
- If you have several skins and can't decide which one to use, click **Rotate** and create a rotation schedule for multiple skins.

STEP 2: LOCATE AND DOWNLOAD SKINS

Skins for Style XP are available from a variety of sources. The best way to find skins is to simply perform a Web search using your favorite search engine. Use the search terms **Windows XP skins** for best results. Pages you visit should note which software is required to install the skins. Style XP is the most popular skin program, but review the site carefully for special instructions.

STEP 3: INSTALL A SKIN

Most skins are downloaded in compressed ZIP files. Extract the files to the following location: **C:\WINDOWS\Resources\Themes**.

If Windows XP is installed in a different location on your computer, make sure the theme files are installed in the **\Resources\Themes** folder for your Windows installation. To extract the ZIP file, locate the file using **My Computer** or Windows Explorer, right-click it, and choose **Extract All**. Follow the instructions on-screen to extract the files. When you get to the screen shown in **Figure 11.4**, make sure you choose the **C:\WINDOWS\Resources\Themes** folder.

When you install the files, one of the files should have the **.theme** filename extension. The **.theme** file should be directly in the **C:\WINDOWS\Resources\Themes** folder. However, when you first extract the downloaded theme, the **.theme** file may be in a subfolder. The skin cannot function properly if the **.theme** file isn't in the correct location. Use **My Computer** or Windows Explorer to browse to the **\Themes** folder, open the subfolder for your new skin if applicable, and copy the **.theme** file from the subfolder up one level to the **C:\WINDOWS\Resources\Themes** folder, as shown in **Figure 11.5**.

> **NOTE**
>
> Filename extensions such as **.theme** may not be shown on your system. See the next technique, "Exploring Windows Your Own Way," to reveal filename extensions.

STEP 4: ACTIVATE THE SKIN

After your new skin is installed in the correct location, activate it using the Style XP control panel. Follow these steps:

- Choose **Start** ➤ **All Programs** ➤ **TGT Soft** ➤ **Style XP** to open the Style XP control panel.
- Click **Themes** on the left side of the window to open theme options as shown in **Figure 11.6**.
- Click the name of the theme you want to use. A preview of the theme appears to the right, as shown in **Figure 11.6**.
- Click **Apply Theme**. Windows XP updates its appearance to use the new skin.

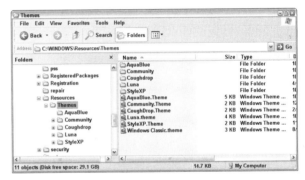

11.5

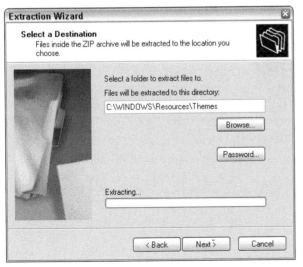

11.4

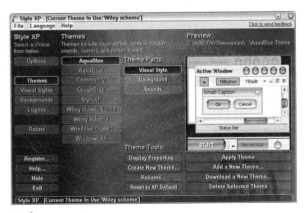

11.6

EXPLORING WINDOWS YOUR OWN WAY

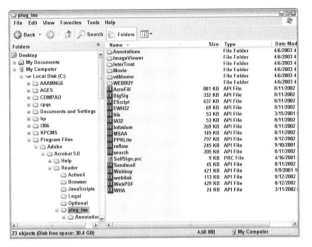

12.1

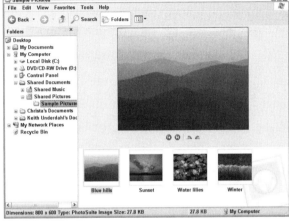

12.2

ABOUT THE FEATURE

Windows XP provides several tools to help you find and organize your files. The most versatile tool is Windows Explorer, and it can be customized to ensure that it provides all of the information you need at a glance.

More than a decade ago, when graphical user interfaces were less common in PCs, locating and managing computer files was a complex task. Software vendors offered tools that did nothing but help you create directories and move files around your disk drives. Of course, file organization programs are no longer necessary because file management and organization is a primary function of Windows. The most powerful and versatile file management tool in Windows XP is Windows Explorer, shown in **Figure 12.1**. Windows Explorer arrays files using simple, intuitive folder trees and browser windows.

You probably already use Windows Explorer on a daily basis to move, rename, copy, delete, and measure the size of files. But is Windows Explorer configured to provide file information the way you want it? Can you learn needed information at a glance, or does everything seem to be a mouse-click or two away? Windows Explorer can be customized to show information the way you want. You can set up Windows Explorer to show primarily

61

data, as shown in **Figure 12.1**, or in some cases you can set up Explorer to preview pictures and other types of media, as shown in **Figure 12.2**. This technique shows you how to customize Windows Explorer to be easier to use and better suited to the way you work.

STEP 1: LAUNCH WINDOWS EXPLORER

You can use several methods to launch Windows Explorer:

- Double-click the **My Computer** or **My Documents** icon on your desktop.
- Choose **Start** ➢ **All Programs** ➢ **Accessories** ➢ **Windows Explorer**.
- Right-click the **Start** button as shown in **Figure 12.3** and choose **Explore** from the context menu that appears. This technique is my favorite because I can access Windows Explorer almost instantly without closing or minimizing any other windows.

STEP 2: REVEAL THE STATUS BAR

One of the most useful parts of Windows Explorer is the Status bar. Unfortunately, the Status bar is not

shown by default in Windows XP. To reveal the Status bar in Windows Explorer, choose **View** ➢ **Status Bar**. The Status bar appears across the bottom of the Windows Explorer window and is shown in **Figure 12.4** and **Figure 12.5**. The Status bar is invaluable because of the information and feedback it provides at a glance, including:

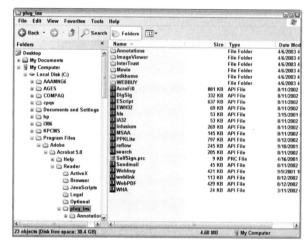

12.4

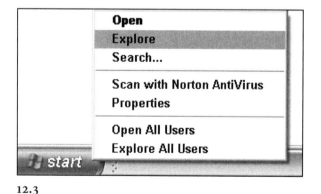

12.3

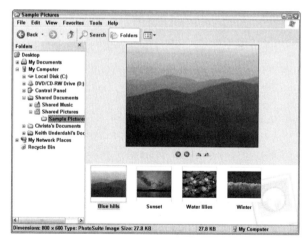

12.5

- The number of items in a folder. If the current folder contains six folders and 17 files, like the folder shown in **Figure 12.4**, the Status bar reads **23 objects**.
- Hidden items. If the folder contains hidden items, that fact is noted in the Status bar.
- Disk free space. The free space on the current disk is displayed. In **Figure 12.4** I am browsing a folder on my C: drive. According to the Status bar, that disk has 30.4GB of free space.
- The total size of items in the current folder. If you select the folder name in the folder list on the left side of the screen, the total size of files in the current folder is listed. In **Figure 12.4**, the current folder holds 4.60MB. That total does not include files located in subfolders.
- If you select a file in the right side of the Windows Explorer window, the Status bar lists the type of the file, the file size, and possibly some other information. In **Figure 12.5**, the dimensions of the graphic are listed as 800 × 600.

STEP 3: SET VIEW OPTIONS

Windows Explorer has many other options that you can set. To set view options:

- Choose **Tools ➢ Folder Options**. The **General** tab of the Folder Options dialog box appears.
- Under **Tasks** choose **Show common tasks in folders** if you want the common tasks bar to appear on the left side of the screen, as shown in **Figure 12.6**. As the name implies, the common tasks bar displays a list of common tasks related to the selected file or folder. If you don't use these tasks very often, you can hide it by choosing **Use Windows classic folders**.

- If you want each folder to open in a new window, choose **Open each folder in its own window**. If you don't like double-clicking, choose **Single-click to open an item**.

STEP 4: REVEAL FILE EXTENSIONS

By default, Windows XP hides file extensions for known file types. In most cases you don't need to see file extensions because Windows displays the file type under each file's icon, or in the **Type** column if you use Details view in Windows Explorer. But in some cases you may want to see file extensions. For example, if you are a Web developer you need to see the exact case used in filenames and extensions because many Web servers are case sensitive. If your Web document refers to a file named **news.gif** but the file name is actually **news.GIF**, the page may not display properly when viewed online.

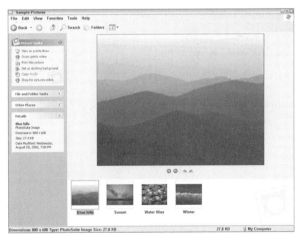

12.6

To reveal file extensions:

- Open the Folder Options dialog box if it is not already open, and click the **View** tab to bring it to the front.
- Remove the check mark next to **Hide extensions for known file types**.
- Click **Apply**. File extensions are now displayed next to each file name, as shown in **Figure 12.7**. Notice in **Figure 12.7** that the file name of the first file is **news.GIF**. This information is crucial to me when I author Web pages.

STEP 5: SHOW HIDDEN FILES

Windows Explorer allows you to browse the files and folders on your computer, but you may be surprised to learn that it probably doesn't show you everything. Windows XP hides certain kinds of files and folders. Most of these items are hidden for good reason.

Hidden items include crucial system files that, if deleted or modified, could make your system inoperable.

Other hidden files are files on CD-ROMs and DVD-ROMs that provide compatibility with other operating systems, such as the Apple Macintosh. The disc in **Figure 12.8**, for example, has a file called **Mac_Installer**. This is a setup program for Macintosh users, and Windows XP normally hides such files. As a Windows user you don't need to see such files, and in fact Macintosh system files can cause errors if they are shown and you try to copy the contents of the disc to your hard drive.

Sometimes you may find it necessary to view hidden files. For example, hardware drivers are usually hidden and if you need to manually move or install a driver, you need to reveal hidden files. To reveal hidden files:

- Open the **View** tab of the Folder Options dialog box if it isn't shown already.
- Under **Hidden files and folders**, choose **Show hidden files and folders**.
- Remove the check mark next to **Hide protected operating system files**.

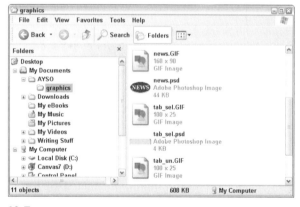

12.7

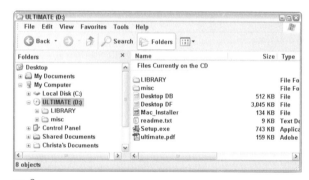

12.8

■ Click **OK** to apply your changes and close the Folder Options dialog box. You can now view hidden files and folders. In **Figure 12.9**, for example, I am viewing the **inf** folder in the **C:\WINDOWS** folder, which is where driver files are stored.

Again, hidden files and folders are usually hidden for good reason. When you are done working with hidden files, I strongly recommend that you change the Windows settings back so that hidden files and folders are hidden again.

STEP 6: MAKE EXPLORER REMEMBER YOUR PREFERENCES

After you spend a lot of time adjusting display settings, you may find it frustrating to have to adjust the

same settings every time you open a new folder. To quickly apply your favorite Windows Explorer settings to all folders:

■ Set up the current folder with your favorite view options. For example, if you prefer **Details** view, make sure it's chosen. Likewise, if you like to use the Status bar, make sure it is displayed.

■ Choose **Tools ➤ Folder Options** to open the Folder Options dialog box, and then click the **View** tab to bring it to the front.

■ **Click Apply to All Folders** to quickly apply the current view settings to all folders. Click **Yes** in the dialog box that appears.

■ Under **Advanced Settings**, make sure the **Remember each folder's view settings** option is checked.

■ Click **OK** to apply your settings and close the Folder Options dialog box.

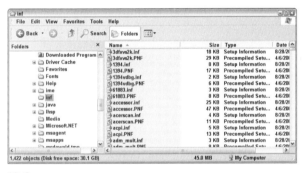

12.9

TIP

If you encounter file copy or read errors while trying to copy files or folders from a CD-ROM or DVD-ROM, make sure that hidden files are hidden.

CHAPTER 3

BOOSTING WINDOWS XP'S PERFORMANCE

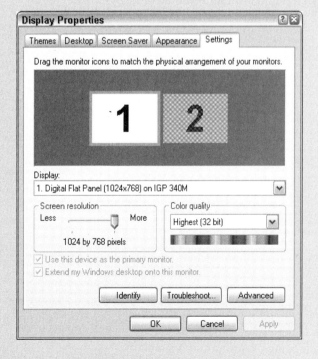

Auto enthusiasts are always seeking to boost performance. With a tweak here, some tuning there, and a few well-chosen accessories, a mundane transportation device becomes a true hot rod ready to blow the doors off any competition.

Your PC may benefit from some hot-rodding as well. If the performance of your computer seems sluggish, you can tune it up and make it faster using some tools and tweaks available in Windows XP. The techniques in this chapter show you how to improve hard drive performance, make your laptop's battery last longer, expand the size of your Windows desktop, and manage the services that run whenever you use Windows XP.

Configure Power Schemes

Automate Disk Maintenance

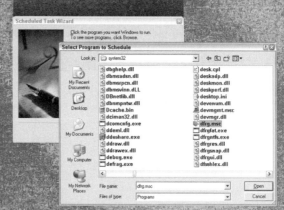

Battery Optimizer

disk defragmenten

Seeing Double With Dual Monitors
Seeing Double With Dual Monitors

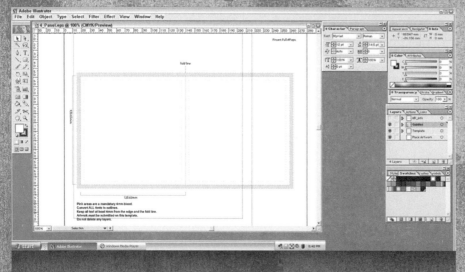

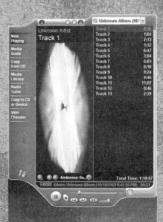

TUNING-UP HARD DRIVE PERFORMANCE

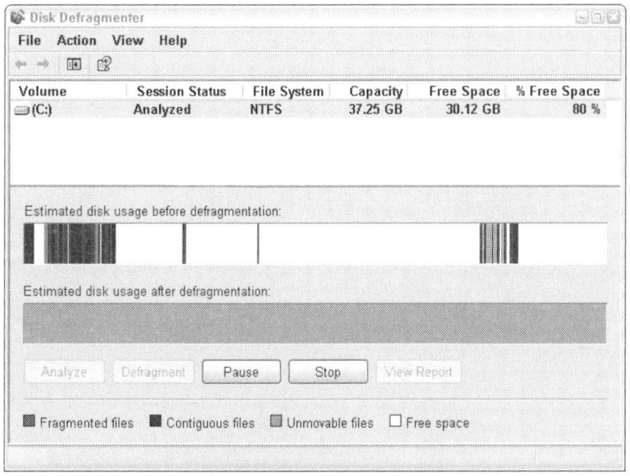

13.1

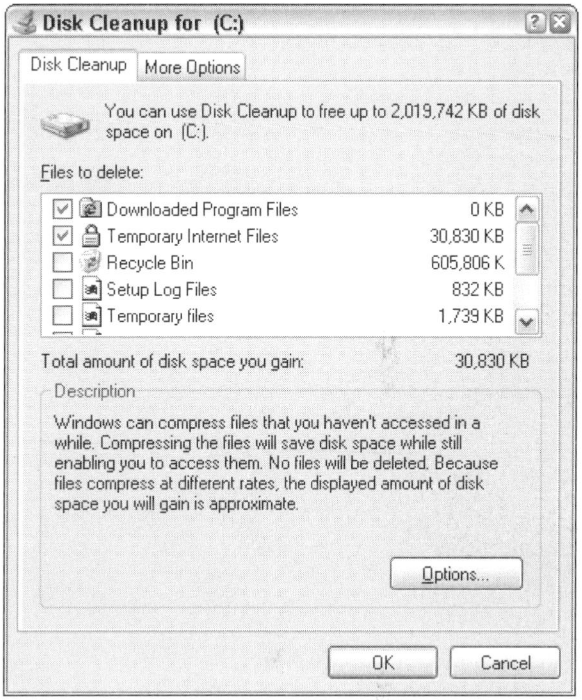

13.2

°ABOUT THE FEATURE

Hard drives still require some maintenance to ensure peak performance. Windows XP includes tools to keep your hard drive running efficiently.

Computer hard drives are often compared to file cabinets because they are primarily used to store and organize files. Like a file cabinet, your hard drive works best if files are organized logically, and if old, unused files are cleaned out from time to time. Unfortunately, modern hard drives are often treated more like gas tanks, with files continuously poured in and taken out without any real maintenance. Eventually this leads to sluggish system performance.

Some people argue that hard drive maintenance is less important today because Windows XP does a better job of hard drive management. Do not listen to these people. Disk errors can still occur, disk caches still fill up, and, as you can see in **Figure 13.1**, hard drives still become fragmented. All of these things make your computer run slower, and they reduce the

amount of free space available, even when running
Windows XP. Hard drive maintenance is still a fundamental part of system maintenance, and Windows XP
provides tools to help you maintain your hard drives,
such as the **Disk Defragmenter** shown in **Figure 13.1**,
and the **Disk Cleanup** tool shown in **Figure 13.2**.

STEP 1: FIND AND REPAIR DISK ERRORS

Hard drive maintenance should always start with a
check for disk errors. This is especially true if you've
recently experienced a system crash or improper
shutdown, conditions which often create disk errors.
Windows XP includes an error-checking tool to help
you detect and repair hard disk errors. To use error-
checking:

- Close all open programs and files, and restart
Windows.
- Open My Computer. If you don't have a **My
Computer** icon on the desktop, choose **Start ➢
My Computer**.
- In My Computer, right-click the icon for the
hard drive that you want to check, and choose
Properties from the context menu that appears.
The Local Disk Properties dialog box appears.
- Click the **Tools** tab to bring it to the front, and
click **Check Now** under **Error Checking**. The
Check Disk dialog box appears as shown in
Figure 13.3.

> **NOTE**
>
> Restarting Windows is important because Error
> Checking may not be able to run if some system
> files are in use. The only way to ensure these files
> are not in use is to restart Windows XP.

- Place check marks next to **Automatically fix file
system errors** and **Scan for and attempt recovery
of bad sectors** if you want errors to be fixed
automatically.
- Click **Start**. The disk check process may begin,
although in many cases the check cannot proceed,
even if you have just restarted Windows. If you see
a message stating that the disk check cannot proceed, click **Yes** to schedule the disk check to run
after the next restart, and then restart Windows.
The disk check runs as part of the startup process.

STEP 2: FREE DISK SPACE

You're probably well aware of the value of available
hard disk space, and you may be surprised at how
much disk space seems to disappear as you use
Windows. Windows XP provides a handy Disk
Cleanup tool that helps you clear unneeded files that
are taking up a lot of space on your hard drive. To use
Disk Cleanup:

13.3

■ Open My Computer if it isn't already open.

■ In My Computer, right-click the icon for the hard drive that you want to clean up, and choose **Properties** from the context menu that appears. The Local Disk Properties dialog box appears as shown in **Figure 13.4**. A pie chart on the **General** tab provides a visual estimate of the amount of used and unused space on your hard drive.

■ Click **Disk Cleanup**. The Disk Cleanup tool scans your hard drive and then displays the Disk Cleanup dialog box as shown in **Figure 13.5**. The Disk Cleanup dialog box lists different kinds of files that can be safely deleted from your computer.

Click an item to view a brief description in the bottom half of the dialog box. The estimated space savings is listed next to each item. In **Figure 13.5**, for example, I can reclaim about 600MB of hard disk space just by emptying the **Recycle Bin**.

■ Place a check mark next to each item that you want to delete. One of the items in the list — **Compress old files** — doesn't actually delete files. Instead, it compresses files that haven't been used for a long time. Compressed files are not deleted and remain available for use.

■ Click **OK**. Click **Yes** when you are asked to confirm the action. Disk Cleanup cleans up the specified files.

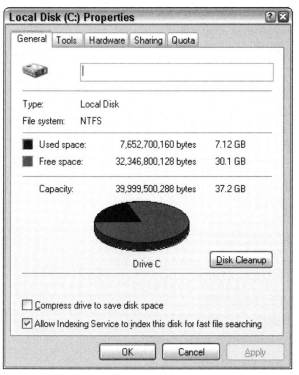

13.4

13.5

STEP 3: DEFRAGMENT THE HARD DISK

When you save a file, Windows must sometimes break files into smaller chunks and save each chunk in different physical locations on the hard drive. Eventually, file fragments are scattered all over the drive. This condition is called *fragmentation*, and it slows down the performance of your computer. Although fragmentation is less of a problem with Windows XP and large, modern hard drives, it still occurs and can still affect performance. Fragmentation is especially bad if you perform tasks that use the hard drive heavily, such as digital video editing.

Windows XP includes a Disk Defragmenter, and you should run it periodically — once per month, for example — on your hard drive. Run Disk Defragmenter after scanning the hard drive for disk errors and running Disk Cleanup as described in the previous steps. To run the Defragmenter:

- Close all open programs.
- Choose **Start** ➤ **All Programs** ➤ **Accessories** ➤ **System Tools** ➤ **Disk Defragmenter**. The Disk Defragmenter appears as shown in **Figure 13.6**.
- Click **Analyze**. Disk Defragmenter analyzes the current condition of your hard drive.
- When the analysis is complete, click **View Report**. A detailed fragmentation report appears as shown in **Figure 13.7**.
- Click **Close** to close the report. The Disk Defragmenter window displays a color-coded graph representing the current fragmentation of your hard drive. If your drive hasn't been defragmented for a while it probably has file fragments

scattered all over the drive, similar to the drive in **Figure 13.6**. Red lines represent file fragments.
- Click **Defragment** to begin defragmentation. Defragmentation takes a long time to run, so it's a good idea to run Disk Defragmenter when you won't need to use the computer for a while.

TIP

Don't run Disk Defragmenter on a laptop computer while running on battery power, even if the battery is fully charged. The hard drive works hard during defragmentation, putting a heavy, prolonged strain on the battery. The battery probably can't last for the whole defragmentation process.

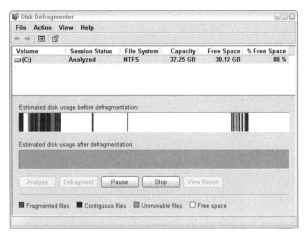

13.6

STEP 4: AUTOMATE DISK MAINTENANCE

Even if you have good intentions and mean to perform hard drive maintenance on a regular basis, it's an easy thing to forget as you go about your daily work. To make sure disk maintenance gets done, schedule disk maintenance tasks to run regularly using the Windows XP Scheduled Tasks Wizard:

- Choose **Start** ➤ **All Programs** ➤ **Accessories** ➤ **System Tools** ➤ **Scheduled Tasks**. The Scheduled Tasks window appears.
- Double-click **Add Scheduled Task**. The Scheduled Task Wizard appears.
- Click **Next**. A list of applications appears.
- Choose **Disk Cleanup**, and click **Next**.

- Choose how often Disk Cleanup runs. I recommend running it monthly. Click **Next** after you have selected an interval.
- Complete schedule information on the next screen. It's best to set Disk Cleanup to run at a time when you aren't actually using the computer, such as late at night. Click **Next**.
- Enter your user name and password as appropriate in the next screen. Click **Next**.
- Click **Finish**. **Disk Cleanup** now appears in your list of scheduled tasks.
- Double-click **Add Scheduled Task** again, and click **Next** when the Scheduled Task Wizard appears.
- You may notice that Disk Defragmenter isn't listed in the Scheduled Tasks Wizard. Click **Browse**. In the Select Program to Schedule dialog box, navigate to the folder **C:\WINDOWS\ SYSTEM32** and choose the file **dfrg.msc** as shown in **Figure 13.8**. Click **Open**.
- Complete the wizard as you did earlier for the Disk Cleanup utility. I recommend scheduling Disk Defragmenter to run about 30 minutes after Disk Cleanup runs.

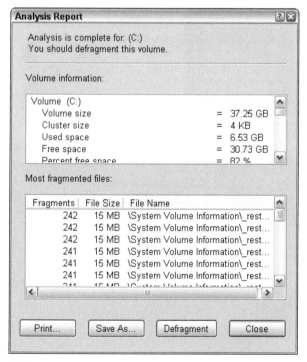

13.7

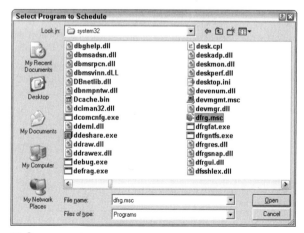

13.8

CREATING MULTIPLE PARTITIONS

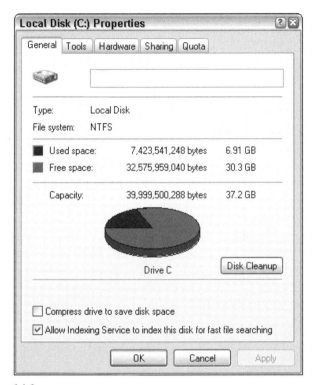

14.1

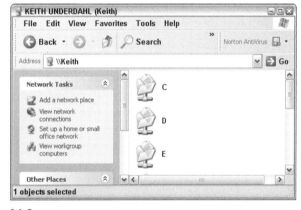

14.2

Windows XP allows you to divide your hard drives into separate partitions, allowing for a variety of special uses.

Most computers have one hard drive, and in modern computers that drive is usually pretty large. Hard drives of 100GB or larger are now common, and in most installations the entire hard drive is set up as a single huge drive. You can, however, divide the drive into separate partitions. Each partition behaves like a separate hard drive. In **Figure 14.2**, drives C, D and drive E are separate partitions on the same hard drive.

Partitioning hard drives has become a contentious issue in recent years. Partitioning a large hard drive into smaller drives does have some advantages, including:

■ Cluster sizes are smaller on smaller partitions. A cluster is a section on the hard drive, and smaller clusters allow for more efficient use of disk space.

■ Partitions can be used to organize programs and data. Some people like to keep Windows XP and programs on one partition, and data files on another partition.

■ If you use your computer as a file server on a network or the Internet, you can set up the computer to only share items on one partition, thereby offering greater protection to data on the other partitions.

■ If you frequently master CDs or DVDs, a separate partition can serve as a temporary disk image for testing and building.

■ Your computer can be set up to dual-boot between different operating systems installed on separate partitions. Some users like to install Windows XP on one partition, and another operating system, such as Linux, on the other partition.

Unless you have a special need such as dual-booting between two operating systems or serving files online, I recommend against partitioning a very large hard drive into smaller drives. Although partitioning does give the theoretical advantage of more efficient disk space usage, that efficiency is less important today thanks to the sheer size of modern hard drives, as well as the effectiveness of the NT File System, or NTFS. NTFS — which is used by the drive shown in **Figure 14.1** — is described in step 1. At some point you may find that the efficiency advantage is offset by the inconvenience of running out of space on the drive that contains your Windows XP installation, for example.

STEP 1: CHOOSE A FILE SYSTEM

Hard drives and partitions are formatted using a specific kind of file system. The file system manages how files and disk space are managed on the drive. The FDISK partition utility that comes with Windows XP allows you to choose one of three different file systems for your disk partitions:

■ **FAT:** Short for *File Allocation Table*, the FAT file system is old and not well suited to most modern hard drives. Cluster size is relatively large on FAT drives, meaning that disk space is not used efficiently. The greatest limitation is that a FAT drive cannot be larger than 4GB. Also, individual files cannot be larger than 2GB. A single 10-minute digital video file can easily exceed 2GB. The FAT file system was often used on older PCs running Windows 95 and is still used on small removable disks such as floppy or Zip disks. I recommend that you not use the FAT file system on drives larger than 512MB.

■ **FAT32:** This is a 32-bit version of FAT and is the file system most often used on computers running Windows 98 or Windows Me. On drives that are more than 512MB, FAT32 makes more efficient use of disk space than FAT because the cluster sizes are much smaller, and FAT32 does not have the 4GB drive size limitation. The maximum size of a FAT32 drive is 2TB — terabytes — or 2,048GB. Although FAT32 is superior to FAT, you should only choose the FAT32 file system if you plan to install Windows 98 or Windows Me on the partition. The version of FDISK that comes with Windows XP does not allow you to use FAT32 on partitions larger than 32GB. Individual files cannot be larger than 4GB on a FAT32 partition.

■ **NTFS:** This file system was introduced with Windows NT 4.0 and is the preferred file system for hard drives and partitions in Windows XP. NTFS partitions can be virtually any size, and the size of individual files is limited only by the size of the partition itself. NTFS also offers superior security and performance. Windows 95, 98, or Me will not run from an NTFS partition.

STEP 2: BACK UP YOUR DATA

Partitioning is a destructive process. If you divide an existing drive into two or more partitions, all of the data currently on that drive is deleted. This has several implications:

- You must back up all data files on the drive that you want to keep. See Technique 19, "Making Regular Backups," in Chapter 4 for more on backing up your data. Even if you aren't partitioning the hard disk that contains your data, it's a good idea to make a backup before partitioning anyway, just in case.
- Programs installed on the drive must be reinstalled. Make sure you have installation disks and files ready so that you can reinstall your programs after partitioning.
- If Windows is installed on the drive you plan to partition, the Windows XP software must be reinstalled as well. After reinstallation you are prompted to activate Windows. If Windows XP is not reactivated within 30 days it ceases to function on your computer. The reactivation prompt provides instructions on how to activate Windows.
- If you must reinstall Windows, you must also reinstall hardware drivers for any special hardware you have, including printers, scanners, cameras, and modems. Gather the installation disks for your hardware before you proceed with partitioning.

STEP 3: SET UP YOUR COMPUTER TO BOOT FROM THE CD-ROM DRIVE

The Windows XP installation CD includes a tool to help you partition hard drives. To use this tool you must boot the computer from the CD instead of from the hard drive. Check the documentation that came with your computer to see how to adjust boot options. On most computers, press the **Delete** key during the memory test that occurs immediately after turning the power on. In the CMOS setup options, make sure the computer is set to boot from the CD-ROM or DVD-ROM drive first, and the hard drive second. CMOS settings control basic hardware parameters for your PC.

STEP 4: BOOT FROM THE WINDOWS XP CD-ROM

Place your Windows XP installation CD in the computer's CD-ROM or DVD-ROM drive and start the computer. Watch the screen carefully, and when you see the message "Press any key to boot from CD," quickly press a key. A blue screen titled "Windows Setup" appears. When you see a screen titled "Welcome to Setup" you are ready to begin.

STEP 5: PARTITION THE DRIVE

Now that Windows Setup is running, you're ready to partition your hard drive. Follow these steps:

- In the "Welcome to Setup" screen, press the **Enter** key. The Windows XP Licensing Agreement appears.
- Press **F8** to agree to Microsoft's terms. Windows setup detects your current installation of Windows, as well as any other Windows installations.
- Press **Esc** because you do not want to repair your current Windows installation. A list of existing partitions appears, as well as a list of unpartitioned space on each drive. Use the arrow keys on the keyboard to select a partition or unpartitioned space.

> **NOTE**
>
> Most drives have small chunks — usually 10MB or less — of unpartitioned space. Small, unpartitioned chunks like this are generally not very useful, but if you have larger chunks of unpartitioned space you can turn it into usable, partitioned disk space.

■ If you want to turn an existing partition into two smaller partitions, you must first delete the existing partition. Select the partition and press **D** to delete it. Press **L** to confirm the deletion.

■ Select an unpartitioned space and press **C**.

■ Enter the size in megabytes of the first partition that you want to create, and then press **Enter**. For example, if you want the first partition to be about 10GB, type **10000** and press **Enter**. This creates a 10,000MB partition, which equals approximately 10GB.

■ Select the remaining unpartitioned space and press **C** again. Enter the size for this partition in megabytes again, or just press **Enter** if you want to devote all remaining space to this partition. Repeat as needed until all unpartitioned space is used.

■ If you deleted the partition that included your Windows XP installation, you need to select the partition where you want to reinstall Windows. Select the partition in the list, and press **Enter**.

■ Specify the file system you chose back in step 1. If you are installing Windows XP on this partition, I strongly recommend that you choose **Format the partition using the NTFS file system**. Only choose a **Quick** formatting option if you are formatting a new hard drive that hasn't been used before.

■ Follow the instructions on-screen to complete formatting and, if necessary, reinstall Windows XP.

STRETCHING LAPTOP BATTERY LIFE

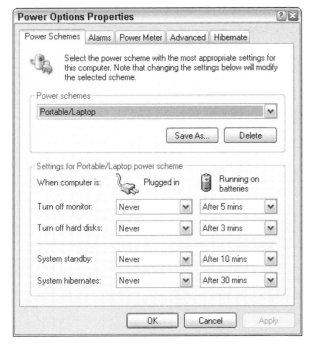

15.1

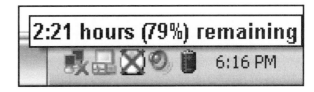

15.2

L aptop batteries have improved tremendously in recent years. Modern laptop batteries last longer, are easier to charge, and are smaller and lighter than ever. Windows XP is also more energy efficient than previous versions of Windows, and it provides tools to help you get the most life out of a battery charge. You can configure power schemes as shown in **Figure 15.1** for maximum battery efficiency.

Windows XP also provides visual feedback to help you determine at a glance how much battery power is left, as shown in **Figure 15.2**. This is an important bit of information to know, but it's only useful if the information is accurate. Windows XP can help you ensure the accuracy of your battery life indicator as well. This technique shows you how to set up Windows XP to get the most use out of your battery, and it shows you how to calibrate the Windows XP battery indicator so that it gives accurate battery life information.

STEP 1: CALIBRATE THE BATTERY

Until a couple of years ago most laptop computers used NiCad — short for nickel-cadmium — batteries that required a great deal of maintenance to keep in top condition. For best performance and life, NiCad batteries had to be discharged completely after each use, and they had to be fully charged before you used them again. Improper charging led to shorter battery life with each charge.

Most modern laptops use NiMH — nickel-metal hybrid — or lithium-ion batteries that are less sensitive to charging technique. Modern batteries can be treated more like gas tanks; you can discharge them as much as you like, and you can recharge them at any time. The maximum charge of NiMH and lithium-ion batteries is also more consistent over the life of the battery, but some variance still occurs from charge to charge.

When you are running on battery power, Windows XP provides a visual battery life indicator in the Windows system tray as shown in **Figure 15.2**. The icon looks like a battery. When you hover the mouse pointer over this icon it provides an estimate of the time and charge percentage remaining in the battery. In **Figure 15.2**, Windows estimates 2 hours and 21 minutes of battery life remaining. The accuracy of this indicator depends on the ability of Windows to accurately measure the remaining power in the battery. If the battery isn't calibrated to your installation

of Windows XP, the battery life icon may provide an inaccurate reading.

If you've recently purchased a new laptop or battery, you should calibrate the battery to Windows XP. To calibrate the battery:

- Plug the computer in to wall power. The computer must be plugged in to calibrate the battery. The calibration can take up to eight hours, and the computer must be plugged in the entire time.
- Choose **Start ➣ All Programs ➣ Utilities ➣ Battery Optimizer**. The Battery Optimizer Wizard appears.
- Click **Next**. The second screen in the Battery Optimizer Wizard asks if you want to test the battery. If you're interested in technical details about your battery, click **Battery Details**. The Battery Details dialog box appears as shown in **Figure 15.3**. Most of the information in this dialog box is more interesting than useful, although if you're not sure what kind of battery you have, just look at what is noted next to **Chemistry**. **LION**, as shown in **Figure 15.3**, is the abbreviation for lithium-ion. Click **OK** to close the Battery Details dialog box.
- Click the **Test Battery** radio button to select it. The battery test takes a few extra minutes but it's an important step. Click **Next** to begin the battery test.

> **NOTE**
>
> Although the computer must be plugged in the whole time that battery calibration is running, you can perform other work while calibration occurs.

■ When the battery test is complete, a report of the test appears as shown in **Figure 15.4**. If the battery is not in good condition as shown in **Figure 15.4**, consider replacing it with a new battery. Click **Next**.

■ Make sure that the **Start now** radio button is chosen, and click **Next**. Battery calibration begins, and the process takes about eight hours. Make sure that the computer remains plugged in to wall power during the entire calibration process.

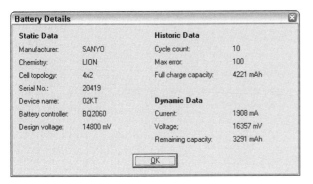

15.3

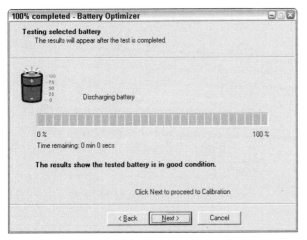

15.4

STEP 2: CHOOSE A POWER SCHEME

Electricity isn't getting cheaper, so chances are you like to save energy whenever possible. Windows XP makes saving power easy by providing power schemes tailored to different operating conditions. Some power schemes make your computer easier to use when wall power is plugged in, while other power schemes use battery power more efficiently. You should review the power scheme settings on your laptop to ensure it's configured the way you want:

■ Open the Windows Control Panel by choosing **Start** ➢ **Control Panel**. If the Control Panel is set up for Category view, click the **Performance and Maintenance** category to open it.

■ Open the **Power Options** icon. The **Power Schemes** tab of the Power Options Properties dialog box appears, as shown in **Figure 15.5**.

15.5

■ Windows XP provides several default power schemes in the **Power Schemes** menu. Choose the scheme that best matches the usage patterns for your computer. For a laptop, you want to choose **Portable/Laptop** save for some rare exceptions. For example, if you are giving a PowerPoint presentation using your laptop you should choose the **Presentation** scheme to ensure that the display doesn't turn off while you discuss part of your presentation with the audience. Likewise, if you will be away from AC power for extended periods, choose the **Max Battery** scheme. As you choose different schemes in the **Power Schemes** menu, notice the specific settings for turning off the monitor or hard drive after periods of inactivity.

■ Fine-tune specific settings, and then click **OK** to apply your changes.

STEP 3: SET UP A LOW BATTERY ALARM

Consider for a moment how long it takes to shut down your computer. Even with a very fast processor, the Windows XP shutdown process can take 30 seconds or more. Now consider what can happen if your computer is not shut down properly. You can lose data or even damage Windows so that it no longer runs properly.

Windows XP displays a battery icon to help you keep an eye on battery power and avoid an improper shut down caused by a dead battery. But it's a small icon, and if you are very busy you may overlook the readout. To augment the icon I recommend that you set up a low battery alarm. To set up an alarm:

■ Right-click the battery icon in the Windows XP system tray, and choose **Adjust Power Properties** from the context menu. The Power Options Properties dialog box appears.

■ Click the **Alarms** tab to bring it to the front as shown in **Figure 15.6**.

■ Make sure that the **Low Battery Alarm** and **Critical Battery Alarm** options are checked. Move the sliders left or right to change the battery percentage at which the alarms trigger. For example, you may want the low battery alarm to activate when 10 percent of battery power remains rather than the default 6 percent.

■ Click **Alarm Action** under **Low Battery Alarm**. The Low Battery Alarm Actions dialog box appears as shown in **Figure 15.7**. If you want an audible alarm to sound when battery power is low, place a check mark next to **Sound alarm**.

■ You can force the computer to Stand By, Hibernate, or Shut Down when the alarm is triggered. However, for the Low Battery Alarm I recommend that you leave the **Alarm Action** option unchecked. This gives you plenty of time to save work and tie up other loose ends before battery

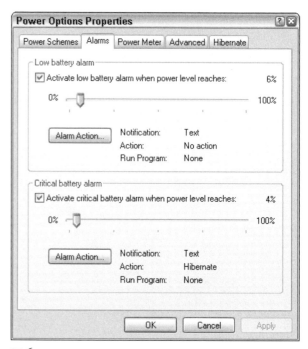

15.6

power is completely gone. You may also run a program with the alarm if you want. For example, if you want your e-mail program to open and check mail before shutting down, place a check mark in the **Run a program** option, and choose the program using the pull-down menu below.

■ Click **OK** to close the Low Battery Alarm Actions dialog box.

■ Click **Alarm Actions** under **Critical battery alarm** and review actions for the Critical battery alarm, just as you did for the low battery alarm. When the Critical battery alarm activates it's a good idea to have the computer shut down or hibernate. Click **OK** to close the Critical Battery Alarm Actions dialog box when you are done reviewing settings.

■ Click **OK** to close the Power Options Properties dialog box.

15.7

STEP 4: HIBERNATE OR STAND BY THE COMPUTER

The best way to cut battery power use is of course to shut the computer down. But shutting the computer down takes time, and starting it up again later takes even more time. Shutting down also requires you to close all open programs. If you don't want to shut the computer all the way down, Windows XP offers two alternatives that save power without forcing you to go through the whole shutdown and restart process.

One alternative is to put the computer in **Stand By**, which is similar to **Sleep** mode in the Macintosh OS. In **Stand By** the computer stays on but goes into a low power-use mode. I usually put my laptop in **Stand By** when I will not be using the computer for the next few minutes or even an hour, say during transport from one office to the next. I like **Stand By** because when I get to my destination I can wake the computer back up and resume working in just a few seconds.

Hibernate mode uses even less power because the computer actually shuts down. When you **Hibernate** your computer, a snapshot of all open files and folders on your computer is taken and saved to the hard drive. When you wake the computer from **Hibernate** mode, this image is restored from the hard drive, and your computer is restored to its exact state before hibernation. **Hibernate** actually saves the entire contents of memory on the hard drive, so it requires an amount of free hard disk space equivalent to the size of system RAM.

Hibernate must be enabled on your computer. To make sure it's enabled:

■ Right-click the **Power** icon in the Windows System Tray and choose **Adjust Power Properties** from the context menu.

- Click the **Hibernate** tab in the Power Options Properties dialog box as shown in **Figure 15.8**. Note the amount of hard disk space required for hibernation.
- Place a check mark next to **Enable hibernation** and click **OK** to close the Power Options Properties dialog box.

To **Hibernate** or **Stand By** your computer, simply choose **Start ➢ Turn Off Computer**. Choose **Stand By** or **Hibernate** from the Turn Off Computer dialog box. To turn your computer back on, press the power button on your computer.

> **NOTE**
>
> If your Power Options Properties dialog box doesn't have a **Hibernate** tab, your computer does not support hibernation.

15.8

SEEING DOUBLE WITH DUAL MONITORS

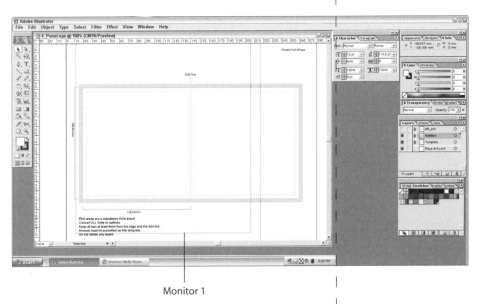 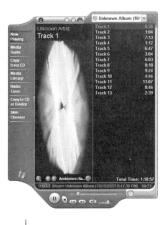

Monitor 1   Monitor 2

16.1

ABOUT THE FEATURE

You can increase your work-space by using two or more monitors on your computer. Windows XP fully supports multiple monitors.

If you've been using Windows for a few years you probably know that you can squeeze more items onto the screen by increasing the resolution setting on your monitor to 1280 × 1024, 1600 × 1200, or even higher. But as you choose higher and higher resolution settings, text, buttons, icons and other items on-screen start to look pretty small. One solution is to buy a bigger monitor. A monitor with a viewing area of 20 inches or more allows you to use higher resolutions without requiring you to squint quite as much. But very large monitors are expensive, especially if you buy a flat-panel monitor, and you may find that even a large monitor still doesn't have quite as much room as you'd like.

An increasingly popular solution to the need for more screen real estate is to use multiple monitors. With the right hardware you can connect two or more monitors to your computer. Placed side-by-side or atop each other, multiple monitors behave like one giant desktop, vastly expanding your digital work area as shown in **Figure 16.1**. Multi-monitor layouts are particularly popular with video editors, because modern video editing programs have a lot of screen elements that all need to be visible at the same time. In fact, the designers of Adobe Premiere Pro developed the interface on the assumption that most users would have two or more monitors.

Even if you aren't a video editor you can benefit from multiple monitors. You may find it handy to have your e-mail program, instant messaging program, and other often-used applications off to the side in one monitor while you work on another program in the other monitor. Such an arrangement means you no longer have to constantly go to the Windows taskbar when you want to switch between programs. Windows XP supports up to ten separate monitors on a single system, and configuring them is easy.

STEP 1: CONFIGURE YOUR HARDWARE

Before you can set up Windows XP to use multiple monitors, you need to have the right hardware. Most obviously, you need more than one monitor. You also need:

- A video card with two or more video ports. Various video cards are now available with multiple monitor support. The card should have individual ports for each monitor.
- Multiple video cards. You may be able to install additional video cards in your computer if your computer has open expansion card slots. Most video cards use AGP slots, which are brown, or PCI slots, which are white.

If you have a laptop, you can probably use two monitors without installing any new hardware. Many laptops have a monitor port in addition to the built-in LCD display. Simply connect a monitor to this port, and you should be ready to work with dual monitors. Check the documentation for your laptop if you're not sure.

Of course, one of the biggest challenges to working with multiple monitors that you may face is desk space. Monitors are big, and your workspace may not have room for more than one monitor. Flat-panel monitors take up less space, and as an added bonus they draw less electricity.

STEP 2: SET UP MULTIPLE MONITOR SUPPORT IN WINDOWS

After your hardware is configured and installed, restart Windows XP. When you first restart Windows, each monitor displays the same basic desktop image. This is because the multiple monitor settings need to be configured. Follow these steps:

- Right-click a blank area of the desktop and choose **Properties**. The Display Properties dialog box appears.

> **TIP**
>
> Modern video cards tend to use a lot of power. Multiple video cards can put too much strain on your computer's power supply, diminishing usability and potentially causing damage. If you plan to install two or more video cards in your computer, upgrade the power supply to match.

> **WARNING**
>
> Internal computer components are fragile and expensive, so if you don't have experience upgrading or repairing computer hardware, you may want to have a PC professional install new video cards or other hardware.

■ Click the **Settings** tab to bring it to the front. As you can see in **Figure 16.2**, each monitor is represented by a separate icon. **Monitor 1** is your primary monitor. Icons that are grayed out, like **Monitor 2** in **Figure 16.2**, represent monitors that are not currently active.

■ Click the icon for a secondary monitor, and place a check mark next to **Extend my Windows desktop onto this monitor**.

■ Click **Apply**. The display changes, and you may be asked by Windows if you want to keep the current display configuration, as shown in **Figure 16.3**. If everything looks okay, click **Yes**. If the display is terribly messed up and you can't see anything, just wait 15 seconds. Windows automatically reverts to the previous settings if you don't click **Yes**.

■ Adjust the **Screen resolution** and **Color quality** settings as needed. Each monitor is different, so experiment with resolution and quality settings that provide the best display on each unit. The size

of each monitor's icon varies depending on the resolution settings. Higher resolution settings mean larger icons. The icons in **Figure 16.4** are the same size because each monitor is set to 1024×768.

■ Click and drag monitor icons around the Display Properties dialog box so that they match the physical arrangement of the monitors in your office. In **Figure 16.4**, for example, I have moved **Monitor 2** to the left of **Monitor 1**.

■ Click **Apply** to apply your changes.

16.3

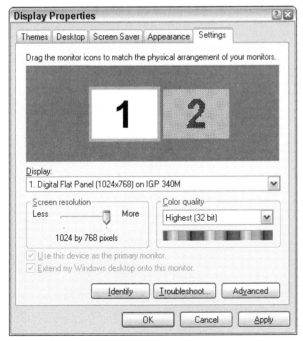

16.2

16.4

STEP 3: SPECIFY A PRIMARY MONITOR

When you have more than one monitor, one monitor is always set as the primary monitor. The primary monitor is where the Windows logon screen appears, and it is the default location for programs when you first open them. To change the primary monitor:

■ Right-click a blank area of the desktop and choose **Properties** to open the Display Properties dialog box if it isn't already open, and click the **Settings** tab to bring it to the front as shown in **Figure 16.4**.

■ If you're not sure which monitor is which in the diagram on the **Settings** tab, right-click a monitor and choose **Identify**. A giant number appears on the actual monitor for a few seconds and then disappears.

■ To set a monitor as your primary monitor, right-click it in the diagram on the **Settings** tab and choose **Primary** from the menu that appears.

■ Click **OK** to close the Display Properties dialog box and apply your settings.

STEP 4: MOVE ITEMS BETWEEN MONITORS

When your multiple monitors are configured, moving items between monitors is a simple click-and-drag affair. To maximize a window in a monitor, click and drag the title bar of the window so that more than half of it is in the desired monitor, and then click the window's **Maximize** button. You can also click and drag window borders to span more than one monitor. In **Figure 16.5**, I have expanded an Adobe Illustrator window across one and a half monitors. This allows me to have the graphic I'm working with on the primary monitor, while the program's various floating palettes are moved to the secondary monitor. The Windows XP taskbar in the lower-left portion of **Figure 16.5** spans the width of the primary monitor. The larger desktop space also allows me to keep my media player program in view on the far right.

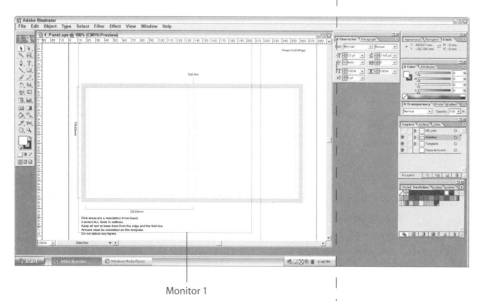
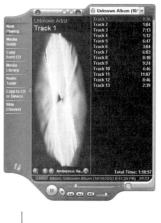

Monitor 1   Monitor 2

16.5

MANAGING SYSTEM SERVICES

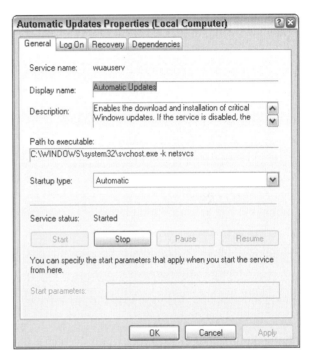

17.2

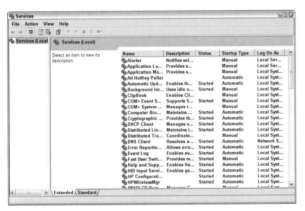

17.1

Windows XP is more than just a graphical interface of windows, toolbars, menus, and icons. Windows must also allow your computer to access external hardware, use network connections, and run other important tools. Windows XP facilitates these activities using tools called *services*. Services start every time you run Windows XP, and they provide for many crucial system functions.

Dozens of services are running on your computer right now. They are listed in the Services control panel, as shown in **Figure 17.1**. Although many of these services are critical, some of them are probably also unnecessary. These unnecessary services consume precious RAM and processor resources while providing no benefit, like leaving the lights on after you leave a room. You can increase available RAM and processor resources by disabling services that you don't use, as shown in **Figure 17.2**.

STEP 1: OPEN THE SERVICES CONTROL PANEL

To manage services you must be logged on to Windows XP with administrator rights. After you are properly logged on, open the Services control panel:

- Choose **Start ➤ Control Panel** to open the Windows Control Panel. If your Control Panel uses category view, open the **Performance and Maintenance** category.
- Open the **Administrative Tools** icon. The Administrative Tools control panel appears.
- Double-click **Services**. The Services control panel opens as shown in **Figure 17.3**. Expand the window as needed to provide a better view.

STEP 2: REVIEW SERVICE PROPERTIES

As you view the list of services in your Services control panel, you may be intimidated by the sheer number of services that are listed. The fact that most of them have cryptic or technical names doesn't help. Fortunately, the Services control panel actually makes it easy to get information about services.

Look at the bottom of the Services control panel. You should notice two tabs, named **Extended** and **Standard**, respectively. The same services are listed on each tab, but the **Extended** tab provides a more informative extended view of service properties. Click the name of a service on the **Extended** tab. A plain-language description of the service appears as shown in **Figure 17.4**. In **Figure 17.4** I'm viewing details of the **Automatic Updates** service.

> **TIP**
>
> Before you start disabling and modifying services, it's a good idea to create a system restore point, as described in Technique 18, "Using System Restore Points," in Chapter 4.

The Services control panel provides other important information about each service:

- **Status:** This column tells you whether the service is started or paused. If the column is blank, the service is not running.
- **Startup Type:** This column tells you whether the service starts automatically, manually, or is disabled.

Need even more information about a service? Right-click it and choose **Properties** from the menu that appears. A Properties dialog box for the service appears as shown in **Figure 17.5**.

17.3

17.4

STEP 3: STOP A SERVICE

Stopping a service is pretty simple. Simply right-click the service in the Services control panel, and choose **Stop** or **Pause** from the menu that appears. However, before you stop a service you need to consider some important factors:

■ Can you positively identify the service? You can probably look at some services and know right away that you don't need them. For example, any

TIP

Most services can be researched on the Internet. Simply enter the name of the service in a Web search engine and see what comes up.

service relating to a piece of hardware that is no longer installed can probably be stopped. If you don't know exactly what purpose the service performs, do not stop it until you have fully researched it and determined that its function is not critical to your system.

■ Are any dependencies affected? Open the Properties dialog box for a service and click the **Dependencies** tab to bring it to the front as shown in **Figure 17.6**. The upper box lists other services upon which this service depends. The bottom box is more important because it lists other services that depend on the current service. These services cease to function if you disable the current service. If I stop the Network Connections service in **Figure 17.6**, the **Internet Connection Firewall (ICF) / Internet Connection Sharing (ICS)** service will not work.

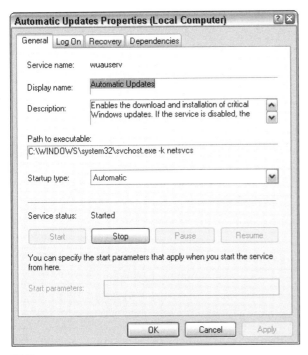

17.5

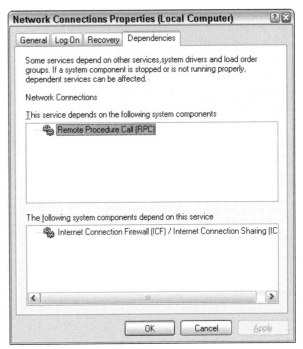

17.6

STEP 4: DISABLE SERVICES AT STARTUP

As I mentioned earlier, some services start automatically when you launch Windows XP. You can stop services, as I showed in the previous step, but the next time you start Windows any services you stopped start again. To prevent this, you can disable unwanted services so that they do not automatically start with Windows. Follow these steps:

- Open the Services control panel, and double-click the service that you want to disable. The Properties dialog box for the service appears, as shown in **Figure 17.5**.
- On the **General** tab, choose **Disable** from the **Startup type** menu.
- Click **OK**. The service is now disabled upon startup.

STEP 5: RESTART A SERVICE

If you want to restart a service, open the Services control panel, right-click the service, and choose **Start** from the menu that appears, as shown in **Figure 17.7**.

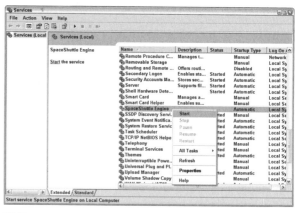

17.7

CHAPTER 4

MAINTAINING YOUR SYSTEM IN TOP CONDITION

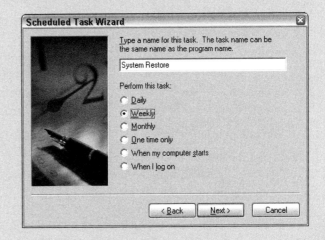

Windows XP is the most powerful and reliable version of the Windows operating system yet offered by Microsoft. Windows XP also requires that you spend less time maintaining the operating system to keep it in top condition. Many important maintenance tasks happen automatically without any input from you.

Of course, some things cannot happen automatically. If you encounter a major system crash or if a program installation corrupts Windows, you must manually fix the problem. Windows XP has some valuable maintenance tools to help you recover from a major problem, and the techniques in this chapter show you how to use them.

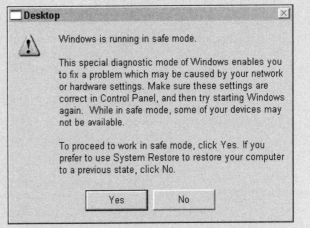

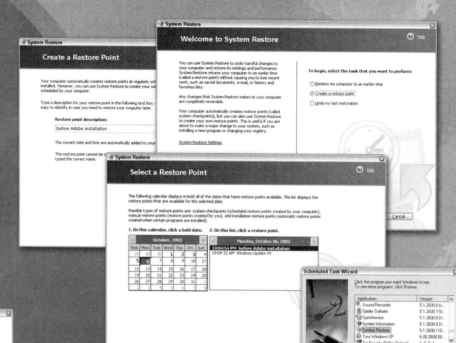

System Restore Points

Making Regular Backups

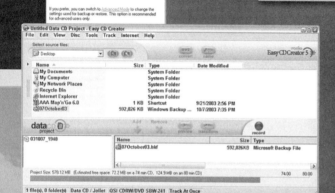

Adding Hardware

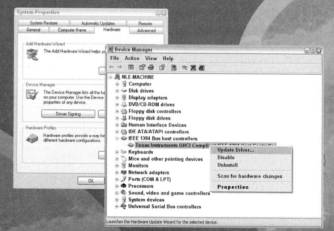

USING SYSTEM RESTORE POINTS

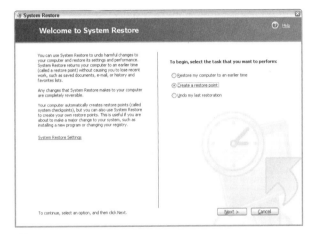

18.1

18.2

Windows XP records the configuration of your computer's software in system restore points. In the event of a system crash or other major problem, you can quickly restore your computer's configuration to a previous system restore point.

D o you ever wish you could go back in time and change a decision you made? In Windows XP, you can! Windows XP includes a feature called **System Restore**, shown in **Figure 18.1**, and as the name implies, this feature can restore your computer to an earlier state. Here's how it works: Windows XP periodically takes a snapshot of your computer. This snapshot, called a *system restore point*, records most installed programs, the current configuration of Windows XP, and other important system components. If your computer encounters a major problem — say, a newly installed program unacceptably modifies your Windows installation — you can return Windows to the state in a saved system restore point as shown in **Figure 18.2**.

As important as what System Restore *does* do is what it *does not* do. System Restore does not move or delete personal files saved since the restore point, nor does it restore deleted personal files. System Restore doesn't completely uninstall recently installed programs. For this reason, when you want to remove an unwanted program use that program's uninstallation utility or the **Add/ Remove Programs** icon in the **Windows Control Panel**. After that, use System Restore to repair damage that the program caused to Windows itself.

STEP 1: ADJUST SYSTEM RESTORE SETTINGS

You may disable System Restore, exclude some drives, or change how much disk space is allocated to System Restore. To adjust System Restore settings:

- Choose **Start ➤ Control Panel** to open the Windows Control Panel. If you see the **Performance and Maintenance** category, click it to open it.
- Double-click the **System** icon, and click the **System Restore** tab to bring it to the front as shown in **Figure 18.3**.

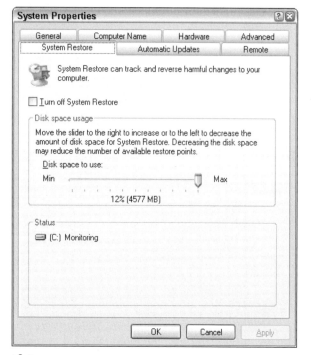

18.3

- If you need to conserve disk space on your computer, move the **Disk space to use** slider left to reduce the amount of space used by System Restore. System Restore requires at least 200MB of disk space to function.
- To disable System Restore, place a check mark next to **Turn off System Restore**. If you disable System Restore, restore points are not automatically created when you update Windows software or perform other tasks that otherwise trigger a restore point.
- If your computer has multiple hard drives and you want to exclude a nonsystem drive from System Restore, click **Settings** next to the drive you want to exclude and place a check mark next to **Turn off System Restore on this drive**.
- Click **OK** to close the System Properties dialog box.

STEP 2: SET A SYSTEM RESTORE POINT

System Restore points are automatically set when you update the Windows XP software. If you are installing a new program, adding new hardware, or making another major system change, you should create a system restore point before proceeding. This ensures that if your system change creates a problem you can restore Windows to the earlier state. To set a system restore point:

- Choose **Start ➤ All Programs ➤ Accessories ➤ System Tools ➤ System Restore**. The System Restore Wizard starts as shown in **Figure 18.4**.
- In the System Restore Wizard, choose **Create a restore point** and click **Next**.
- Type a description for the restore point, as shown in **Figure 18.5**.
- Click **Create**. System Restore creates a restore point that is identified both by the description you provide as well as the date and time of the creation.
- Click **Close** to close the System Restore Wizard.

STEP 3: SCHEDULE A SYSTEM RESTORE POINT (OPTIONAL)

Your system can crash at any time, and major problems can come from seemingly nowhere. To prevent potential calamity, you should set system restore points periodically even if you don't install new software or update Windows. You can set restore points manually as described in the previous step, or you can schedule system restore points to be set automatically:

■ Choose **Start ➤ All Programs ➤ Accessories ➤ System Tools ➤ Scheduled Tasks**. The Scheduled Tasks window appears.

■ Double-click the **Add Scheduled Task** icon. The Scheduled Task Wizard appears.
■ Click **Next**. A list of applications on your computer appears.
■ Scroll down the list of applications and choose **System Restore** as shown in **Figure 18.6**.
■ Click **Next**.
■ Choose an interval for the scheduled task. The example in **Figure 18.7** shows System Restore scheduled to run weekly.
■ Click **Next**.

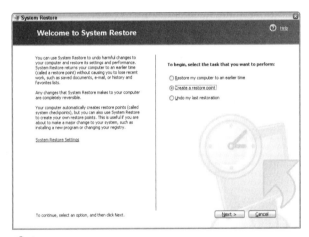

18.4

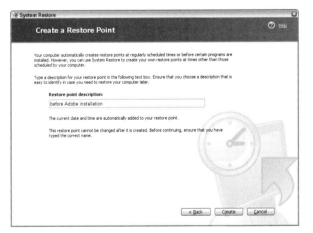

18.5

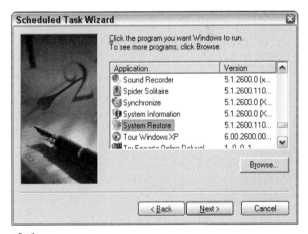

18.6

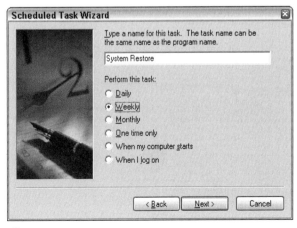

18.7

- Specify a starting time and day, if appropriate. Windows XP creates system restore points quickly, but you should schedule the task to occur when your computer is on but not heavily used.
- Click **Next**, and enter your user name and password in the next screen. You must have administrator rights on the computer to run System Restore.
- Click **Next**, and then click **Finish**. System Restore now appears in the list of scheduled tasks, as shown in **Figure 18.8**.

STEP 4: RESTORE THE COMPUTER TO AN EARLIER STATE

If your computer does not function properly after a program installation, Windows XP software update, or system crash, use the System Restore Wizard to restore Windows to a previous restore point.

- Close all open applications.
- Choose **Start** ➢ **All Programs** ➢ **Accessories** ➢ **System Tools** ➢ **System Restore**. The System Restore Wizard appears.

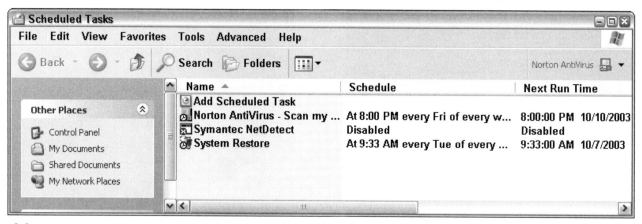

18.8

■ Choose **Restore my computer to an earlier time** and click **Next**. A list of saved restore points appears as shown in **Figure 18.9**.

■ Click a date with a **boldface** number in the calendar on the left. Boldface dates have saved restore points.

■ Choose a restore point from the list on the right and click **Next**.

■ Read the warnings and click **Next** again. Windows restarts during the restoration process.

STEP 5: UNDO A SYSTEM RESTORATION (OPTIONAL)

If you are unhappy with a system restoration, you may undo it. Simply open the System Restore Wizard by choosing **Start** ➤ **All Programs** ➤ **Accessories** ➤ **System Tools** ➤ **System Restore**, choose **Undo my last restoration**, and click **Next**. Read the warnings and click **Next**. The last restoration is undone and your computer restarts.

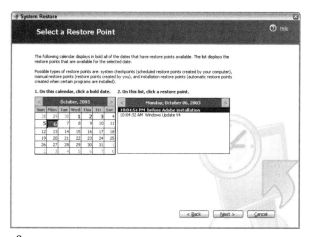

18.9

NOTE

If you are unable to start Windows XP normally after a system crash, see Technique 20, "Running in Safe Mode," for steps on running System Restore and other troubleshooting tools in Safe Mode.

MAKING REGULAR BACKUPS

19.1   19.2

Make backup copies of important files to ensure you don't accidentally lose work that is difficult or impossible to replace. The Windows XP Backup or Restore Wizard makes it easy to back up important data.

Few mishaps in modern work or personal life are as costly and frustrating as the loss of an important file. In the blink of an eye you can lose hours, days, or even weeks of work. Many things can cause data loss. Sometimes files are corrupted or accidentally deleted. Hardware problems such as hard drive failures can also cause data loss.

The exact causes of data loss are less important than what you should do about it. To prevent data loss, you should make backup copies of your most important files. Windows XP includes a handy **Backup or Restore Wizard** — shown in **Figure 19.1** — that guides you through the process of backing up important files. If you later need to restore lost files, the Backup or Restore Wizard also guides you through the restoration process, as shown in **Figure 19.2**.

STEP 1: LAUNCH THE BACKUP OR RESTORE WIZARD

To launch the Backup or Restore Wizard, follow these steps:

- Choose **Start** ➢ **All Programs** ➢ **Accessories** ➢ **System Tools** ➢ **Backup**. The Backup or Restore Wizard appears as shown in **Figure 19.3**.
- Click **Next**.
- In the Backup or Restore screen, choose **Back up files and settings** and click **Next**.
- In the screen shown in **Figure 19.4**, choose what you want to back up. Each setting provides a summary of backup items. If you are the only user on the computer and all of the things you want to back up are in **My Documents**, choose **My documents and settings**. This backs up the **My Documents** folder, Internet favorites, desktop

TIP

This technique shows you how to use Windows XP's Backup tool. You may also want to consider a third-party backup program such as DriveBackup! from NTI at www.ntius.com. Programs such as DriveBackup! simplify the backup process by automating backups to CDs, DVDs, or even network drives, as well as simplify the restoration process should you ever need to do it.

NOTE

If Backup isn't installed on your system, you can install it from the Windows XP CD-ROM. Locate the installation file NTBACKUP.MSI in the folder VALUEADD\MSFT\NTBACKUP. Double-click the installation file and follow the instructions on-screen to install Backup.

items, and Internet cookies. If more than one person uses the computer and you want to back up everyone's data, choose **Everyone's documents and settings**. If you want to pick and choose what to back up, choose **Let me choose what to back up**, as selected in **Figure 19.4**.

- Click **Next**. If you chose **Let me choose what to back up**, you see a dialog box similar to **Figure 19.5**. Place a check mark next to each folder or item that you want to back up. Click the plus-signs to expand the lists of drives and folders. **Figure 19.5** shows **My Documents** being backed up, as well as

19.3

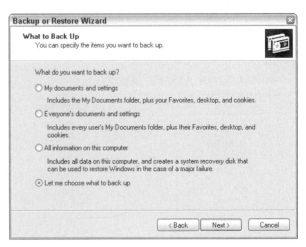

19.4

a folder called **AGES** on the **C:** drive. Click **Next** when you are done choosing items to back up.

■ Click **Browse**. Navigate to a location where you want to save the backup file, and type a descriptive name for the file. I recommend that you name the backup file based on the current date, such as **23July04**, or on the content, such as **Summer03pictures**. Click **Save** to close the Save As dialog box, and then click **Next** in the Backup or Restore Wizard.

■ Review the backup settings and click **Finish** if everything looks correct. If not, click **Back** and change settings as needed. When you click **Finish**, the backup begins and a dialog box similar to **Figure 19.6** shows the progress of the backup.

NOTE

The **All information on this computer** option creates a backup of everything on the computer. This option usually isn't necessary, though you may want to choose it if you have a lot of software installed and you think it may be difficult or impossible to reinstall in the event of a major system crash.

STEP 2: ARCHIVE THE BACKUP FILE

The backup files created by the Windows Backup or Restore Wizard are extremely valuable. However, a backup file doesn't do you any good if it's stored on a hard drive that just died. You should always save the backup file in another physical location, such as a CD-R, DVD-R, second hard drive, or even a network hard drive.

If you plan to use CD-Rs, keep in mind that a 700MB disc actually only holds about 690MB. When

TIP

If you're not sure how much data is stored in a folder, open **My Computer** or **Windows Explorer**, right-click the folder in question, and choose **Properties** from the context menu that appears. The **General** tab of the Properties dialog box that appears lists the size of the folder.

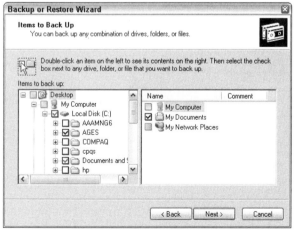

19.5

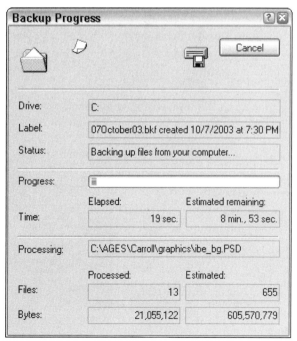

19.6

the Backup or Restore Wizard creates a backup file, the file is the size of the items stored in it because backed-up items are not compressed. For example, if your **My Documents** folder contains 850MB of data and you back it up, the size of the backup file is 850MB. This file won't fit on a single CD-R, so you may need to back up individual folders in the **My Documents** folder separately.

To place a backup file on a CD-R, your computer needs a CD-R or CD-RW drive and CD mastering software. In **Figure 19.7**, I am using Roxio Easy CD Creator to burn a backup file to a CD-R. If you have a DVD-R drive, you can burn backup copies onto 700MB CD-Rs or 4.7GB DVD-Rs. The huge capacity of blank DVD-Rs makes them ideal for storing large backup files.

STEP 3: RESTORE DATA FROM A BACKUP

Thanks to the Windows XP Backup or Restore Wizard, you can restore data as easily as you back it up. To restore data:

- Choose **Start** ➢ **All Programs** ➢ **Accessories** ➢ **System Tools** ➢ **Backup** to launch the Backup or Restore Wizard, and click **Next** in the first screen of the wizard.
- Choose **Restore files and settings** and click **Next**. The **What to Restore** window appears as shown in **Figure 19.8**.

- Click **Browse** and locate the backup file from which you want to restore.
- Place check marks next to items that you want to restore. In **Figure 19.8** I am only restoring the folder called **AGES**. If you want to restore everything in the backup file, place a check mark next to the name of the backup file in the left side of the wizard.
- Click **Next**.
- Review the restoration settings, and click **Finish** if everything looks correct. Click **Back** if you want to change any settings. A Restore Progress dialog box appears and shows the status of the restoration.
- Click **Close** when the restoration is complete.

> **NOTE**
>
> If your DVD burner is labeled as a DVD-R drive, make sure you buy blank media labeled "DVD-R." Likewise, if you have a DVD+R drive you must use media labeled "DVD+R." Newer hybrid DVD+/-R drives can use both types of media.

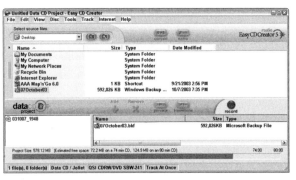

19.7

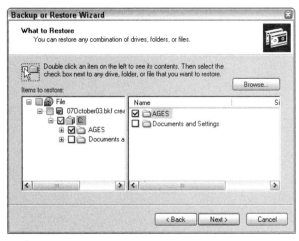

19.8

RUNNING IN SAFE MODE

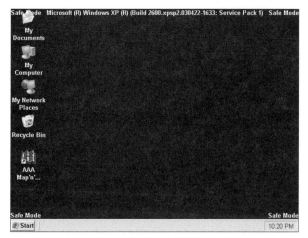

20.1

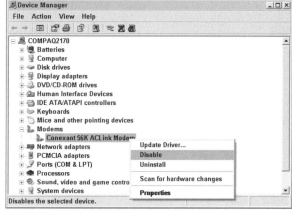

20.2

ABOUT THE FEATURE

Safe Mode is a special startup mode that lets Windows XP load with a minimum of software drivers. This helps troubleshoot system problems and is sometimes the only way to get a problematic computer to start.

When Windows XP starts, it doesn't just launch the Windows software. Various startup programs and hardware drivers are also loaded. Drivers allow Windows XP to communicate with the hardware on your system.

Sometimes a bad driver or startup program disrupts the flow of data traffic in Windows, so Windows XP provides a special startup mode called **Safe Mode** that helps you identify problem items, or at least get Windows started if it will not start normally. For example, if you just installed a new program and now Windows XP won't start properly, you can start the computer in Safe Mode as shown in **Figure 20.1** and disable or uninstall the offending program.

Likewise, you can use Safe Mode to identify which hardware driver may be causing a problem and, if necessary, disable problematic devices as shown in **Figure 20.2**. Safe Mode only loads drivers for the most basic components, including the monitor, keyboard, hard drives, and a few other critical components. If Windows XP starts successfully in Safe Mode, you can rule out a failure in one of these basic components.

STEP 1: START WINDOWS XP IN SAFE MODE

If Windows is currently running, restart the computer using the **Turn Off Computer** option in the **Start** menu if possible. If you are unable to restart the computer normally, hold down the power button for five seconds. The computer eventually turns off. Wait a moment, and then press the power button again to turn the computer back on. To start in Safe Mode:

- Watch the screen carefully as the computer starts. When the memory test is complete, press and hold **F8**. If you see a message that says **Please select the operating system to start**, press **F8** again.
- You should now see a screen titled **Windows Advanced Options Menu**. Use the arrow keys on your keyboard to select **Safe Mode**, and then press **Enter**.
- A screen appears prompting you to select an operating system. If you have more than one operating system installed, choose Windows XP. Otherwise, just press **Enter**. Windows XP Safe Mode loads.

NOTE

Some computers do not show a memory test on-screen when they first start. Instead, you may see a splash screen showing the name of your computer's manufacturer along with a list of keys you can press to enter computer setup. If **F8** is not listed, wait for the screen to disappear. When it disappears, press and hold **F8**.

TIP

If your mouse doesn't work, press the **Tab** key until the desired button or icon is highlighted, and then press **Enter**.

- At the log-on screen, log on to Windows as normal. After logging on you see a dialog box like the one shown in **Figure 20.3** that reminds you that you are currently running in Safe Mode. Click **Yes** to continue running Safe Mode.

One of the first things you probably notice about Safe Mode is that the display is ugly. The screen background is black, as shown in **Figure 20.4**. The screen resolution is set to a low 640×480, and your monitor may flicker. These display problems are a necessary evil of Safe Mode, and they occur because only very basic video display drivers are loaded.

Your network connections won't work in Safe Mode, either. As you may have noticed in the **Windows Advanced Options Menu**, it is possible to start Safe Mode with networking support, but for normal troubleshooting you should launch Safe Mode without network support.

STEP 2: TROUBLESHOOT HARDWARE ISSUES (OPTIONAL)

If Windows XP seems to start and work okay in Safe Mode, you can probably rule out basic problems like a hard drive failure or a severely corrupted Windows installation. If you installed new hardware immediately before the problem occurred, uninstall the drivers and

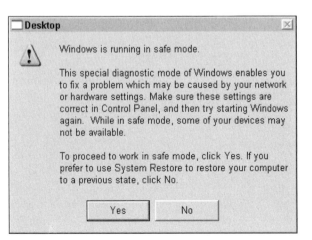

20.3

software associated with that software while running in Safe Mode. Check the following:

- Was a new **Start Menu** folder installed? If so, open it and look for an uninstallation utility, and run it if present.
- Choose **Start ≻ Control Panel** and double-click the **Add or Remove Programs** icon in the Control Panel.
- Look for installed programs that are associated with the offending hardware, and remove them if present. Close the **Add or Remove Programs** window when you're done.
- Double-click the **System** icon in the Control Panel, and then click the **Hardware** tab to bring it to the front.
- Click **Device Manager** to open the Device Manager window as shown in **Figure 20.5**.
- Locate the name of the device that you installed. If you installed a new modem, for example, click the plus sign next to **Modems** to reveal a list of installed modems as shown in **Figure 20.5**. If you did not recently install a new device, look for anything that has a yellow exclamation icon next to it. A yellow exclamation icon indicates a problem with that component. Right-click the name of the offending hardware, and choose **Disable**

from the menu that appears. You may also choose **Uninstall**, but for troubleshooting purposes you can just temporarily disable the device.

- Close **Device Manager**, and restart your computer. Does Windows XP start normally? If so, then the piece of hardware you disabled was probably the culprit. Reopen the Device Manager, reenable the device, and restart the computer. If the problem returns, restart in Safe Mode, disable the device again, and restart in normal mode again. This time, try updating the driver for the component. If the problem persists, you may need to physically remove the device.

Of course, the exact troubleshooting steps you take vary with each new scenario, but by following these basic steps you can use Safe Mode to identify many problem components.

STEP 3: DISABLE STARTUP PROGRAMS (OPTIONAL)

If you believe that your system problems are caused by a new program rather than hardware, Safe Mode can still help. Start in Safe Mode as described previously, open the **Add or Remove Programs** icon in the Control Panel, and uninstall the software you installed immediately before the problem occurred.

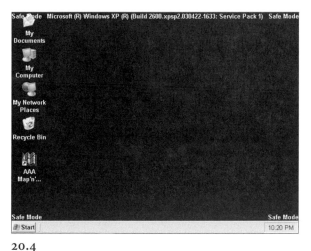

20.4

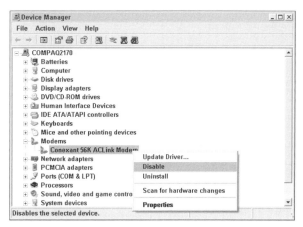

20.5

After uninstalling the program, restart the computer. Does the problem persist? If so, restart in Safe Mode again, and then choose **Start ➤ Run**. In the Run dialog box, type **msconfig** as shown in **Figure 20.6** and click **OK**. The System Configuration Utility appears. Click the **Startup** tab to bring it to the front, and disable startup items as described in Technique 2, "Controlling Startup Items," in Chapter 1.

STEP 4: RUN SYSTEM RESTORE (OPTIONAL)

You can run System Restore in Safe Mode. This may be the best option if Windows recently encountered a problem and you are unable to identify the cause. As described in Technique 18, System Restore restores your computer's settings to the last saved restore point, thereby turning your computer back in time to a configuration it had before the recent problem occurred. To run System Restore in Safe Mode:

■ Choose **Start ➤ All Programs ➤ Accessories ➤ System Tools ➤ System Restore**.

■ In the System Restore window, choose **Restore my computer to an earlier time** and click **Next**.

■ Complete the system restoration as described in Technique 18, "Using System Restore Points," earlier in this chapter.

NOTE

You cannot undo a system restoration performed while running Windows XP in Safe Mode.

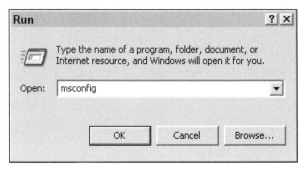

20.6

INSTALLING THE RECOVERY CONSOLE

21.1

21.2

Windows XP provides an advanced troubleshooting and repair tool called the Recovery Console. You can run the Recovery Console to repair system problems that otherwise prevent you from starting Windows.

In the previous technique I show you how to start Windows XP in Safe Mode to help troubleshoot startup and system problems. But even if the problem is so severe that Windows won't even start in Safe Mode, all hope is not lost. Windows XP provides another troubleshooting tool called the Recovery Console. If Windows does not start normally or in Safe Mode, you can run the Recovery Console from your hard drive or the Windows XP CD-ROM to try to repair the problem. The Recovery Console can extract system files from the Windows installation CD to replace damaged or missing files on your hard drive.

The Recovery Console is a more advanced tool and requires more advanced skill to use. You perform Recovery Console tasks using a command prompt as shown in **Figure 21.1**, so you should have some experience working from a DOS-style command prompt before you try to use the Recovery Console. This technique shows you how to install the Recovery Console on your hard drive, how to do some basic Recovery Console tasks, as shown in **Figure 21.2**, and how to uninstall the Recovery Console.

STEP 1: INSTALL THE RECOVERY CONSOLE

Although you can run the Recovery Console from your Windows XP CD-ROM, I recommend that you install it on the hard drive, just in case a system crash or hardware failure prevents you from using the CD-ROM drive. To install the Recovery Console:

■ Make sure your computer's Internet connection is on, if possible. An Internet connection isn't mandatory to install the Recovery Console, but it allows Windows to check the Microsoft Web site for the latest version of the Windows XP Recovery Console.

■ Place your Windows XP disc in the CD-ROM drive. If the disc came with your computer it may be marked "Operating System Disc" by the OEM manufacturer. If a "Welcome to Microsoft Windows XP" window appears, click **Exit** to close that window.

■ Choose **Start ➤ Run** to open the Run dialog box.

■ In the **Open** field, type **D:\i386\winnt32.exe /cmdcons** as shown in **Figure 21.3**. If your CD-ROM drive has a different letter than **D:**, replace **D:** with the appropriate letter.

■ Click **OK**.

■ When you see the Windows Setup dialog box describing the Recovery Console, click **Yes** to install the console. If your computer is connected to the Internet, a Windows Setup dialog box appears as shown in **Figure 21.4**. Windows Setup checks for and downloads updated software.

■ When Recovery Console installation is complete, a message appears telling you that installation was successful. Click **OK** to close the dialog box.

21.3

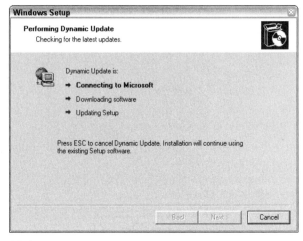

21.4

STEP 2: RUN THE RECOVERY CONSOLE FROM THE HARD DRIVE (OPTIONAL)

As I mentioned in the previous step, if you install the Recovery Console on your hard drive you can use it even if a system problem prevents you from using the CD-ROM drive. To run the Recovery Console from the hard drive:

- Turn on your computer. If Windows XP is already running, restart the computer. During startup, a screen appears asking you to select an operating system to start.
- Use the arrow keys to select **Microsoft Windows Recovery Console** and press **Enter**. The Recovery Console starts.
- The Recovery Console asks you which Windows installation you want to log onto. Normally you only have one option, labeled **1: C:\WINDOWS**, unless you have more than one version of Windows installed. Type the number of the installation you want to log onto and press **Enter**.
- Type the administrator password and press **Enter**. If you do not have a password set up for the Windows XP administrator account, just press **Enter**. When you type the correct password and log on, the Recovery Console presents a command prompt.

STEP 3: RUN THE RECOVERY CONSOLE FROM THE WINDOWS XP CD-ROM (OPTIONAL)

If you don't have the Recovery Console installed on your hard drive, you should still be able to run it from the Windows XP CD-ROM. To run Recovery Console from the CD:

- Place the Windows XP CD in your computer's CD-ROM drive, and then restart the computer.
- When you see the screen that says **Press any key to boot from the CD-ROM**, press the space bar or any other key. A blue screen titled "Windows Setup" appears.
- When Windows Setup is completely loaded, press **R** to run the Recovery Console.
- The Recovery Console asks you which Windows installation you want to log onto. Normally you only have one option, labeled **1: C:\WINDOWS**, unless you have more than one version of Windows installed. Type the number of the installation you want to log onto and press **Enter**.
- Type the administrator password and press **Enter**. If you do not have a password set up for the Windows XP administrator account, just press **Enter**. When you type the correct password and log on, the Recovery Console presents a command prompt.

STEP 4: USE THE RECOVERY CONSOLE

As I mentioned earlier, the Recovery Console assumes you have some experience working from a command prompt. Some tasks you can perform while running the Recovery Console include:

- Type **help** at the command prompt and press **Enter**. A list of available commands appears.
- To gain help on a specific command, type **help** and then the name of the command. For example, if you want to know what the RD command does, type **help rd** and press **Enter**. A description of the command appears, along with other relevant information such as attributes that can be used

with the command. **Figure 21.5** displays help information on the **ren** command.

■ To see a list of files in the current directory, type **dir** and press **Enter**. Press the space bar to scroll down the list of files a screen at a time.

■ Use the **CD** command to change directories. If you are in the **C:\WINDOWS** directory and you want to browse the **\INF** subdirectory, type **cd inf** and press **Enter**. Type **cd ..** to move back up one level in the directory tree.

> **WARNING**
>
> Do not use any command unless you are absolutely sure what it does. All actions taken while using the Recovery Console are final and not undoable.

21.5

■ If you want to browse the contents of another drive, type the drive letter followed by a colon and press **Enter**. If your CD-ROM drive is drive D:, type **d:** and press **Enter**.

■ To close the Recovery Console and restart Windows XP, type **exit** and press **Enter**.

STEP 5: UNINSTALL THE RECOVERY CONSOLE (OPTIONAL)

Although installing the Recovery Console on your hard drive is handy in some situations, you may not like having to choose whether to boot Windows XP or the Recovery Console every time you restart your computer. To stop this, uninstall the Recovery Console:

■ Open My Computer or Windows Explorer, and click the icon for your C: drive. If you have Recovery Console installed on a different drive, open that drive instead.

> **WARNING**
>
> Make sure you only delete the exact items listed here. If you delete the wrong item while hidden and protected system files are displayed, Windows XP could become inoperable.

- If you do not see a folder called **cmdcons** at the root level of your hard drive, choose **Tools ➢ Folder Options** and click the **View** tab in the Folder Options dialog box. Under **Advanced Settings** click the **Show hidden files and folders** radio button, and remove the check mark next to **Hide protected operating system files**. Click **OK** to close the Folder Options dialog box.

- Delete the folder **cmdcons**.

- Delete the file **cmldr**. As with the **cmdcons** folder, the **cmldr** file is located at the root level of the hard drive.

- Right-click the **boot.ini** file and choose **Properties** from the menu that appears. This file is located at the root level of your hard drive. The **.ini** extension may not be displayed, but the icon may also say "Configuration Settings" under the file name. The icon image should look like a gear in front of a pad of paper. Remove the check mark next to **Read-only** in the Properties dialog box and click **OK**.

- Double-click the **boot** file. It should open in Notepad as shown in **Figure 21.6**.

- Delete the line **C:\CMDCONS\BOOTSECT.DAT="Microsoft Windows Recovery Console" /cmdcons** as shown in **Figure 21.6**.

- Choose **File ➢ Save** and then close Notepad.

- Right-click the **boot** file again and choose **Properties**. Place a check mark next to **Read-only** and click **OK**. You may also want to open the Folder Options dialog box again and rehide hidden and protected system files.

21.6

ADDING HARDWARE

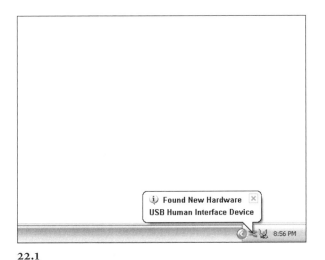

22.1

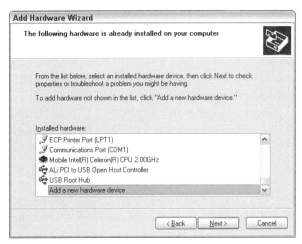

22.2

ABOUT THE FEATURE

Windows XP supports a wide selection of hardware, and installing most new components is very easy. But even if the hardware is old or unsupported, it may still be possible to get it to work with Windows XP.

Since the release of Windows 95, Microsoft has promised that **Plug-and-Play** technology would make hardware installations quick and easy. The concept behind Plug-and-Play is that Windows automatically detects new hardware when it is installed. In **Figure 22.1**, a new USB device has been detected. Necessary drivers are automatically installed, and the new device is ready for use almost immediately.

Plug-and-Play actually works pretty well in Windows XP, but it doesn't work 100 percent of the time. And even when Windows does appear to detect and configure new hardware automatically, the device may not be configured for optimal performance. When Windows XP installs and configures hardware manually, as shown in **Figure 22.2**, it usually uses drivers built in to the Windows software. But the manufacturer of the device probably offers better, more up-to-date drivers. These drivers may be available on a CD-ROM that came with the device, or it may be available on the manufacturer's Web site. Whether you are adding a new network card to your computer or attaching a new USB mouse, this technique shows you how to make sure the installation is successful.

STEP 1: CONNECT HOT-SWAP HARDWARE

Until about five years ago it was necessary to turn your computer off every time you installed new hardware. But you can connect and disconnect many modern devices without shutting down the computer. These devices are called *hot-swappable*. Most hot-swap devices use the USB — Universal Serial Bus — port. Virtually all modern computers have at least one USB port. Common USB devices include printers, mice, digital cameras, and external modems.

Devices that use the IEEE-1394 — also called Firewire — port are also hot-swappable. Firewire ports are less common on Windows PCs and are usually used for digital camcorders or external hard drives.

To install a USB or Firewire device, simply plug it into the appropriate port using a proper cable. Some external devices may also need a separate power cord, and if so, you need to plug it in as well. When you connect a new USB or Firewire device for the first time, a message appears in the Windows system tray as shown in **Figure 22.3**.

WARNING

Make sure you read the documentation that comes with your new hardware and follow any special installation instructions provided.

NOTE

If your computer doesn't have a Firewire port, you can add one by installing an IEEE-1394 expansion card, sometimes called a digital video capture card.

After a few moments you may see a second message stating that the new device has been installed. However, this does not necessarily mean that it is ready to use. If the device came with an installation disc, place it in the CD-ROM drive now and follow the instructions provided with the device to complete installation. In some cases you may be able to use the device just fine without any further installation. USB mice, for example, usually work right away after you plug them in.

STEP 2: INSTALL DEVICES ON A SERIAL OR PARALLEL PORT

Although most modern external devices use a USB or Firewire port, many older devices like printers, scanners, and mice use a parallel or serial port. You can still use these devices with Windows XP, providing your computer has the appropriate ports. Many serial and parallel devices are not Plug-and-Play. To install a serial or parallel device:

- Shut down the computer and make sure the power is off.
- Connect the cable between the device and your computer.
- Connect the device's power cord and make sure the power is turned on.
- Restart Windows.
- When Windows restarts, run the Add Hardware Wizard as described in step 4.

22.3

STEP 3: INSTALL INTERNAL HARDWARE

Internal hardware is more complicated to install because you must open the case and expose the computer's delicate internals. If you've never installed an expansion card or other internal device, consult a professional. Many stores that sell expansion cards also offer professional installation for a nominal fee. When installing internal hardware:

- Make sure the computer's power is off.
- Ground yourself against a bare-metal surface of the case before touching the expansion card or other internal components. Even a small amount of static electricity in your finger can destroy the microscopic circuitry in modern PC components.
- Carefully follow installation instructions that came with the device to ensure proper installation.
- Replace the cover before turning the computer's power back on.

Plug-and-Play should work with most internal components, but some configuration may be necessary. When Windows XP restarts, run the Add Hardware Wizard as described in step 4.

STEP 4: RUN THE ADD HARDWARE WIZARD

The Add Hardware Wizard helps you install hardware that may otherwise be difficult to set up. This wizard usually runs automatically when Windows XP detects new hardware. To use the Add Hardware Wizard:

- If your new hardware came with an installation disc, place it in the drive now. If an installation program on the disc begins to run, use it instead of the Add Hardware Wizard.
- If the Add Hardware Wizard doesn't start automatically, choose **Start** ➢ **Control Panel** to open the Control Panel. If the Control Panel currently displays category view, click the **Switch to Classic View** link on the left side of the screen. Then double-click the **Add Hardware** icon.

- Read the first screen of the Add Hardware Wizard and click **Next**. Windows attempts to search for your new hardware.
- In the next screen choose **Yes, I have already connected the hardware** and click **Next**.
- Scroll down the list of devices and see if your new device is listed. If the device is listed, select it. If it isn't, choose **Add a new hardware device** from the bottom of the list as shown in **Figure 22.4**. Click **Next**.
- In the next screen, choose **Search for and install the hardware automatically** and click **Next**. Windows XP attempts to find the new hardware. If the hardware is found, Windows XP automatically installs it. But if you see a message stating that no new hardware was detected, click **Next** to install it manually.
- Choose the category into which your device fits. If it doesn't match any of the listed categories, choose **Show All Devices**. Choose the manufacturer and model of the device. If neither the manufacturer nor model of the device is listed, click **Have Disk** and browse to the device's installation disk in your floppy or CD-ROM drive.
- Click **Finish** to complete the Add Hardware Wizard.

22.4

STEP 5: UPDATE DRIVERS

Hardware vendors periodically update drivers for their devices to ensure the best functionality with Windows. If you have a device that you believe is not running perfectly, check the manufacturer's Web site for updates. If you obtain an updated driver for a device, installing it is easy:

- Click the **System** icon in the Windows Control Panel and click the **Hardware** tab to bring it to the front.
- Click **Device Manager**. The Device Manager appears as shown in **Figure 22.5**.
- Click the plus sign to expand the relevant category, right-click the device you want to update as shown in **Figure 22.5**, and choose **Update Driver**. The Hardware Update Wizard appears as shown in **Figure 22.6**.

- Choose **Install the software automatically** and click **Next**. Follow the instructions on-screen to update the driver. If the driver that is already installed is newer than the one you are trying to install, or if Windows is unable to locate a newer driver, the wizard advises you that no update is necessary.

NOTE

If you downloaded a new driver from the Internet or have the new driver on a disc, you can **install it from a list or specific location** instead. Browse to the appropriate file and follow the instructions on-screen to update the driver.

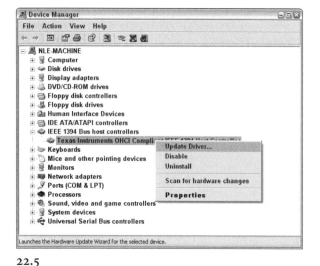

22.5

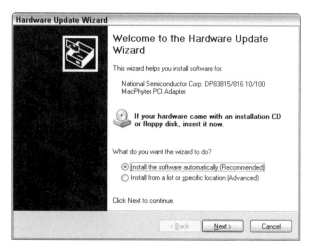

22.6

CHAPTER 5

MANAGING YOUR NETWORK

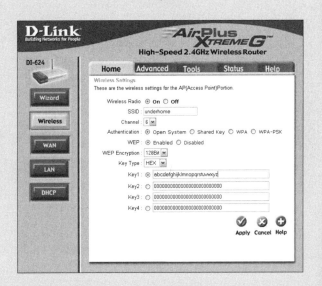

Not so long ago, computer networks were only found in businesses and in the basements of the most die-hard computer geeks. Networking gear was expensive, networks were difficult to configure and maintain, and most home users only had one computer anyway. All that is changing as networking becomes more affordable and easier to manage. A large part of this is driven by the fact that many home users now have more than one computer. It also helps that simple yet powerful networking technologies in Windows XP mean that your small business doesn't have to hire a highly specialized network administrator to manage your small-business network. Almost anyone with a solid Windows XP foundation can administer a small- to medium-sized network today.

Networking computers together has many benefits. Files can be easily shared between computers. Multiple users can access a single database; for example, one server computer can house your customer database, and with the right software that database can be accessed simultaneously by multiple sales staff working on different computers. Networks also allow you to share hardware resources like printers and disk drives. And of course, computers on a network can share a single Internet connection. The techniques in this chapter show you how to make the most of networking in Windows XP.

Sharing Your Internet Computer

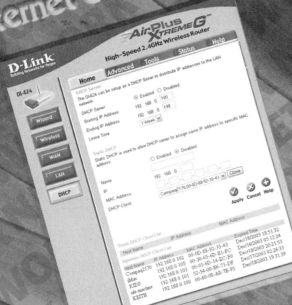

Using Wireless Networking

Using Network Diagnostic Tools

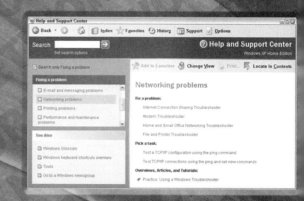

Networking with a Macintosh

CONFIGURING YOUR NETWORK

23.1

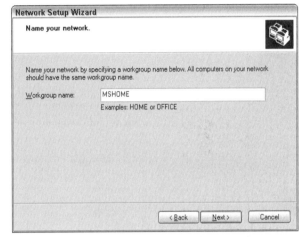

23.2

With each new release of Windows, Microsoft has improved the networking capabilities built into the operating system. Windows XP offers the most powerful set of networking features of any mass-market Windows version, allowing you to easily set up and manage a network of two or 20 computers.

Computers can be connected using one of two basic networking architectures:

- **Peer-to-peer network.** This is the simplest and most common method for home and small office networks. Computers on a peer-to-peer network talk directly to and share resources directly with other computers on the network, without having to go through a server. **Figure 23.1** shows computers on a typical small peer-to-peer network. The techniques in this book focus primarily on peer-to-peer networking.
- **Client-server network.** Larger corporate networks usually use this type of network. A server computer manages all network resources,

which can then be utilized by other computers — called *clients* — on the network. Windows XP Professional Edition can act as a network server, but if you need this type of network you should consider using a more advanced server operating system such as Microsoft Server 2003. Client-server networks usually require the specialized skills of a knowledgeable and experienced network administrator.

Before you can set up networking in Windows, you must have the right networking hardware. Each computer needs a network adapter, and you need a network hub to connect all of the computers together. When your network hardware is set up, you can configure network settings in Windows XP. This technique shows you how to set up a basic small network and get your computers talking to each other using Windows XP. Windows XP makes network configuration easier than ever, as shown in **Figure 23.2**.

STEP 1: SET UP YOUR NETWORK HARDWARE

To have a network, your computers must be able to connect to each other. First, each computer needs a *network interface card*, or NIC for short. Most modern computers have a network card already installed, but you should check the documentation for your computer to be sure. Several types of network adapters are available:

- **Ethernet.** This is the most common type of network adapter. If your computer has an Ethernet adapter, the connector on the back of the computer looks like a wide telephone connector. A network cable connects the Ethernet adapter to your network's hub.
- **Wireless.** Wireless network adapters are increasingly common, and they allow greater flexibility because you don't have to run network cables all over your home or office. Some newer laptops include built-in wireless network adapters. See

Technique 26, "Using Wireless Networking" later in this chapter for more on using wireless network adapters.
- **Phone line or electricity line.** Some network adapters allow you to set up a network using the phone or electricity lines in your home or office. Although this option eliminates the need to run special network cables, I recommend using wireless network adapters instead. Industry trends now favor wireless over obscure phone and electric line networking, meaning that wireless networks are more likely to be supported in future hardware and software configurations.
- **External adapters.** If your computer doesn't have a network adapter and you can't or won't install one, you can connect an external network adapter — Ethernet or wireless — to your computer's USB or IEEE-1394 port. External adapters tend to be more expensive, but they help you avoid performing surgery on your computer's internals.

In addition to network adapters, you also need a hub. The hub is the central device through which all of the networked computers connect. Several different kinds of hubs are available:

- **Hub.** The most basic hubs are simply called hubs. Hubs broadcast network traffic to all ports. Hubs are simple to use because they require no configuration, but they are also slower because of the way data is broadcast.
- **Switch.** A switch determines which port should receive data and transmits it only to that port. A switch offers improved speed and performance compared to a hub.
- **Router.** Like a switch, a router sends data to the appropriate port. Routers also allow different kinds of networks to connect to each other. For example, your DSL or cable modem can connect to the router and share the Internet connection directly to all computers on the network. This arrangement greatly increases the security of

your network, because incoming attacks from the Internet usually cannot get past the router. If you are buying new network hardware, I strongly recommend that you buy a router instead of a hub or switch.

■ **Wireless access point.** Often called a WAP for short, a wireless access point is a radio that allows wireless network adapters to connect to the Internet. WAPs are usually built-in to other network components such as a router. If you're buying a new router, spend a few extra dollars to get one that includes a WAP. This allows much greater expandability to your network in the future.

When you buy a hub, make sure it has enough ports to accommodate all of your computers. Multiple hubs can be connected to each other to infinitely expand your network, but a single hub with more ports is ultimately cheaper and easier to configure. And of course, if your hub includes a WAP, the number of ports is less important because an almost infinite number of wireless adapters can connect to the WAP.

After you purchase your networking gear, follow the manufacturer's instructions to install and connect the network hardware.

STEP 2: CONFIGURE THE INTERNET HOST COMPUTER

If you connect to the Internet using a modem connected directly to one of your computers — regardless

---

TIP

If you just want to network two computers together and each computer has an Ethernet adapter, you can connect them directly without using a hub. To do this, you must use a special *crossover* cable to connect the two Ethernet ports. Crossover cables are available at many computer and electronics stores.

---

of whether the modem is dial-up, DSL, or cable — that computer is your Internet host computer. This is the computer you should configure first. If your modem connects to your router instead of directly to a computer, it doesn't really matter which computer you configure first.

The Windows XP Network Setup Wizard walks you through the process of setting up your network. Run the Network Setup Wizard on your host computer first:

■ Log in as an administrator if you aren't already.
■ Choose **Start ➢ Control Panel** to open the Windows Control Panel. If your Control Panel uses Category view, open the Network and Internet Connections category.
■ Click the **Network Connections** icon.
■ In the list of Network Tasks on the left side of the screen, click **Set up a home or small office network**. The Network Setup Wizard begins. The exact screens that appear vary depending on your configuration. Eventually you get to a screen that resembles **Figure 23.3**. The default workgroup name is always **MSHOME**, as shown in the figure. Each computer on your network must have the same exact workgroup name. I recommend that you change this name to something other than

23.3

MSHOME. Exactly what you choose is not important; just make sure that you write it down. Also,
keep in mind that the workgroup name is case
sensitive. This means that **mynetwork** and
MYNETWORK are not the same.

■ Complete the wizard as directed on-screen. You
may be asked to create a network setup floppy
disk. This disk makes network setup easy on the
other computers on your network, but only if
those other computers actually have floppy drives.
Some newer computers — particularly laptops —
don't have floppy drives. A network setup disk can
come in handy, but it is not absolutely mandatory.

STEP 3: CONFIGURE ADDITIONAL COMPUTERS

The easiest way to set up the other computers on
your network is to use a network setup floppy disk.
The network setup floppy — if you created one —
automatically configures network settings on computers running Windows 98, Windows Me, and Windows
XP. To use the network setup floppy:

■ Place the floppy disk in the disk drive of a
computer on your network.

■ Open My Computer or Windows Explorer, and
then click the icon for the floppy disk drive.

■ Double-click the file **netsetup.exe**, as shown in
Figure 23.4.

■ Follow the instructions on-screen to complete
network setup.

23.4

If you have computers running other operating systems, or if you did not create a setup floppy, you need to configure network settings manually on each computer. On computers running Windows Me or Windows XP you can run the Network Setup Wizard. Make sure the workgroup name is the same name that you set on the first or host computer. To manually change the workgroup name for a computer, open the Windows Control Panel and follow these steps:

- In Windows XP, click the **System** icon and click the **Computer Name** tab to bring it to the front. Click **Change**. The Computer Name Changes dialog box appears as shown in **Figure 23.5**. Make sure that the Workgroup name is correct.
- In Windows 98 or Me, click the **Network** icon and click the **Identification** tab to bring it to the front. Make sure the Workgroup name is correct.

After your basic network is configured, you should be ready to start using the network. See other techniques in this chapter for more on sharing your Internet connection, sharing files and folders, and more.

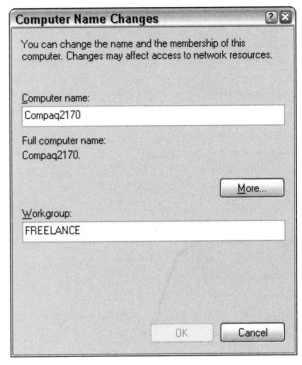

23.5

SHARING YOUR INTERNET CONNECTION

24.1

24.2

Since the Internet went mainstream in 1994 it has become one of the primary reasons that many people own a computer at all. Consider for a moment how much you use the Internet. If you're like many other modern PC users, you use the Internet to communicate, research, work, and shop. This means that one of the most important uses — if not *the* most important use — for your network is to share your Internet connection. When you share your Internet connection across the network, each computer on the network can access the Internet simultaneously, all while using a single connection to the online world.

How you share your Internet connection depends on the configuration of your network and modem. If you have a DSL or cable broadband modem that connects directly to your network router, the router manages sharing of the Internet connection, as shown in **Figure 24.1**. If your modem is installed in or connects directly to one computer on your network — the Internet host computer described in Technique 23, "Configuring Your Network" — Windows manages connection sharing using a feature called Internet Connection Sharing — or ICS for short — as shown in **Figure 24.2**. The following steps explain the technologies that make connection sharing possible, as well as show you how to share your connection using Windows ICS or a network router.

STEP 1: CONFIGURE THE ICS HOST

If you already have a network set up but Internet Connection Sharing wasn't enabled when you configured the network, you can set up ICS at any time. The

> **NOTE**
>
> Some Internet service providers — ISPs — charge additional fees for connections shared across your network. This service model is outdated, but it still exists and you should carefully review the service agreement with your provider to ensure you aren't subject to additional fees. Also, even ISPs that do allow shared Internet connections don't provide technical support for shared connections, so if you have trouble don't expect them to help.

computer that connects to the Internet is the ICS host computer, and all other computers on the network are ICS clients. I strongly recommend that the ICS host be a Windows XP computer because it is more secure and easier to configure than older versions of Windows.

Set up ICS on the host computer first:

■ Make sure that the Internet connection on the ICS host functions properly.
■ Choose **Start ➢ Control Panel** to open the Windows Control Panel. If your Control Panel uses Category view, open the **Network and Internet Connections** category.
■ Click the **Network Connections** icon. A list of network connections on your computer appears. Remember, your Internet connection is considered a network connection.
■ Right-click your Internet connection and choose **Properties** from the context menu that appears. If you connect to the Internet using a dial-up modem, the connection is listed under the **Dial-up** category. If you connect using a broadband DSL modem, the connection is listed under the **LAN or High-Speed Internet** category.

> **TIP**
>
> I recommend that you also check the option under Internet Connection Firewall to protect your Internet connection. See Technique 35, "Protecting Your Internet Connection with Firewalls" in Chapter 6 for more on using firewalls.

■ In the connection Properties dialog box, click the **Advanced** tab to bring it to the front.

■ Place a checkmark next to **Allow other network users to connect through this computer's Internet connection** as shown in **Figure 24.3**.

■ Click **OK** twice to close the dialog boxes.

STEP 2: SHARE A CONNECTION USING A ROUTER

If you have a DSL or cable broadband Internet connection, the best way to share your Internet connection is to connect the broadband modem directly to a router. Routers actually have built-in computers that control router functions. One function of the router's computer should be a Dynamic Host Configuration Protocol — DHCP for short — server, which performs roughly the same function as Windows ICS. I

explain DHCP servers in greater detail later in this technique.

Check your router's documentation for exact instructions on how to connect your broadband modem and share the Internet connection with the network. You should also consult the documentation from your ISP for any special instructions. Usually

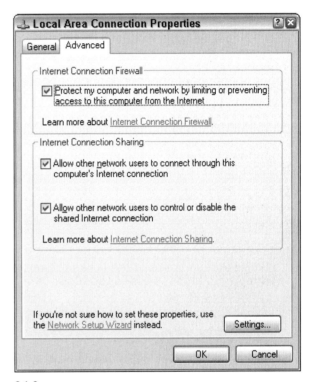

24.3

WARNING

Change the administrative password for your router as soon as possible. The default passwords for common routers are uniform and widely known, making it easy for hackers to compromise your network if you keep the default password.

you log on to the router using your Web browser. In **Figure 24.4** I have logged on to my D-Link router using Internet Explorer. The Internet Protocol — IP — address for the router is **192.168.0.1**, and the router's control panel is password-protected.

Make sure that the router's DHCP server is enabled, as shown in **Figure 24.4**. I recommend that you set the starting IP address at 100, as shown in the figure, and the ending address at 199. This allows your router to theoretically share your Internet connection with up to 100 different computers on your network.

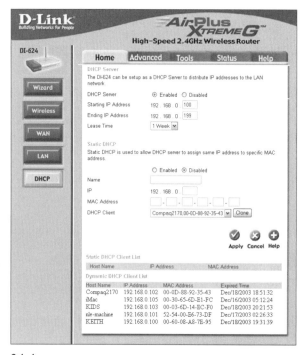

24.4

STEP 3: CONFIGURE CLIENT COMPUTERS

Each computer on your network has a numeric address called an *Internet Protocol* — or *IP* — address. A typical IP address for a computer on a small Windows network is **192.168.0.104**. The first three parts of that address — **192.168.0** — are always the same. The last number identifies an individual computer on the network. The host computer is always **192.168.0.1**.

Each computer that shares the Internet connection must have a unique IP address. The best way to ensure that each computer has a unique address is to assign addresses automatically using a Dynamic Host Configuration Protocol — DHCP — server. The DHCP server is actually a software program that runs on the Internet connection host computer. The DHCP server automatically assigns IP addresses to each computer on the network. When a new computer signs on to the network, it queries the DHCP server and obtains a unique IP address from the server. When properly configured, the DHCP server

> **NOTE**
>
> Remember, only follow these steps on client computers. You don't need to set up automatic IP addressing on the ICS host computer. Also, you don't need to follow these steps on any Windows computers on which you run an ICS setup disk.

runs transparently and automatically in the back-ground. Windows ICS serves as a DHCP server on your host computer. If your router handles connection sharing, a DHCP server runs on the router.

Just as the Internet connection host must run a DHCP server, each computer on the network must be set up to obtain an IP address automatically from the DHCP server. Virtually any modern operating system, including Linux and Macintosh, can obtain an IP address automatically from a DHCP server. Most of your computers are probably already set up to obtain IP addresses automatically, especially if you run a network configuration disk on them. But if your client computers cannot access the shared Internet connection, you should manually check to ensure that they are set up for automatic IP configuration. On a Windows computer, follow these steps:

■ Open the Windows Control Panel. On a Windows XP computer that uses Category view, open the **Network and Internet Connections** category.

■ Click the **Network Connections** icon.

■ Right-click the network connection that you use to connect to your local network and choose **Properties** from the context menu that appears. A Properties dialog box for the connection appears.

■ In the list of protocols, choose **Internet Protocol (TCP/IP)**, as shown in **Figure 24.5**, and click **Properties**. The Internet Protocol (TCP/IP) Properties dialog box appears.

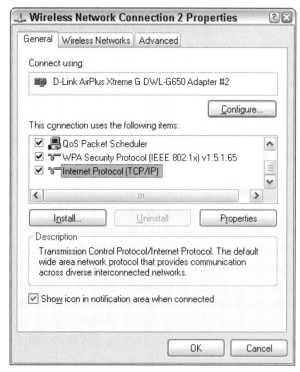

24.5

■ Choose **Obtain an IP address automatically**, as shown in **Figure 24.6**, and click **OK**. Click **OK** again to close the network connection Properties dialog box.

On a Macintosh computer you need to open the TCP/IP control panel and configure the operating system to automatically obtain an IP address from a DHCP server. This allows a Macintosh running system 8.5 or better to share your Internet connection whether you share it using a router or Windows ICS.

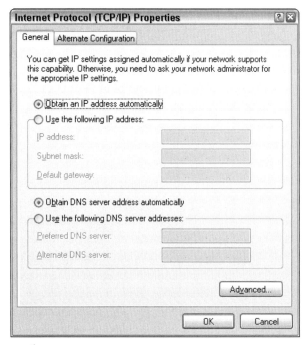

24.6

NETWORKING WITH A MACINTOSH

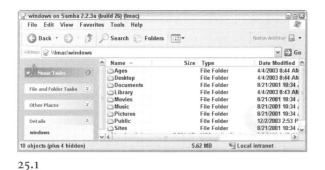

25.1

25.2

I t's no secret that Microsoft Windows remains the world's most popular operating system for personal computers. But Apple continues to sell excellent computers running the Macintosh operating system, and Macs are still preferred by many people.

If you have a Macintosh, there's no reason your Mac should feel like an orphan when you set up a network between your Windows PCs. Tools built-in to the latest Macintosh operating systems help your Mac connect to your Windows network and share resources just like any other PC. Virtually all modern Macs have built-in Ethernet cards, so all you need is a standard Ethernet cable to connect your Mac to your network hub or router. After just a few simple network configuration steps you can access your Mac from Windows, as shown in **Figure 25.1**, and you can access a Windows PC from your Mac, as shown in **Figure 25.2**.

Networking between PCs and Macs has been possible for many years using special networking software. But if your Mac runs OS 10.2 or better you can network with Windows XP without installing any special software.

The necessary tools are built right in to the Macintosh operating system beginning with version 10.2, also called Jaguar. The steps in this technique assume you have OS 10.2 or better. OS 10.1 and earlier versions of the Mac OS don't have Windows File Sharing, a necessary feature if you plan to share files through the graphical user interface. If you haven't upgraded to OS 10.2 or higher yet, I strongly recommend that you do so if your Mac supports it.

STEP 1: CREATE USER ACCOUNTS

Macintosh OS X — the nomenclature often used to refer to version 10 and higher of the Mac operating system — controls computer access using user accounts very similar to the user accounts in Windows XP. When you want to access a Mac from a Windows PC, you must log on to the Mac using a valid user name and password for an account on the Mac. Likewise, when you try to connect to a Windows PC from a Mac, you must log on to the PC using a valid Windows account and password.

On your Windows PC, simply create a user account as normal. On your Macintosh, log on to an account with administrative rights, create a new user account if you want, and then follow these steps:

- Choose **System Preferences** from the **Apple** menu to open the System Preferences window.
- Click the **Accounts** icon under **System**.

> **NOTE**
>
> Mac OS X is based on UNIX. Because of this, user account names and passwords are case sensitive. Make sure you enter names and passwords in the proper case when you try to log on to a Mac from Windows XP.

- Click an account to select it. Choose the account that you want to use when you log on to the Mac from a Windows PC.
- Click **Edit User**. The Edit User pane slides down from the Accounts window as shown in **Figure 25.3**.
- Place a checkmark next to **Allow user to log in from Windows** and click **OK**. You may be prompted to enter a new password for the account. In **Figure 25.3**, I'm using an account with the user name "Windows."
- Close the Accounts window.

STEP 2: START WINDOWS FILE SHARING

Version 10.2 or higher of the Macintosh operating system includes a feature called Windows File Sharing that allows you to easily share files with Windows PCs. To start Windows File Sharing:

- Open the System Preferences window if it isn't open already, and then click the **Sharing** icon.
- In the Sharing window, place checkmarks next to **Personal File Sharing**, **Windows File Sharing**, and **Remote Login** as shown in **Figure 25.4**.

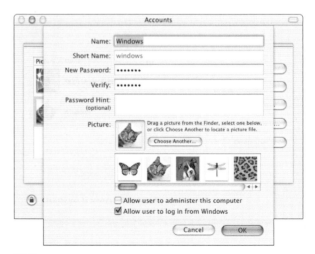

25.3

■ Change the **Computer Name** if you want. In **Figure 25.4** my computer is simply named *iMac*. This is the name that other computers on the network can see.

Make a note of the network address shown in the Sharing window. If the address starts with 192.168.0 but is not 192.168.0.1, close the Sharing window. Windows File Sharing is started and ready to use. But if the address does *not* start with 192.168.0, or if the address is 192.168.0.1, you need to configure your Macintosh to obtain an IP address from your network's DHCP server. As I describe in Technique 24, "Sharing Your Internet Connection," the DHCP server helps computers on your network share an Internet connection by assigning each computer on the network a unique IP address.

The computer that hosts the DHCP server always has the IP address 192.168.0.1. If you use Windows Internet Connection Sharing — ICS — the ICS host computer serves as a DHCP server. If you have a broadband modem connected to a router, the computer inside the router serves as the DHCP server. The Mac OS doesn't really care what kind of computer

acts as the DHCP server so long as you have your Mac configured to automatically obtain an IP address from the server. Follow these steps:

■ Click **Edit** next to the network address in the Sharing window. The Sharing window closes and the Network window appears.

■ Choose **Automatic** in the **Location** menu, and choose **Built-in Ethernet** in the **Show** menu.

■ Click the **TCP/IP** tab to bring it to the front.

■ Choose **Using DHCP** from the **Configure** menu, as shown in **Figure 25.5**. When you choose **Using DHCP**, the address for the router is automatically set to 192.168.0.1, and the subnet mask is set to 255.255.255.0. You can leave the rest of the fields blank unless the configuration instructions for your router advise different settings.

■ Click **Apply Now**, and then restart your computer. After the computer restarts, open **System Preferences**, click the **Network** icon, and review the IP Address listed on the **TCP/IP** tab. It should begin with 192.168.0. As you can see in **Figure 25.5**, my computer has been assigned the IP address 192.168.0.105.

25.4

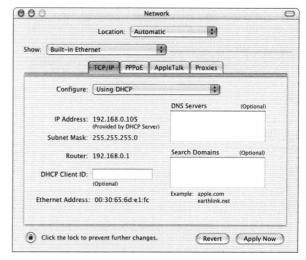

25.5

STEP 3: SET THE WORKGROUP NAME

Windows networks organize computers into workgroups. Your Macintosh will be much easier to access on the network if it has the same workgroup name as your Windows PCs. The default Windows workgroup name in the Macintosh OS is "WORKGROUP," which probably is not the correct workgroup name for your network. To change the Mac's workgroup name:

■ Open the hard drive containing your system software, and then open the **Applications** folder.
■ In the **Applications** folder, open the **Utilities** subfolder and double-click the **Directory Access** utility to open it.
■ Click the lock icon at the bottom of the Directory Access utility to unlock it. Enter an administrator password when you are prompted to do so.
■ Click **SMB** on the **Services** tab to select it, and then click **Configure**.
■ Open the **Workgroup** menu. If you see the name of your Windows workgroup listed, choose it. Otherwise, type the correct workgroup name in the **Workgroup** field. In **Figure 25.6**, I've entered the workgroup name "FREELANCE" because that is the workgroup name used by my Windows computers.
■ Click **OK** to set the workgroup name, and then click **Apply** in the Directory Access utility to apply your changes. Close the Directory Access utility when you're done.

STEP 4: CONNECT TO YOUR MAC FROM WINDOWS

When your Mac is properly configured, accessing it from Windows XP is pretty easy. When you open **My Network Places**, available Macs have the name

"Samba" at the beginning of the computer name. In **Figure 25.7**, my Mac is listed second from the top. Double-click the Mac to access it. When you first access the computer, a logon screen appears as shown in **Figure 25.8**. Enter the user name and password for

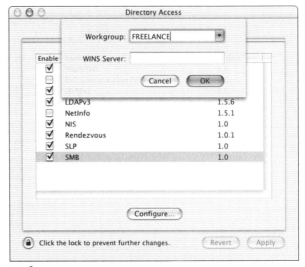

25.6

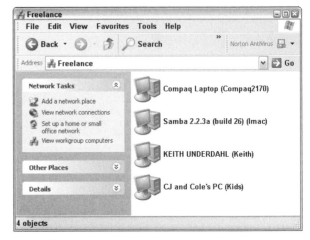

25.7

your account on the Mac. Remember, you must enable Windows access for this account on the Mac, as described in step 1. When you are logged on, you can access resources available to your user account on the Mac. In **Figure 25.9**, I'm browsing folders on my Mac from Windows.

25.8

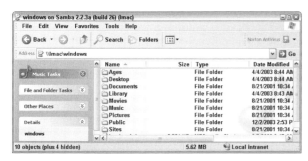

25.9

STEP 5: CONNECT TO WINDOWS FROM YOUR MAC

To connect to a Windows PC from your Mac, follow these steps:

- Choose **Go ➣ Connect to Server**. The Connect to Server dialog box appears.
- If you see the workgroup name for your Windows network, double-click it to open it. You should see a list of computers currently available on your network, as shown in **Figure 25.10**.

25.10

■ Click the name of the computer to which you want to connect, and click **Connect**. The SMB/CIFS Filesystem Authentication dialog box appears.

■ Type the user name and password for your account on the computer to which you are trying to connect, as shown in **Figure 25.11**, and click **OK**. An SMB Mount dialog box appears.

■ Choose a volume that you want to mount. Items in the list of things you can mount include your **My Documents** folder, the **SharedDocs** folder, and other shared items from the Windows computer to which you are connecting.

■ Click **OK**. The selected item mounts on your computer as if it were a disk drive or volume. Simply double-click the volume to access it. In **Figure 25.12**, I'm accessing the **My Documents** folder on one of my Windows PCs from my Mac.

25.11

25.12

USING WIRELESS NETWORKING

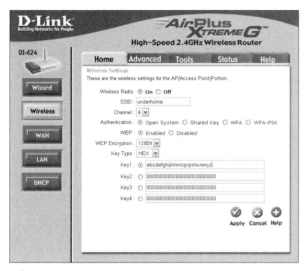

26.1

26.2

When I bought my first network hub a few years ago it was a simple little hub with five Ethernet ports, and at the time I couldn't imagine ever needing more than five ports. Times change, of course, and networks grow. Before I knew it I had more computers than ports. Also, the physical location of computers in my home was dictated by where I was willing and able to route an Ethernet cable. I was ready for a better solution.

Wireless networking is that better solution. Wireless networking gear is now affordable and widely available, making it a truly viable alternative to Ethernet networking gear. Wireless networking offers two main advantages:

■ You aren't limited by the number of ports on the network hub.
■ You don't have to climb up in the attic or go through other extraordinary means to route network cables all over your home or office.

If you plan to buy new networking gear in the near future, go wireless. Modern networking gear is powerful and easy to use with Windows XP. This technique helps you choose and configure wireless networking gear, including wireless access points as shown in **Figure 26.1** and wireless network cards as shown in **Figure 26.2**.

STEP 1: CHOOSE WIRELESS GEAR

The first piece of gear you need is a wireless access point, or WAP. WAPs usually have built-in routers or hubs. I recommend that you purchase a router that includes both a wireless access point and traditional Ethernet ports. You also need a wireless network adapter for each computer that you want to network wirelessly. Some laptops have wireless adapters built-in, but you can also purchase wireless adapters separately. For a laptop, use a wireless network adapter that fits in your computer's card bus or PCMCIA slot. For a desktop computer, you can purchase wireless network cards that install in a PCI slot.

Several different wireless standards are currently on the market. The most common wireless standards are:

■ **802.11b.** This standard — sometimes called *WiFi* — has been around for a couple of years and offers a maximum data rate of 11 Mbps. 802.11b gear is widely available but is quickly being superceded by 802.11g.

■ **802.11g.** This is basically a faster version of 802.11b, and is also sometimes called WiFi. Most 802.11g gear claims a maximum data rate of 54 Mbps, but even higher speeds are possible. 802.11b network adapters can be used with 802.11g access points. 802.11g gear is slightly more expensive, but the higher speeds justify the expense. I recommend using 802.11g gear.

■ **Bluetooth.** This was designed primarily for networking with PDAs, cell phones, and other personal electronic gear. The maximum data rate is only 2 Mbps, so this technology is not really suitable for primary networking between PCs.

If you're buying new wireless gear, 802.11g is the standard to choose. It offers the greatest performance, reasonable cost, and the brightest prospects for hardware support in the foreseeable future. I recommend an 802.11g access point that is part of a router that also includes firewall and several Ethernet ports.

STEP 2: INSTALL THE HARDWARE

You should follow the manufacturer's instructions to install your wireless networking hardware. However, there are some general installation guidelines that you should follow:

■ Make sure your Internet connection is configured and works properly before setting up your new wireless network. The network will be much easier to configure if you aren't trying to configure a new broadband modem or other Internet connection at the same time.

■ If you have a wireless access point/router, connect at least one computer to an Ethernet port and use that computer to configure the router and wireless settings.

■ Check the manufacturer's Web site for updates after installation is complete. Hardware manufacturers often provide free, downloadable updates for existing hardware. For example, shortly after I purchased my D-Link DI-624 WAP/router, I downloaded an update that increased the maximum speed of the wireless network from 54 Mbps to 102 Mbps. If you have a WAP/router, the administrative control panel may be able to access the manufacturer's Web site directly to check for updates, as shown in **Figure 26.3**. As you can see in the figure, my firmware — the router's built-in software — is current as of October 13, 2003.

STEP 3: CONFIGURE WIRELESS SETTINGS

When you set up your wireless network, one of the things you must do is specify a service set identifier, or SSID. The SSID can be thought of as a name for your wireless network, similar to the workgroup name on a Windows network. The SSID on your access point and all wireless clients must be the same. Wireless access points always come with a default SSID, and you should change it to your own SSID immediately. The SSID can be up to 32 characters. In **Figure 26.4**, I've set the SSID on my WAP/router to

underhome. Although your SSID should be unique, it's important to keep in mind that an SSID by itself doesn't provide any real security to your wireless network.

Wireless clients on your network must share the same SSID as the WAP. Wireless network adapters usually install a utility program similar to the one shown in **Figure 26.5**, a configuration utility for the D-Link DWL-G650 wireless adapter card on my laptop. I access this utility by double-clicking the wireless utility icon in the Windows system tray, in the lower-right corner of the screen. As you can see in **Figure 26.5**, the wireless adapter has the same SSID as the access point in **Figure 26.4**.

STEP 4: ENCRYPT YOUR NETWORK

Wireless networking can make your life easier because you can access your network from any location that is within broadcast range of the radio waves sent by your wireless access point. Unfortunately, you cannot control where the radio waves go, which means that *anyone* within broadcast range can theoretically access your network. For most wireless gear, that broadcast range is usually 100 to 150 feet depending

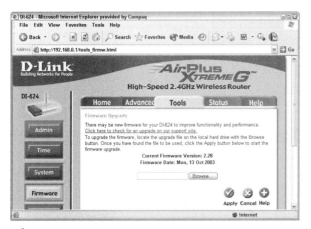

26.3

26.4

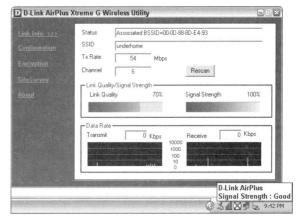

26.5

on major signal obstructions like steel, cement, or brick walls. Consider for a moment what lies within a 150-foot radius of your WAP. That range may encompass neighbors, other businesses, or even the street or parking lot out front. Anyone who is in broadcast range and has the right equipment — a laptop and a wireless network card — can intercept data traveling over your network. They can also use your wireless network to access the Internet for free. This can get you in trouble with your ISP and increase your Internet service fees, and if the unauthorized user downloads illegal content using your Internet connection, you could even be criminally liable.

Protecting your data from wireless breach is critical, especially if you live or work in close quarters with others. Wireless networks can use encryption to protect your data from unauthorized use. Several different types of encryption are used in modern wireless gear:

■ **WEP — Wired Equivalent Privacy.** This protocol relies on a 26-character, 128-bit key to secure your wireless network. Each computer must have the same 26-character key. In **Figure 26.6** I've enabled WEP and entered a key in the **Key1** field that is the alphabet. The WAP and each wireless network adapter must have the same key. Unfortunately, anyone within broadcast range of your access point can *sniff* your key using hacker programs that can be easily downloaded from the Internet. Because of this, WEP is an encryption scheme that only keeps honest people honest. Anyone within range who really wants to get on your network can easily defeat WEP with minimal computer skills.

■ **WPA — WiFi Protected Access.** Also called 802.11i, this encryption protocol is superior to

WEP because the key is more carefully encrypted in broadcast traffic, and WPA authenticates users so that only authorized users can access the network.

■ **WPA-PSK — WPA-PreShared Key.** This uses the same encryption method of WPA, but authentication is made using a simple password. WPA-PSK offers good security and is easy to configure, making it ideally suited to home and small-business networks.

When purchasing wireless gear, choose components that support WPA encryption. If you have existing wireless gear that only supports WEP encryption, check the manufacturer's Web site for updates. Some companies offer firmware upgrades that add WPA encryptions. Follow the manufacturer's instructions to configure encryption on your network.

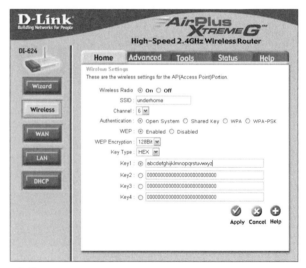

26.6

SHARING FILES

27.1

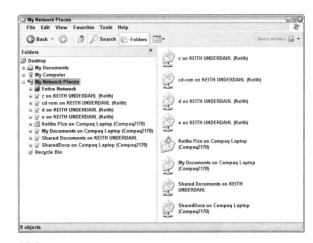

27.2

File sharing is a primary purpose for most networks, especially in a business environment. Windows XP helps you control which files you share over your network and which files you keep private.

For decades the most common type of network was a sneakernet. That's computer geek lingo for the practice of sharing files between computers by copying them onto floppy disks and walking the disk to another computer in a different room. Needless to say, sneakernetting is inefficient, slow, and inconvenient.

A properly configured network makes file sharing a lot easier, and Windows XP includes tools that give you complete control over file sharing. You use folders to control which files are shared, as shown in **Figure 27.1**, and you can browse shared folders on other network computers using Windows Explorer, as shown in **Figure 27.2**. This technique shows you how to quickly and easily share files over a Windows network.

STEP 1: SHARE A FOLDER

If you have some files you want to share on your network, Windows XP makes sharing them easy. You can share any folder on your hard drive on the network, even if the folder is in your personal **My Documents** folder. To share a folder:

- Open My Documents or Windows Explorer, and browse to the folder that you want to share on your network.
- Right-click the folder, and choose **Sharing and Security** from the context menu that appears, as shown in **Figure 27.3**. A Properties dialog box for the folder appears with the **Sharing** tab in front. In **Figure 27.3**, I'm sharing the **My Pictures** folder in my **My Documents** folder so that other network users can access my pictures. Only the **My Pictures** folder is shared. Other **My Documents** items aren't shared.
- Place a checkmark next to **Share this folder on the network**, as shown in **Figure 27.4**.
- Type a name for the folder in the **Share name** field. This is the folder name that other network users see. In some cases you may find it necessary to provide a more descriptive name. In my example, simply sharing the folder as My Pictures isn't very useful because *My* could refer to anyone who uses this computer. In **Figure 27.4** you can see that I've given the Share name Keiths Pics.
- If you want to allow others to edit or delete files in your shared folder, place a checkmark next to **Allow network users to change my files**. If you

leave this option unchecked, other users can only view or copy your files.
- Click **OK** to close the Properties dialog box.

STEP 2: USE THE SHARED DOCUMENTS FOLDER

Another quick way to share items with other network users is to place them in the **Shared Documents** folder on your computer. By default, the **Shared Documents** folder is shared with other network users. If you don't want the **Shared Documents** folder on your computer to be shared over your network, follow these steps:

- Right-click the **Shared Documents** folder, and choose **Sharing and Security**. The **Shared Documents** folder is located in **C:\Documents and Settings\All Users\Shared Documents**.

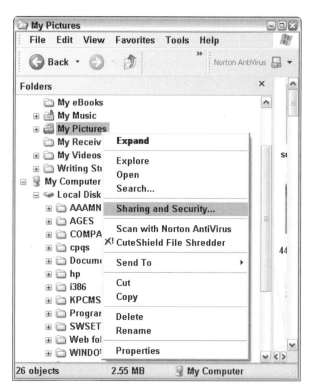

27.3

> **NOTE**
>
> If your network includes Windows 95, 98, or Me computers, the folder name must be 12 characters or less. You should also avoid punctuation or other special characters.

- Remove the checkmark next to **Share this folder on the network**. This option is checked by default for the **Shared Documents** folder.
- Click **OK** to close the dialog box and apply your changes.

STEP 3: SHARE A DRIVE

You can share disk drives on your network just as you share folders. I strongly recommend that you not share your whole hard drive on the network because that gives free access to your whole computer to anyone with network access. In the worst case, hackers could access your computer over the Internet and disrupt important system files or steal data and personal

information. Even if hackers seem like a remote danger, free access also means that other authorized network users could accidentally delete important files. However, you may want to share other kinds of drives. For example, if your computer has a DVD-ROM or floppy drive, you may want to share that drive on the network so that other computers that don't have floppy or DVD drives can access the drives.

To share a drive, right-click the drive in My Computer, and choose **Sharing and Security**. The **Sharing** tab of the drive Properties dialog box appears as shown in **Figure 27.5**. Click the warning to reveal sharing settings. Place a checkmark next to **Share this folder on the network**, and click **OK**.

27.4

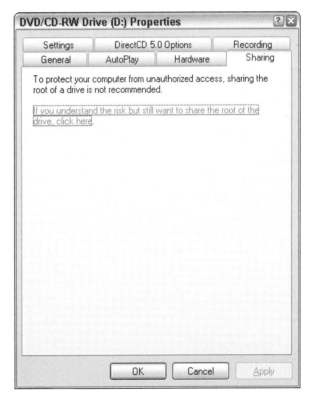

27.5

STEP 4: ACCESS NETWORK FOLDERS AND DRIVES

You can easily access shared folders on other computers using Windows Explorer or My Network Places. Choose **Start ➤ My Network Places** to see a list of shared resources on the various computers on your network as shown in **Figure 27.6**. Any currently available resources can be accessed just like any other folder on your computer.

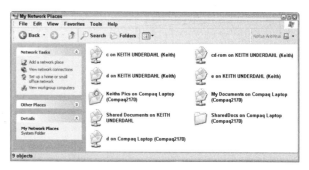

27.6

SHARING PRINTERS

28.1

28.2

Networks allow you to share various resources, including printers. If a printer that is attached to one computer is shared, any computer on the network can print on that printer.

Previous techniques in this chapter show you how to share files or an Internet connection over a network. You can also share other resources, including printers and scanners. This comes in handy especially with printers, because you may not feel like buying — or you cannot afford to buy — a separate printer for each computer in your home or office. When a printer is shared, anyone on the network can print to it.

This technique shows you how to share a printer on your computer, as shown in **Figure 28.1**, and I show you how to access a shared printer on another network computer, as shown in **Figure 28.2**.

STEP 1: INSTALL A PRINTER

Before you can share a printer it must be installed and working properly on your computer. If you have a USB printer, Windows probably detects the printer when you first connect it, as shown in **Figure 28.3**. Windows XP may be able to install the printer automatically, but for best results you should follow the manufacturer's recommended installation procedure.

When the printer is successfully installed, a printer icon appears in the Windows system tray, which is the area in the lower-right corner of the screen next to the clock. Make sure that you print a document or a test page of some type to ensure that the printer is working properly.

STEP 2: SHARE A PRINTER

After your printer is installed and working properly, you can share it with other network users. Follow these steps:

- Choose **Start ➢ Printers and Faxes** to open the Printers and Faxes window. This window includes a list of all printers and faxes available on your system, including network printers that have been previously shared.
- Right-click the name of the printer you want to share, and choose **Sharing** from the context menu that appears. A Properties dialog box for the printer appears with the **Sharing** tab in front.
- Choose **Share this printer**, as shown in **Figure 28.4**.
- Enter a **Share name** for the printer. This is the name that other network users see, so make the name descriptive. In **Figure 28.4**, I've named my printer **laptop-HP** because it's a Hewlett-Packard printer connected to my laptop. The **Share name** should be 12 characters or less to ensure compatibility with other operating systems.

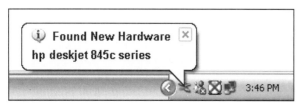

28.3

- If any of your network computers run an operating system other than Windows XP, click **Additional Drivers**. The Additional Drivers dialog box appears, as shown in **Figure 28.5**.
- Place a checkmark next to each operating system that is present on your network, place your Windows XP CD in the CD-ROM drive, and click **OK** to close the Additional Drivers dialog box. Windows begins to install drivers from the Windows XP CD-ROM.
- Click **Close** to close the Properties dialog box for your printer. Your printer can now be shared, as indicated by the open hand on the printer's icon in the Printers and Faxes window.

STEP 3: USE A SHARED PRINTER

Before you can print to a shared printer that is installed on a different network computer, you must add that network printer to your computer's list of

28.4

available printers. To add a printer, make sure the computer with the printer is running and connected to the network, and then follow these steps:

- Choose **Start ➤ Printers and Faxes** to open the Printers and Faxes window.
- On the left side of the Printers and Faxes window, click **Add a printer** under **Printer Tasks**. The Add Printer Wizard begins.
- Click **Next** in the first wizard screen.
- Choose **A network printer, or a printer attached to another computer** in the second wizard screen, and click **Next**.
- Choose **Browse for a printer**, and click **Next**. A list of network computers and shared printers appears.
- Choose the network printer that you want to add. In **Figure 28.6**, I'm choosing an HP Deskjet printer on the Compaq 2170 computer. Click **Next** to proceed, and click **Yes** in the warning message that appears. Windows automatically acquires the necessary printer drivers from the computer on which the printer is installed.

- Choose whether you want to make the printer your default printer, and click **Next**. Click **Finish** to complete the wizard.

The new network printer can be used just like any other printer installed on your computer. When you print a document, choose the network printer in the **Printer Name** menu of the program's Print dialog box, as shown in **Figure 28.7**.

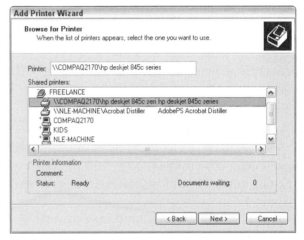

28.6

28.5

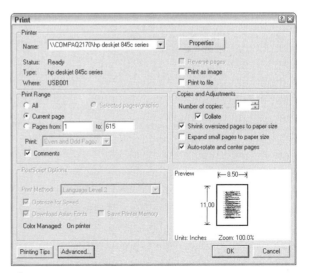

28.7

RUNNING YOUR OWN WEB SITE

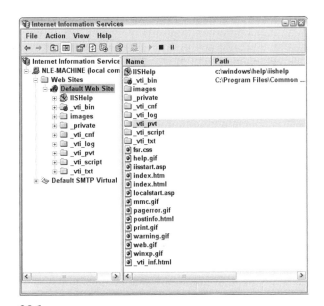

29.1

29.2

Just as the Internet can be thought of as a giant network, you can look at your private network as a miniature version of the Internet. If you have Windows XP Professional Edition you can even host your own Web sites on your network, which can then be accessed by anyone on your network using a Web browser, as shown in **Figure 29.2**. Windows XP Professional includes a tool called Internet Information Services — or IIS for short — that allows you to set up a Web server on your XP-Pro computer. You may find this especially useful on a small-business network, where you want all employees to be able to access documentation or other daily-use files without having to set up folder-access permissions or other complex network rules. If you're a Web developer, IIS — the IIS control panel is shown in **Figure 29.1** — can also help you test more-advanced features of your Web site before going live.

Internet Information Services does have some limitations. As I said, IIS is only available with the Professional Edition of Windows XP. IIS allows only ten clients to access your site at a time, and it is not suitable for hosting a Web site on the Internet. If you plan to do online Web hosting, you should use a Server version of Windows. But if all you want to do is run a Web site on your local network, IIS is the perfect tool for the job. This technique shows you how to install and begin using IIS on your network.

STEP 1: INSTALL INTERNET INFORMATION SERVICES

Internet Information Services is the feature of Windows XP Professional that allows you to host Web pages and other online features. To install IIS, follow these steps:

- Place your Windows XP Professional installation disc in the CD-ROM drive. If Windows XP setup starts automatically, click **Exit**.
- Open the Windows Control Panel, and then click the **Add/Remove Programs** icon. The Add/Remove Programs window appears.
- Click **Add/Remove Windows Components** on the left side of the Add/Remove Programs window. Windows XP Setup begins, and the Windows Components Wizard appears.
- Place a checkmark next to **Internet Information Services** as shown in **Figure 29.3**.
- Click **Next**. Windows installs IIS. Click **Finish** when the wizard is complete.

STEP 2: CREATE WEB CONTENT

After IIS is installed you can add some content to your Web site. The default location for Web content is **C:\Inetpub\wwwroot**. Anything stored in that folder will be available on your Web site. Use Windows Explorer or My Computer to open that folder now. Notice that it already includes some files, as well as a subfolder called **images**. Copy image files that you want to share on your site into this **images** folder.

Now you are ready to create a home page for your Web site. Use your favorite Web page creation tool such as Dreamweaver, FrontPage, or a text editor to create a home page. If you've never created a Web page before, open Notepad and type the following lines of HTML:

```
<HTML>
<HEAD>
<TITLE>My Home Page</TITLE>
</HEAD>
<BODY>
<CENTER>
<IMG SRC="images/PIC0010.jpg">
<H1>My Home Page</H1>
<P>Welcome! <A HREF="images/">Click
    here to browse the "images"
    folder.</A></P>
</CENTER>
</BODY>
</HTML>
```

In the markup, replace the filename **PIC0010.jpg** with the filename of one of your own image files. When you're done typing, choose **File ≻ Save**. In the Save As dialog box, browse to the folder **C:\Inetpub\ wwwroot**, name the file **index.htm**, and click **Save**.

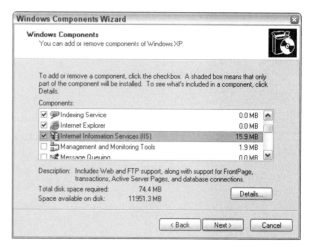

29.3

Now use Windows Explorer or My Computer to open the **C:\Inetpub\wwwroot** folder again, and double-click the **index.htm** file to open it. The file opens and looks something like **Figure 29.4**, but with your own image file in place of the one shown here. If you see a red **X** instead of the correct image, make sure you typed the filename correctly and that the image file is located in **C:\Inetpub\wwwroot\images**.

Create additional Web pages as your time allows and needs warrant. You can create additional sub-folders in the **C:\Inetpub\wwwroot** folder if needed. If your Web site includes many files and folders it's a good idea to use subfolders to keep things organized.

NOTE

Images should use the JPEG, GIF, or PNG format if you plan to use them on your Web site.

29.4

STEP 3: ADJUST SITE PROPERTIES

Internet Information Services gives you a great deal of control over your personal Web site. I don't have room here to cover every property and settings change that you can make in IIS, but there are a couple of changes that I find useful:

- Choose **Start ➤ All Programs ➤ Administrative Tools ➤ Internet Information Services**. The IIS control panel opens as shown in **Figure 29.5**.
- On the left side of the IIS control panel, click the plus sign next to the local machine, click the plus

TIP

Although Windows XP and IIS are not case-sensitive, you should get in the habit of typing file-names in HTML in the same case that is used in the actual filenames. If you upload your Web pages to a Web server that runs Linux or another case-sensitive operating system, links that use improper case may not work.

29.5

sign next to **Web Sites**, and then click **Default Web Site** to view its contents on the right.

■ Right-click **Default Web Site**, and choose **Properties** from the context menu that appears. The Default Web Site Properties dialog box appears.

■ Click the **Documents** tab to bring it to the front. This tab lists filenames for default documents on your site. If a user opens a directory on your site but does not specify a filename, the default document appears if one is present. If you like to use a filename for your home page that doesn't appear in the list, click **Add** and type the filename you want to add. Use the arrow keys next to the filename list to move your preferred default filename to the top of the list. In **Figure 29.6**, I've added **index.html** and moved it to the top of the list.

■ Click **OK** to close the Default Web Site Properties dialog box.

Another change you may want to make is to allow directory browsing. One of the best reasons to host a Web site on your network is to share files. If you store files in subfolders of your Web site folder, other network users can access those files, but by default they can't browse the list of files in a given folder. This means that users must know the exact location and filename for a file they want to access, or you have to create a Web page with a link to each file. To simplify file access, follow these steps:

TIP

When IIS is first installed, **index.htm** is included in the list of default filenames, but not **index. html**. I strongly recommend that you add **index. html** to your own list of default filenames because it is such a common filename for home pages.

■ In the IIS control panel, right-click the folder that you want to allow other users to browse and choose **Properties** from the context menu. A Properties dialog box for the folder appears.

■ On the **Directory** tab, place a checkmark next to **Directory browsing**.

■ Click **OK** to close the Properties dialog box.

With directory browsing enabled, network users can easily access all of the files in the folder. If a user types the address for the folder but does not provide a filename, a list of files in that directory appears, as shown in **Figure 29.7**. The list isn't beautiful, but it does allow easy access to all of the files in a given folder. In **Figure 29.7**, I've shared my **images** folder so that anyone on the network can browse my list of image files.

29.6

STEP 4: VISIT THE SITE

You can access an IIS Web site using a Web browser program on any computer on the network. To access the site from another computer, simply type **http://** followed by the name of the computer hosting the IIS site. To visit a specific page on the side, add a / and then the filename of that page you want to visit. A computer running Windows should be able to access the site using the computer's name on the network. In **Figure 29.8**, for example, I've accessed the default Web page on the computer named **nle-machine**. In **Figure 29.7**, I am browsing the subfolder **/images/** on that same computer.

In some cases you may need to use the computer's IP address instead of its name. For example, in **Figure 29.9** I'm accessing the same page shown in **Figure 29.8**, but this time I'm accessing it from a Macintosh running an operating system version that is not compatible with Windows XP computer naming. Thus, I access the site by typing the host computer's IP address, which in this case is **192.168.0.101**. Technique 24, "Sharing Your Internet Connection," shows you how to determine the IP address of a computer on your network.

29.8

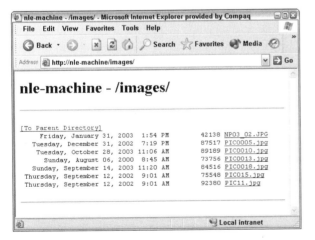

29.7

29.9

TECHNIQUE **30**

DIAGNOSING NETWORK PROBLEMS

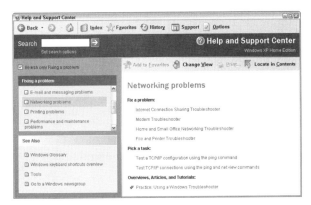

30.1

30.2

ABOUT THE FEATURE

If your network isn't working exactly as it should, there are many tools at your disposal to help you troubleshoot and solve the problem.

Networking has become much easier in recent years, and Windows XP makes setting up and using a network as simple as ever. Setting up a Windows XP network is basically automatic: All you do is run some basic network setup wizards, and your network should be up and running.

Of course, just because network configuration *should* be easy doesn't mean it always *is* easy. One or more computers may not be able to access the network. Your shared Internet connection may not work. Whatever the problem, various tools can help you diagnose and repair your network problems. These tools include graphical programs like Windows troubleshooters as shown in **Figure 30.1**, as well as powerful command line tools as shown in **Figure 30.2**.

157

STEP 1: CHECK THE BASICS

If you're experiencing network problems, you should start with the basics. It sounds simplistic, but even the most experienced user can overlook a basic problem. The first things to check include:

- **Workgroup name.** Does each computer have the same workgroup name, as shown in **Figure 30.3**? Click the **System** icon in the Windows Control Panel, and click the **Computer Name** tab. Is the workgroup name correct? In **Figure 30.3** the workgroup name is "FREELANCE." Each computer on your network should have the same workgroup name. Click **Change** to change the workgroup name.
- **Hardware.** Are all network adapters installed and cables connected properly? Is the hub or router plugged in and powered on? Click the **System** icon in the Windows Control Panel, click the **Hardware** tab, and click **Device Manager**. If you see a red X on the network adapter, or if your actual adapter isn't listed under **Network adapters**, then the network adapter may not be installed or working properly.

> **NOTE**
>
> Remember, workgroup names are case-sensitive. This means that the workgroup names "FREELANCE" and "freelance" are not compatible.

- **Cables.** Obviously the first thing to check is that cables are properly connected between your Ethernet adapter and your hub or router. Also, do you have the right kind of cable? If you have a crossover cable — a special kind of Ethernet cable designed to connect two computers directly to each other without a hub — that cable will not work between an Ethernet adapter and a hub. You must use standard Ethernet cables between adapters and hubs or routers. Fortunately, crossover

30.3

cables are unusual. To check for a crossover cable, or to simply check for a defective cable, swap the suspect cable with one from another network computer that you know works correctly. If you have a router, the router's built-in software may have diagnostic tools like the one shown in **Figure 30.4** to help test cables to make sure they are the correct type and are working properly. Check the router's documentation for more information.

■ **Firewall.** If you have a firewall program running, disable it. Does the network function correctly after disabling the firewall? If so, consult the documentation for more on making your network

compatible with the firewall. When you perform further troubleshooting, make sure that any firewall — including the Windows ICS Firewall — is disabled. See Technique 35, "Protecting Your Internet Connection with Firewalls," for more about firewalls.

■ **Shared resources.** Are resources on network computers shared? Even though a computer is connected to the network and the network is working properly, you can't access hard drives, printers, or other resources if they are not shared. See Technique 24, "Sharing Your Internet Connection"; Technique 27, "Sharing Files"; and Technique 28, "Sharing Printers," for more on sharing resources with the network.

STEP 2: RUN A WINDOWS NETWORK TROUBLESHOOTER

Windows XP includes troubleshooters that are designed to help you diagnose common network problems. In my experience, the built-in Windows troubleshooters rarely do more than walk you through the basics described in the previous step, but they may still prove valuable in some situations. To use a Windows troubleshooter, choose **Start ➤ Help and Support** to open the Help and Support Center. Click the **Fixing a Problem** help topic, and then click

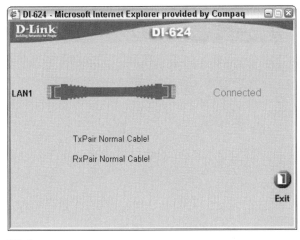

30.4

Networking Problems in the list that appears on the left. A list of troubleshooters appears on the right, as shown in **Figure 30.5**. Your Help and Support Center may look different if it was customized by your computer's manufacturer. Click the name of a troubleshooter to run it, and follow the instructions on-screen to troubleshoot your problem.

STEP 3: PING NETWORK COMPUTERS

Windows XP includes more advanced tools to help you collect information about your system, information that may prove useful as you try to identify a problem. One of these advanced tools is the **ping** command, which you can run from the command line or MS-DOS prompt of any Windows-based computer. The **ping** command sends a signal across a network connection, allowing you to perform a basic check on a network connection even if you can't seem to access the network using the Windows graphical interface.

Ping sends signals using IP addresses. I explain IP addresses in Technique 24, "Sharing Your Internet Connection." Each computer on your network should have a unique IP address. To determine the IP address of a computer, follow these steps:

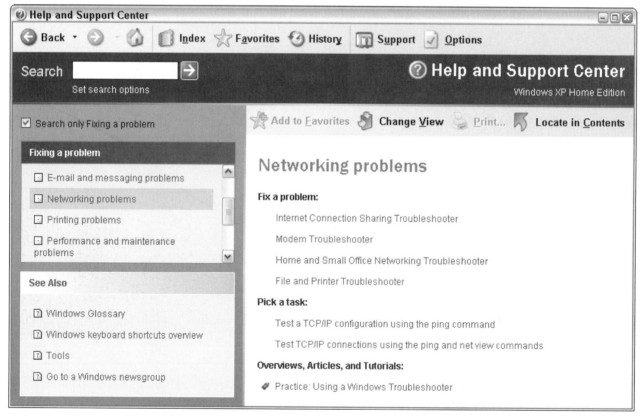

30.5

- In Windows XP, choose **Start** ➤ **All Programs** ➤ **Accessories** ➤ **Command Prompt**. In other versions of Windows, such as Windows 98 or Windows Me, open the **MS-DOS Prompt** from the **Accessories** menu instead of **Command Prompt**.
- At the command prompt, type **ipconfig** and press **Enter**. IP configuration information about the computer is listed, as shown in **Figure 30.6**. Make a note of the IP address of each computer on your network.

Each IP address should be unique. If any computers have the same IP address, make sure that Internet sharing client computers are set up to obtain an IP address automatically, as described in Technique 24. Also, keep in mind that the IP address for a specific computer may change if you restart that computer. Make a note of the IP address for each computer and keep all of them running while you perform the **ping** test.

To ping another computer on your network, open the command prompt and type **ping 192.168.0.103** where **192.168.0.103** is the IP address of the computer you want to ping. If you see successful ping replies, as shown in **Figure 30.7**, then the computers can communicate with each other over the network. If the ping is not successful, the network connection is not

functioning, probably due to a hardware problem. If the ping is unsuccessful, type **ping 127.0.0.1**, and press **Enter**. If you are unable to successfully ping **127.0.0.1**, a loopback address on the current computer, then the network protocol software — usually the TCP/IP protocol — is not properly installed on this computer. Run the Network Setup Wizard again on this computer to reinstall network protocol software.

STEP 4: USE THE NET VIEW COMMAND

The **net view** command allows you to survey shared network resources from the command prompt. Open the command prompt, type **net view**, and press **Enter**. A list of computers that are currently on and available

> **TIP**
>
> If you have a software firewall running on one of your Windows computers, make sure it's disabled before using the **ipconfig**, **ping**, or **net view** commands.

30.6

30.7

on your network appears as shown in **Figure 30.8**. Computers that don't appear in the list are not currently available on the current network connection. This may be because a computer is not running, or it is not configured properly for networking.

To view shared resources on a specific computer, type **net view** followed by a space, two backslashes, and the

name of the computer shown when you first ran **net view**. For example, in **Figure 30.9** I typed **net view \\KEITH** to display a list of shared resources on the computer named **KEITH**. Resources that don't appear in the list aren't shared or are not currently available.

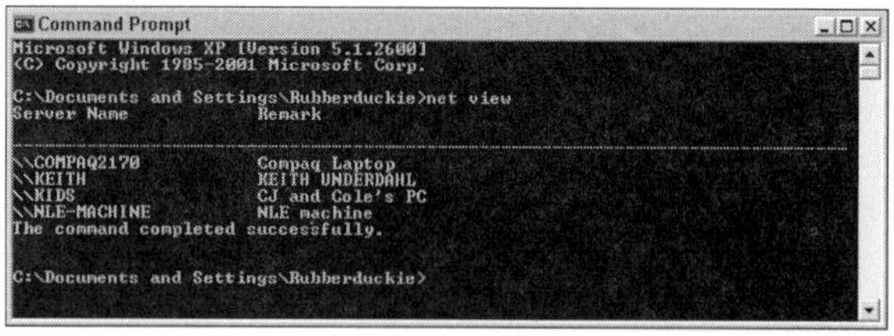

30.8

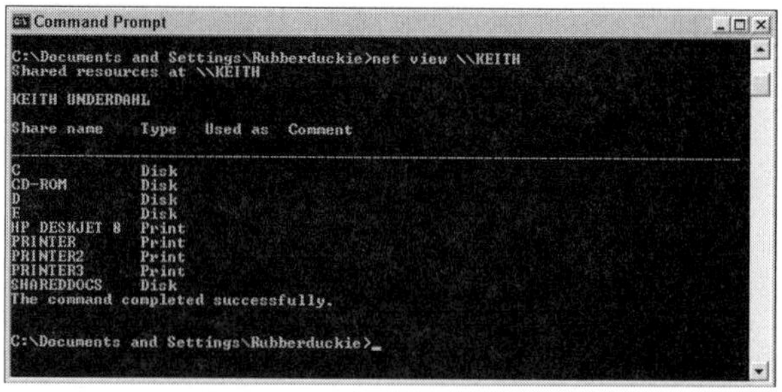

30.9

CHAPTER

6

TIGHTENING UP SECURITY

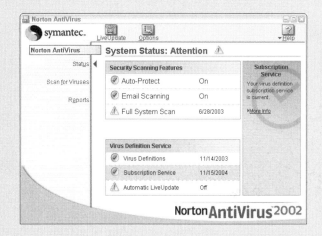

Every couple of weeks it seems that another new computer virus or security flaw threatens computers running Windows. Because Windows is the most common operating system, it stands to reason that hackers and others who threaten the security of your computer target it most often. Security threats can expose your sensitive data, reveal personal information, and violate your privacy.

Security threats come from many sources. Viruses can destroy or expose data. Intruders can access your computer through your Internet connection. Unauthorized persons with physical access can log on to an unprotected computer and view your data or damage Windows. Windows XP provides tools to protect your computer, and various third-party tools are ready to help as well. The techniques in this chapter show you how to maintain the security of your computer.

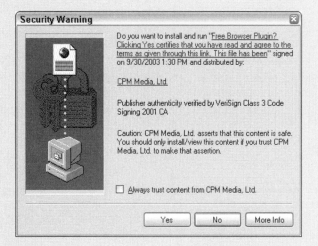

MANAGING PASSWORDS

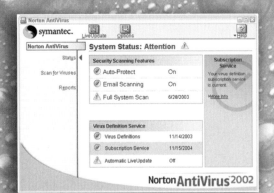

Virus Protection

Firewalls

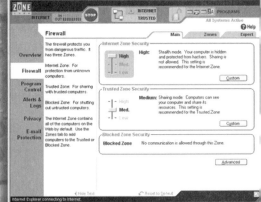

Finding and Destroying Spyware

MANAGING PASSWORDS

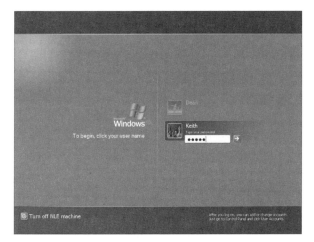

31.1

31.2

ABOUT THE FEATURE

Access to programs, files, and Windows itself can be controlled with passwords. Windows XP gives you control over how passwords are used.

ecurity on your computer starts with passwords. Passwords have been an important security measure for centuries, whether soldiers on a battlefield or computers in an office use them. Passwords are effective tools because if you don't have the right password, you don't get in. As shown in **Figure 31.1** you can use passwords in Windows XP to protect access to programs, files, and even Windows itself.

Of course, passwords aren't perfect. Some passwords are easily guessed, and even the most obscure, cryptic password can be compromised. Windows XP Professional Edition allows you to control the length and nature of passwords as shown in **Figure 31.2**, and you can control how long passwords are valid. Windows XP also helps you deal with the headache of a forgotten password.

STEP 1: SET UP USER PASSWORDS

The first and most important security measure you should take to protect your computer is to set up passwords for each user account. User account passwords add an extra step to the login process, but they ensure that you can control physical access to your computer. User account passwords prevent unauthorized persons from using the computer, and they prevent authorized users from accessing the personal files of other users. And, of course, account passwords also ensure that only the administrator can make major system changes such as accessing settings or installing new programs. To set up user account passwords:

- Log on to Windows as an administrator if you are not already.
- Choose **Start** ➣ **Control Panel** to open the Windows Control Panel.
- Click the **User Accounts** icon. The User Accounts control panel appears.
- Click **Change the way users log on or off**. Logon and logoff options appear.
- Remove the check mark next to **Use the Welcome screen** as shown in **Figure 31.3**.
- Click **Apply Options**. Windows now uses a classic-style login dialog box that forces users to use a password when they log on.

If you prefer to continue using the Windows XP Welcome Screen at log on, you need to manually set up an account for each user account. To do so:

- In the **User Accounts** control panel, click an account. A list of options for that account appears.
- Click **Create a password**.
- Type a password for the account, retype it, and enter a password clue, as shown in **Figure 31.4**. When you type a clue, keep in mind that anyone with physical access to the computer can see the clue. In **Figure 31.4** I have used the clue, "What is the name of your brother's boat?" Anyone who knows the answer to this question can get the password.

> **TIP**
>
> Passwords in Windows XP are case sensitive, so mixing case makes passwords even more secure. Just make sure you remember the case you use in your passwords!

31.3

31.4

STEP 2: ADJUST PASSWORD SETTINGS (WINDOWS XP PROFESSIONAL ONLY)

One of the advantages of Windows XP Professional Edition is that you have greater control over password behavior than if you have Windows XP Home Edition. You can specify a minimum length for passwords, mandate complex passwords, and you can make passwords expire after a certain period of time. To adjust password settings:

■ Choose **Start** ➢ **Control Panel** to open the Windows Control Panel. If the Control Panel currently uses Category view, click the **Performance and Maintenance** category to open it.

■ Click the **Administrative Tools** icon. The Administrative Tools control panel appears.

■ Click the **Local Security Policy** icon. The Local Security Settings window appears.

■ In the folder tree on the left side of the Local Security Settings window, click the plus sign next to **Account Policies**, and then click **Password Policy**. The Password Policy window appears on the right, as shown in **Figure 31.5**, with a list of password policies.

■ Double-click a policy to adjust settings. For example, if you double-click **Maximum password age**, a window appears that allows you to change the maximum age for passwords, as shown in **Figure 31.6**.

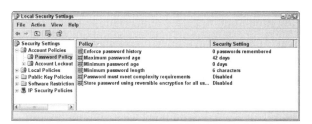

31.5

STEP 3: MAKE A PASSWORD RESET DISK

What do you do if you forget your password? You could consult your computer's administrator and ask for a new password to be assigned. But what if you *are* the computer administrator? A lost password could be a disaster, but it's an easily preventable disaster. Windows XP allows you to create a password reset

TIP

To make passwords very difficult to guess, enable the "Password must meet complexity requirements" option in the Local Security Settings window as shown in Figure 31.2. With this option enabled, passwords cannot contain part of the user's user name, they must be at least six characters long, and they must contain special characters such as a mix of upper- and lowercase letters, numbers, and punctuation characters such as $, %, or !.

31.6

disk for each user account. If you forget your password, simply use the password reset disk to reset the password and access your account. Each user should create a password reset disk for his or her account.

Your computer must have a removable disk drive such as a floppy drive or Zip drive to create a password reset disk. To create a password reset disk, place a blank disk in your removable disk drive and follow these steps:

- Choose **Start** ➢ **Control Panel** to open the Windows Control Panel.
- Click the **User Accounts** icon. The User Accounts control panel opens. If you are logged on as an administrator, click the name of an account for which you want to create a password reset disk.
- Under **Related Tasks** on the left side of the window, click **Prevent a forgotten password**. The Forgotten Password Wizard appears.
- Click **Next** twice, and enter your current account password when prompted to do so.
- Click **Next** again after entering your password. Windows creates your password reset disk.
- Click **Next** and **Finish** when the creation process is complete.

WARNING

A password recovery disk could be used by anyone to access the computer. To prevent unauthorized access, make sure that all password reset disks are stored in a locked, secure location.

Store the password reset disk in a safe place. You can use the same password reset disk to reset your account, even if you change the password after creating the disk. If you ever forget your password, Windows XP prompts you to reset your password using the reset disk. Follow the instructions on-screen to reset the password using your password reset disk.

STEP 4: CHANGE A PASSWORD

If you ever suspect that your password has been compromised, you should change it. It's also a good idea to change your password periodically. Security experts recommend that you change your password every 30 to 60 days. As I showed earlier in this technique, if you have Windows XP Professional Edition you can force all users to create new passwords on a regular basis. To change your password:

- Choose **Start** ➢ **Control Panel** to open the Windows Control Panel.
- Click the **User Accounts** icon. The User Accounts control panel opens. If you are logged on as an administrator, click the name of an account for which you want to create a password reset disk.
- Click **Change my password**.
- Type your current password, and then type and retype your new password. Provide a password hint if you want.

CONTROLLING FILE ACCESS

32.1

32.2

Think for a moment about all the files on your computer. Are you willing to let just anyone view, change, or even delete those files? Windows XP helps you control access to your files to ensure their security.

Of course, the level of security you need varies depending on what kind of file it is. Some files — such as music, video, or picture files — you may want to share with others on your computer. Windows provides several levels of security for files stored on your computer. This technique shows you how to control file access by sharing files, as shown in **Figure 32.1**, or hiding files, as shown in **Figure 32.2**.

STEP 1: USE FOLDERS TO CONTROL ACCESS

File access control in Windows XP relies on folders. To share or hide files, you actually share or hide the folders in which the files reside. Thus, it is important for you to use folders to organize your files. For example, if you have several files that all need to be private, put them all in the same folder and make that folder private.

Folder location is also important. To control access to a folder, it must be in the Windows XP user profile folders. User profile folders are all contained within the **\Documents and Settings** folder on your hard drive. Folders outside of the **\Documents and Settings** folder can be accessed by anyone who uses your computer, and there isn't anything you can do about it. Thus, make sure you save your important files in your user profile folders. Items in the user profile folder that can be secured include:

- **The desktop and all items stored in desktop folders.** If you create a new folder on your desktop, it can be secured. However, this does not apply to shortcuts to root-level folders that may be on your desktop.
- **Favorites.** Internet favorites can be shared or made private.
- **My Documents.** This folder is where you should store most of your work.
- **Start Menu.** Custom Start Menu items can be secured.

> **NOTE**
>
> To use Windows XP's file security features, your hard drive must be formatted using the NT file system, or NTFS. For more on NTFS, see Technique 14, "Creating Multiple Partitions," in Chapter 3.

To view a complete list of user profile items, right-click **Start** in the taskbar and choose **Explore** from the menu that appears. A Windows Explorer window appears as shown in **Figure 32.3**. All folders and files within the **\Documents and Settings** folder are user profile items. Folders not in this folder can be accessed by anyone using this computer. For example, in **Figure 32.3** the folders **\AAAMNG6**, **\AGES**, and **\COMPAQ** can be accessed by anyone who uses this computer.

STEP 2: SHARE A FOLDER WITH OTHER COMPUTER USERS

You probably have some items that you want to share with anyone who uses your computer. For example, you may want to share music and picture files with others. To make a folder free for anyone to access, place it in the **Shared Documents** folder. **Shared Documents** is just like **My Documents**, but as the name implies, it is shared by all users regardless of their access level to the computer. By default, the **Shared Documents** folder is also shared on your network if you have one.

The **Shared Documents** folder can be accessed through My Computer. As you can see in **Figure 32.4**, **Shared Documents** is one of the items listed when

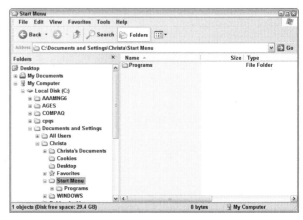

32.3

you first open My Computer. **Shared Documents** also appears in the pane on the left side of the My Computer window, right under **My Network Places** and **My Documents**, so you can click-and-drag items to it from anywhere in My Computer.

STEP 3: MAKE A FOLDER PRIVATE

Remember that in Windows XP there are two kinds of users: Those with administrator access and those with restricted access. Users with administrator access can access virtually any folder on the computer, including items in your own **My Documents** folder. Restricted users can only access their own **My Documents** folder as well as the **Shared Documents** folder.

You can make your folders private, even from administrators. To make a folder private:

■ Open My Computer or Windows Explorer and locate the folder that you want to make private.
■ Right-click the folder and choose **Properties** from the menu that appears. A Properties dialog box for the folder appears.

> **NOTE**
>
> To share files and folders on a network, see Technique 27, "Sharing Files," in Chapter 5.

32.4

■ Click the **Sharing** tab to bring it to the front.
■ Place a check mark next to **Make this folder private**, as shown in **Figure 32.5**.
■ Click **OK** to close the Properties dialog box.

After you have made a folder private, only you can access it. Other users of the computer can see the name of the folder, but if someone tries to open the folder, an "Access is denied" message appears, as shown in **Figure 32.6**.

32.5

32.6

STEP 4: HIDE DESKTOP ITEMS AND FAVORITES

If you often use the Windows desktop to store sensitive items, you should make your desktop private. Likewise, you may want to hide your Internet favorites from prying eyes around the home or office. You can hide desktop items and favorites just like you hide other folders:

- Choose **Start** ➢ **My Computer** to open My Computer, and then click the icon for your hard drive.
- Open the **Documents and Settings** folder, and then open the folder for your user account. A list of items appears, as shown in **Figure 32.7**. The list includes **Desktop** and **Favorites** folders.

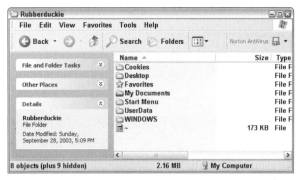

32.7

- Right-click **Desktop** or **Favorites**, and choose **Properties** from the menu that appears.
- Click the **Sharing** tab to bring it to the front, and place a check mark next to **Make this folder private**, as shown in **Figure 32.8**.
- Click **OK** to close the Properties dialog box.

32.8

UPDATING WINDOWS SOFTWARE

33.1

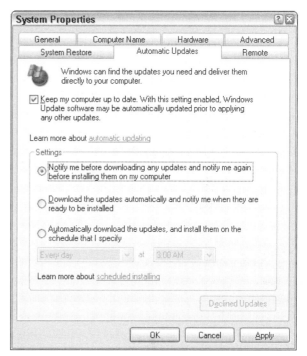

33.2

When Windows XP was released in 2002, it was the most advanced, secure version of Windows ever. But even the best operating system in the world can't be perfect, and it was only a matter of time before new potential security holes were discovered or exploited. Because of this, Microsoft cannot simply release the Windows software into the world and forget about it. Microsoft programmers constantly tweak the XP software to add improvements and address new security concerns.

It is of paramount importance that you regularly update your operating system software. Fortunately, keeping Windows XP current with the latest improvements from Microsoft is easy thanks to a tool called Windows Update. Windows Update connects your computer to the Microsoft Web site, as shown in **Figure 33.1**. Necessary upgrades are identified based on your current Windows installation, and those upgrades are then downloaded and installed on your computer in a near-seamless process. This technique shows you how to use Windows Update effectively to ensure your Windows XP installation stays in top condition. It also shows you how to make updates happen automatically, as shown in **Figure 33.2**.

STEP 1: UNDERSTAND HOW WINDOWS UPDATE WORKS

Windows Update connects your computer to the Microsoft Web site, and information about your computer is transmitted to Microsoft as part of the update process. Information that Microsoft collects from your computer includes:

- **The exact version number of your Windows XP installation and Internet Explorer.** This ensures that only updates that apply to your copy of Windows are installed. Windows Update uses the Internet Explorer program, even if that is not your default Web browser.
- **Version numbers for other relevant software.** If Windows Update updates any other software on your computer, version numbers for those programs are collected.

> **TIP**
>
> If you just bought a new computer, run Windows Update immediately. Your computer's installation of Windows XP probably hasn't been updated since the computer was first manufactured, which may have been several months ago. Countless updates have probably become available during that time.

- **Plug-and-Play Hardware ID numbers.** This allows Windows Update to provide updates that may help your hardware run better.
- **Regional and language settings.** This allows Windows Update to communicate effectively with you and also maintain your current settings.
- **Windows XP Product ID and Product Key.** Windows Update ensures that you have a valid, licensed copy of Windows. If you do not have a valid copy, Windows Update will not run.

With all this information about your computer being collected, it's understandable that you may have some privacy concerns. Microsoft states that it does not collect any personal information about you — such as your name or e-mail address — from the computer, nor does it use any of the collected information to identify you.

STEP 2: LAUNCH WINDOWS UPDATE

Before you run Windows Update, you should save your work and close any open programs because many updates require you to restart your computer. To launch Windows Update, choose **Start ➢ All Programs ➢ Windows Update**. Windows Update begins as shown in **Figure 33.3**. If you want more information about Microsoft's privacy policies, click

33.3

Read our privacy statement. Otherwise, click **Scan for updates**. Windows checks your computer and then searches the Microsoft Web site for available updates.

STEP 3: REVIEW THE LIST OF AVAILABLE UPDATES

When Windows Update is done looking for updates, a list of available updates appears. The list is divided into three categories:

- **Critical Updates and Service Packs.** Consider these updates mandatory. Critical updates usually plug security holes or repair major problems that could make Windows XP unstable.
- **Windows XP.** These are updates to Windows XP that are less critical but still recommended.
- **Driver Updates.** These are updated drivers for hardware that may or may not be installed on your computer.

Click an update category in the Windows Update category on the left side of the window to review a list of updates in that category. In **Figure 33.4**, Windows Update found zero critical updates, 16 Windows XP updates, and three driver updates. In the figure, I am reviewing Windows XP updates. To add an update to the list of items that you want to download and

install, click **Add** under the update's name and description. To remove an update from the list, click **Remove**.

Each update's description includes a download size and time estimate for the download. The top of the Windows Update window keeps a running tally of the number of updates you have selected. In **Figure 33.4** I have selected seven updates.

STEP 4: INSTALL THE UPDATES

When you are done reviewing and selecting updates, click **Review and install updates** at the top of the Windows Update window. A summary of updates appears as shown in **Figure 33.5**. A summary of the download size and estimated download time appears at the top of the window.

> **NOTE**
>
> Some updates must be installed separately. If so, a note stating this fact appears in the update's description. If an update says that it must be installed separately, install it first. You can rerun Windows Update to install other updates.

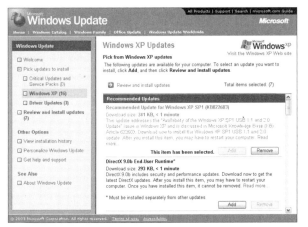

33.4

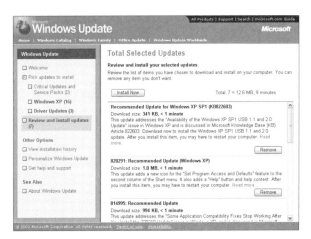

33.5

If you change your mind at the last minute about any of the changes, click **Remove**. Otherwise, click **Install Now**. If any of the updates require you to accept a license agreement, a dialog box appears containing the agreement. Click **Accept** to accept the agreements. A progress window shows the progress of the download and installation, as shown in **Figure 33.6**. Many updates require you to restart your computer after installation, so be prepared to restart when Windows Update is complete.

33.6

STEP 5: SCHEDULE AUTOMATIC UPDATES

Chances are, Windows Update already runs automatically on your system from time to time. It's a good idea to automate Windows Update on a periodic basis because updating Windows XP is an easy task to forget. Automatic updates only download and install critical updates; noncritical Windows XP and driver updates need to be downloaded and installed manually using Windows Update, as described above.

To enable automatic updates or change settings, follow these steps:

■ Choose **Start** ➤ **Control Panel** to open the Windows Control Panel. If your Control Panel is set up to show category view, open the **Performance and Maintenance** category.

■ Click the **System** icon. The System Properties dialog box appears.

■ Click the **Automatic Updates** tab to bring it to the front, as shown in **Figure 33.7**.

■ Place a checkmark next to **Keep my computer up to date** if it isn't checked already. This enables automatic updates. With this enabled, Windows Update automatically detects when your computer is connected to the Internet. When a connection is detected, Windows Updates checks the Microsoft Web site for updates.

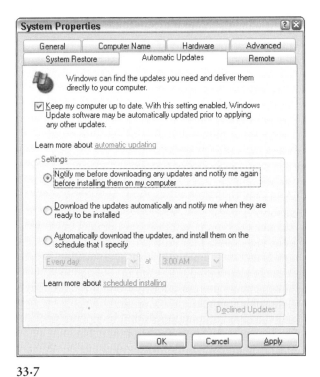

33.7

■ Choose an option under **Settings**. In **Figure 33.7**, I have chosen the first option. With this option, a **Windows Update** icon appears in the Windows system tray, which is the area in the lower-right corner of the screen next to the clock. When the **Windows Update** icon appears, as shown in **Figure 33.8**, click it and follow the instructions on-screen to download and install updates. If you would rather have Windows download the updates automatically, choose the middle option under **Settings**. You can also choose the third option if you want to specify your own schedule.

■ Click **OK** to close the System Properties dialog box.

33.8

GUARDING YOUR SYSTEM AGAINST VIRUSES

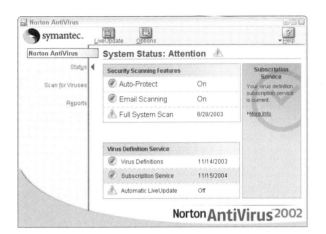

34.1

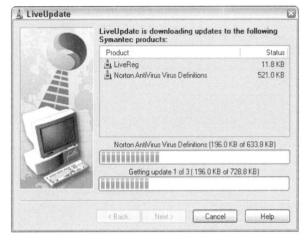

34.2

Depending on whom you ask, computer viruses have been around for at least 20 to 30 years. The first virus to infect personal computers as we know them today — called Brain — appeared in 1986, and the rest, as they say, is history. Today, hundreds of thousands of virus infections occur every day, and by using the Internet a modern virus can spread around the world within minutes of release. Viruses are the most common and persistent security threats that your computer faces. Some viruses merely create annoyances, while others violate your privacy or even damage your computer.

Windows XP is the most secure version of the Windows operating system ever, but it still doesn't include antivirus software. To protect your computer and the data it contains, you must use third-party antivirus software, as shown in **Figure 34.1**; you must keep your antivirus software updated, as shown in **Figure 34.2**; and you must exercise sound practices when using your computer.

STEP 1: USE SOUND ANTIVIRUS PRACTICES

Antivirus software is absolutely essential on any modern computer. But antivirus software is only one part of your campaign to keep your computer virus-free. Most viruses only infect your computer after you take some action to cause the infection. Some sound practices that can help you avoid viruses include:

■ Be extremely wary of files attached to e-mails. E-mail has become the most common method of virus distribution. Viruses often infect the address book of an e-mail program, replicating and resending itself to others in the address book. Such viruses rarely damage your computer, but when enough copies abound, all replicating and e-mailing themselves to more recipients, Internet servers get choked by the traffic and grind to a halt. Microsoft Outlook and Outlook Express are most often targeted by these e-mail viruses, but virtually all other e-mail programs are vulnerable to attack as well. If you receive a file attachment in e-mail and it comes from an unknown source, delete it without opening it. Even if the attachment appears to come from someone you know, if you weren't expecting the file and aren't sure exactly what it is, contact the sender before opening it and find out if the attachment is legitimate.

■ Suppress the Preview pane in your e-mail program. If you use Outlook or Outlook Express for

e-mail, the program includes a Preview pane to display e-mail messages, as shown in **Figure 34.3**. In the top half of the screen I've selected the message titled "Re: Technical Support" and a preview of that message appears in the Preview pane below. Some other e-mail programs have Preview panes as well. The Preview pane is potentially dangerous because some viruses can infect your computer simply by opening the e-mail message. When a message appears in the Preview pane, that message is opened. To disable the Preview pane in Outlook Express, choose **View ➤ Layout**. The Window Layout Properties dialog box appears. Remove the checkmark next to **Show preview pane**, and click **OK**.

■ Delete obvious spam and chain mail. Before you open any e-mail, scan through the list of subject lines and senders in your e-mail program. Delete messages that are obviously unsolicited commercial mail or chain letters before you even open them. In **Figure 34.3**, for example, one of my e-mails is called Happy Screensaver, a suspicious name, and that e-mail includes an attachment, as indicated by the paper clip icon. If I don't know the sender or was not expecting him or her to send me a screen saver, I should delete this message without opening it. The next two messages also

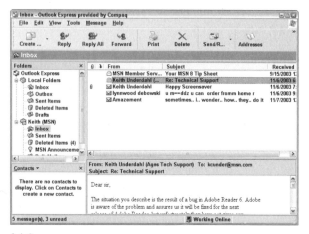

34·3

appear to be spam, so I'll delete those too.
If you use Outlook Express, see Technique 41,
"Safeguarding E-mail in Outlook Express" for
more on making that program virus-safe.

■ Do not download files or programs from ques-
tionable or unknown Web sites. If you visit a Web
site and see a message such as the one shown in
Figure 34.4, do not click **Yes** to install the program
unless you are absolutely sure that you recognize
the program and want to install it. Even if you do
want to install the program, I strongly recommend
that you not enable the option to always trust content from the publisher. This provides an extra
safeguard because your computer asks for permis-
sion each time a new program tries to install.

STEP 2: INSTALL ANTIVIRUS SOFTWARE

The cornerstone of your antivirus campaign must be
a good antivirus program. An antivirus program
serves two important functions:

■ Monitor all current activities, and warn of
potential virus activity as it occurs

34·4

■ Scan your computer on demand, searching for,
identifying, and eliminating potential infections

Your computer may already have antivirus software
installed. An antivirus program is often included on
new computers. If you don't have antivirus software,
you can purchase it virtually anywhere that computers and software are sold. Some popular antivirus
programs include:

■ McAfee VirusScan — www.mcafee.com
■ Norton AntiVirus — www.norton.com
■ Panda Antivirus Platinum — www.
pandasoftware.com

Any antivirus program is better than none at all, so
you can hardly make a bad choice. Whatever program you choose, make sure that it specifically offers
Windows XP compatibility and that online updates
are available. Antivirus programs sometimes come
bundled with other tools, such as firewalls or system
utilities. A firewall is definitely a good thing to have,
as I describe in the next technique, but there are some
excellent free firewall programs available for personal
use. And the system utilities included with some popular antivirus programs often cause more problems
than they resolve.

When you have chosen and installed an antivirus
program, you should make sure that it is configured
to constantly guard your computer. Your antivirus
program probably has a system tray icon, as shown in
Figure 34.5. To open the control panel for your
antivirus program, right-click the system tray icon
and choose an option to open the program.

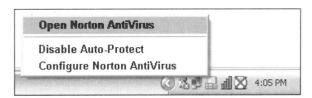

34·5

Although each program is different, most have an auto-protect setting similar to Norton Antivirus, which is shown in **Figure 34.6**. Make sure that automatic protection is enabled. If it isn't, click **Options** and enable auto-protection. You should also enable e-mail protection if it's available. E-mail protection usually scans incoming messages and warns you about possible incoming viruses.

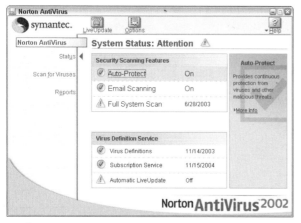

34.6

STEP 3: SCAN YOUR SYSTEM

Even with automatic protection enabled, you should perform a complete system scan periodically to make sure that a virus hasn't snuck onto your system somehow. To scan your system:

- Open your antivirus program as described in the previous step.
- Click the **Scan** or **Scan for Viruses** button. Again, every program is different, but most have a button to help you quickly start a system scan.
- Choose what you want to scan if a list of items appears. In **Figure 34.7**, I can choose to scan my whole computer, removable drives, floppy drives, or only specific files or folders.
- Click **Scan** to begin scanning. The scan process may take a while, depending on what you choose to scan. When the scan is complete, a report appears listing the virus infections that were found, if any, as well as a report on what action was taken. Depending on the program as well as the extent of any damage that was found, you may be given instructions on how to repair the damage.

STEP 4: UPDATE YOUR ANTIVIRUS SOFTWARE

Antivirus software works by searching your computer for signs of known viruses. Part of the antivirus software is a definitions list that contains information about all known viruses. If your definitions list isn't up-to-date, your antivirus program cannot identify new viruses that may infect your system. New viruses appear every day, so keeping your antivirus definitions list current is crucial.

At the very least, you should update your antivirus definitions weekly. Most antivirus programs allow you to schedule automatic updates, and you can download the updates from the Internet. The updates are usually small so they download quickly.

Updating your antivirus software is easy. Open the antivirus program as described earlier, and look for an update button. If your antivirus program has an automatic update feature, open the appropriate settings dialog box and enable automatic updates as well. In **Figure 34.8**, I have enabled automatic LiveUpdate in Norton Antivirus.

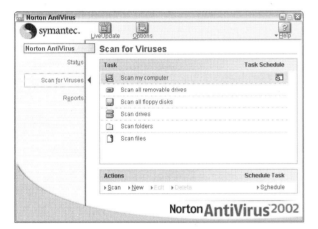

34.7

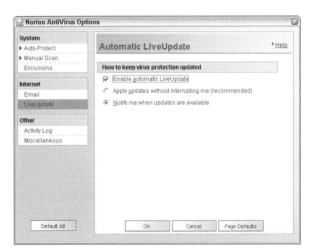

34.8

PROTECTING YOUR INTERNET CONNECTION WITH FIREWALLS

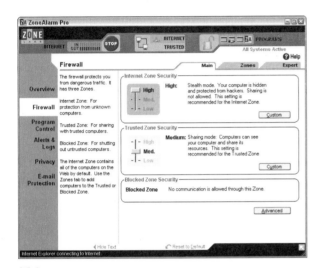

35.1

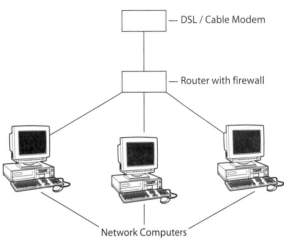

— DSL / Cable Modem

— Router with firewall

Network Computers

35.2

ABOUT THE FEATURE

Firewall programs guard your Internet connection so that intruders cannot use it to access your computer.

I n cars and trucks, the panel between the engine compartment and the passenger compartment is called a firewall. The firewall is so named because it keeps engine fires and other dangers away from the passenger compartment. Likewise, modern building construction often incorporates firewalls, which are special flame-resistant walls designed to isolate fire damage and reduce danger.

Software designers have carried the firewall concept over to computers. No, I'm not talking about fire prevention. But if your computer is connected to the Internet, it is susceptible to dangers that can enter your computer from the online world. Using your Internet connection, hackers can gain access to your computer, steal files, read sensitive personal data, and even cause damage or plant viruses. Firewall programs prevent such intrusions, and in this day and age many experts consider a firewall to be nearly as important as antivirus software. This is especially true if you have a broadband connection such as DSL or cable because fast, always-on connections attract hackers to your computer.

Three basic levels of firewalls are available to you. These are:

■ The Windows XP Firewall
■ A third-party firewall program, as shown in **Figure 35.1**
■ A hardware firewall, as shown in **Figure 35.2**

Which level of firewall you use depends on your budget and needs. The following steps detail each level and show you how to use them.

STEP 1: ACTIVATE THE WINDOWS XP FIREWALL

Windows XP comes with a built-in firewall program. The Windows XP Firewall is better than nothing, but only just. The main problem is that although the Windows XP Firewall can block unauthorized access to your computer from an outside source, it does not stop programs on your computer from transmitting data without your knowledge. This means that a hacker could plant a program on your computer, which then transmits data back to the hacker. These programs are sometimes called *spyware*. For example, the program could record all of your keystrokes — even when you type passwords or credit card numbers — and then transmit those keystrokes to a third party.

Another potential problem with the Windows XP Firewall is that it can disrupt normal network activities like printer and file sharing. Only use the Windows XP Firewall on the computer that actually connects to the Internet. If you use Internet Connection Sharing to share your Internet connection over your network, do not enable the XP Firewall on client computers.

But, as I said, the Windows XP Firewall is better than nothing, and if you don't have any other kind of firewall you should activate it now so that you at least have some protection from Internet intrusions. To activate the Windows XP Firewall:

■ Choose **Start** ➢ **Control Panel** to open the Windows Control Panel. If your Control Panel is set up for Category view, open the **Network and Internet Connections** category.
■ Click the **Network Connections** icon. A list of network connections appears, as shown in **Figure 35.3**.
■ Click the network connection that you use to connect to the Internet to select it. On the computer shown in **Figure 35.3**, I've chosen **Wireless Network Connection 2** because that is the connection I currently use to connect to the Internet. If you connect using a dial-up modem, the connection should be listed under the **Dial-up** category in Network Connections. Otherwise, you probably connect to the Internet using a connection under **LAN or High-Speed Internet** category.

35.3

■ Click **Change settings of this connection** under Network Tasks on the left side of the screen. Alternatively, right-click the connection you want to protect and choose **Properties** from the menu that appears. A Properties dialog box for the connection appears.

■ Click the **Advanced** tab to bring it to the front.

■ Under Internet Connection Firewall, place a checkmark next to **Protect my computer**.

■ Click **OK** to close the dialog box.

STEP 2: INSTALL A FIREWALL PROGRAM

Various software vendors now offer powerful, easy-to-use firewall programs that you can install and use in Windows XP. Third-party firewalls offer many advantages over the Windows XP Firewall, including:

■ Internet access can be individually controlled and configured for each program on your computer.

■ Third-party firewalls can control both incoming and outgoing traffic.

■ Internet "lock" features can quickly lock down your Internet connection, immediately stopping all data flow over the connection and blocking it until you unlock the firewall again.

TIP

As I mention in Technique 30, "Diagnosing Network Problems" in Chapter 5, firewalls can sometimes interfere with network configuration. If you're having difficulty getting your network to function correctly, temporarily disable your firewall while you troubleshoot.

■ Some firewalls incorporate Internet content filtering tools to help you control which Web sites can and cannot be accessed on your computer.

■ Thwarted attacks are logged so that you can review potential hacker activity. Some firewalls even help you track down and identify the hackers who are trying to violate your system.

■ Several firewall products help you block pop-up ads and other online annoyances.

Most antivirus software vendors now also offer firewalls, although they are sometimes simply marketed as Internet security tools. Several companies specialize in firewall programs. In **Figure 35.4**, I am using a program called ZoneAlarm Pro that is available from Zone Labs at www.zonelabs.com. Zone Labs offers a free version of ZoneAlarm that lacks some of the more advanced features and controls of ZoneAlarm Pro, but even the free ZoneAlarm program is an improvement over the Windows XP Firewall.

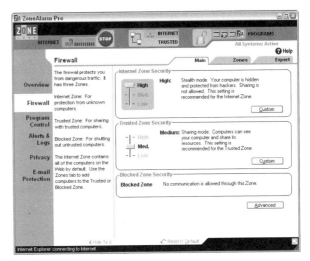

35.4

STEP 3: USE A HARDWARE FIREWALL

The most reliable and secure firewall you can use on your computer or small network is a hardware firewall. Hardware firewalls are usually built into a network router. The network arrangement may resemble **Figure 35.5**. If you have a network in your home or office, chances are you use a hub or router to connect all of your computers together. I recommend that you use a router that incorporates a firewall. These firewalls have a special WAN port into which you connect your broadband DSL or cable modem. The firewall in the router then stands between the modem and your computers, as shown in **Figure 35.5**.

Although each router is different, you usually control the router and its firewall using an administrative control panel. In **Figure 35.6**, I have logged on to the firewall control panel for my D-Link router using Internet Explorer, per the documentation that came with the router. Here I can enable or disable the firewall, or add special rules that, for example, allow access from a computer at a specific IP address. Such a rule would allow an authorized remote user to access my network over the Internet.

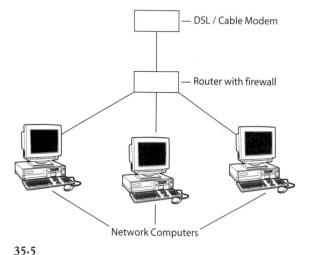

35.5

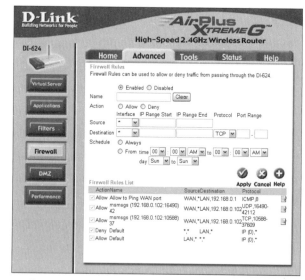

35.6

ENCRYPTING FILES

36.1

36.2

Computer security experts agree that no single solution guarantees the safety of your data. Password-protected access control, firewalls, and antivirus software should all be parts of an overall security plan. Hackers may figure out how to defeat one of your security measures, but if you have security in *depth*, which means many layers of security, your information is far better protected.

If you have Windows XP Professional Edition, another level of security that is available to you is file encryption, as shown in **Figure 36.1**. Files can be encrypted using a feature called Encrypted File System, or EFS. If a file is encrypted using EFS, it can only be accessed and used by an authorized user. This means that even if someone defeats your firewall or otherwise gains access to the files on your hard drive, he or she still cannot access the data contained in encrypted files. When used properly, file encryption can block access to data even if the unauthorized user gains physical access to the computer.

Access to encrypted files is controlled using user-specific certificates. When you want to access an encrypted file, your user certificate allows you to decrypt the file. This technique shows you how to activate and use EFS, as well as how to share encrypted files, as shown in **Figure 36.2**.

STEP 1: ENCRYPT A FOLDER

Windows XP Professional allows you to encrypt files or folders. Encryption is transparent to you when you use the computer, but other users of your computer or other network users cannot access the encrypted files. Although you can encrypt individual files, it's strongly recommended that you encrypt whole folders and store your important files in encrypted folders. This is because some programs create temporary files

> **NOTE**
>
> If you work on a network administered by someone else, consult the administrator before using file encryption. Your administrator may have special instructions or policies that you must follow before you encrypt files.

> **NOTE**
>
> Encryption can only be used on disks that use the NT File System, or NTFS. Your hard drive probably uses NTFS. See Technique 14, "Creating Multiple Partitions," for more details on file system types.

as you work. For example, when you work on a Microsoft Word document, Word periodically creates temporary files on your hard drive that are actually whole copies of the current document. If you encrypted just the original file, the temporary files created by Word are unencrypted. But if you encrypt the folder containing the original document, that document as well as any temporary files created in the folder by Word are also encrypted.

To encrypt a folder, follow these steps:

- Open My Computer or Windows Explorer, and browse to the folder that you want to encrypt. Do not open the folder, but rather browse to the folder level just above the folder that you want to encrypt.
- Right-click the folder and choose **Properties** from the context menu that appears. A Properties dialog box for the folder appears.
- On the **General** tab of the Properties dialog box, click **Advanced**. The Advanced Attributes dialog box appears as shown in **Figure 36.3**.

36.3

■ Place a checkmark next to **Encrypt contents to secure data**, and click **OK** to close the Advanced Attributes dialog box.

■ Click **OK** to close the Properties dialog box. You may be asked to confirm the changes. If so, click **OK** to confirm the changes.

Any files stored in the encrypted folder are encrypted. Subfolders in an encrypted folder are encrypted as well. Other users cannot access files in your encrypted folders. In **Figure 36.4**, I've tried to open a text file in a folder encrypted by another user.

NOTE

Remember, if other users can log on to your computer using your user account, they can access your encrypted files. For file encryption to be truly effective you must password-protect your user account, and you must keep your password secure.

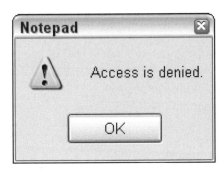

36.4

STEP 2: SHARE AN ENCRYPTED FILE

Normally, you are the only person who can access files that you encrypt. But you can share encrypted files with other trusted users if you want. To share an encrypted file:

■ Right-click the encrypted file that you want to share, and choose **Properties**. Note that you can only share individual files; you cannot share an entire encrypted folder.

■ Click **Advanced** to open the Advanced Attributes dialog box.

■ Click **Details** next to the **Encrypt contents to secure data** check box. The Encryption Details dialog box appears, as shown in **Figure 36.5**.

36.5

- Click **Add**. The Select User dialog box appears, as shown in **Figure 36.6**.
- Choose the user with whom you want to share access, and click **OK**. Repeat until you've shared the document with each desired user.
- Click **OK** to close all of the open dialog boxes.

Each person that was added to the list can now access the encrypted file. Users who are not on the list still don't have access.

> **NOTE**
>
> Make sure that the encrypted file you want to share is in a shared folder. If the file is in one of your private **My Documents** folders, other users still can't access it due to basic Windows file sharing rules. Shared encrypted files should be in the **Shared Documents** folder, or in a folder outside the **Documents and Settings** folders.

STEP 3: DECRYPT A FILE OR FOLDER

Just as the government periodically declassifies old secrets, you can remove encryption from files or folders so that anyone can access them again. To remove encryption from a file or folder:

- Browse to the file or folder using Windows Explorer or My Computer.
- Right-click the file or folder, and choose **Properties** from the context menu that appears.
- Click **Advanced** on the **General** tab of the Properties dialog box.
- In the Advanced Attributes dialog box, remove the checkmark next to **Encrypt contents to secure data**, and click **OK**.
- Click **OK** to close the Properties dialog box. The Confirm Attribute Changes dialog box appears, as shown in **Figure 36.7**.
- Click **OK** to confirm the changes.

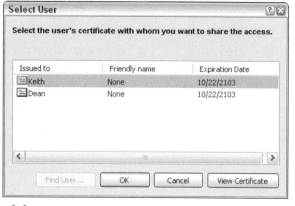

36.6

36.7

PERMANENTLY REMOVE FILES FROM YOUR HARD DRIVE

37.1

37.2

ABOUT THE FEATURE

Even if you delete files and empty the Windows Recycle Bin, traces of files can remain on the hard drive. This technique shows you how to make sure files and other data are truly deleted.

Consider for a moment all the sensitive data on your computer. Virtually everything you do is stored on your computer's hard drive, and in the wrong hands your data could cause a lot of trouble.

Why not just delete the files, and then empty the Windows XP Recycle Bin? Although files that are emptied from the Recycle Bin become inaccessible while using Windows, the files are probably still on your hard drive. They remain in place on the physical hard drive until another file comes along and replaces it in exactly the same physical location on the hard drive. If you have a very large hard drive, old data can sit hidden for a long, long time. Special file recovery utilities can recover these lost files, even if only fragments of the files remain.

You have several options to make sure that files are truly erased from your hard drive. Some options — like defragmenting the hard drive as shown in **Figure 37.1** — are easy, while others require that you do more work or use third-party software, such as the program shown in **Figure 37.2**. Just how far you're willing to go to remove old files depends on how damaging the files could be if they fell into the wrong hands.

STEP 1: DELETE THE FILES

If you don't have a file deletion utility, you need to delete files the old-fashioned way. If you *do* have a file deletion utility, or you want to use one, skip ahead to step 3. Otherwise, continue reading here.

As you know, when you delete files from the hard drive they first go to the Windows XP Recycle Bin, as shown in **Figure 37.3**. The Recycle Bin acts as an easy safety check, allowing you to easily recover files that you deleted by accident. To truly delete a file from Windows, you need to empty the Recycle Bin. The easiest way to do this is to right-click the **Recycle Bin** icon on the Windows desktop, and choose **Empty Recycle Bin** from the menu that appears.

STEP 2: DEFRAGMENT YOUR HARD DRIVE

When you delete a file in Windows, the data actually remains on the physical hard drive until new data is written over it. One simple, cheap way to overwrite

some old data is to defragment your hard drive. When you defragment the hard drive, files are actually reorganized on the physical drive to new locations. This often — but not always — overwrites old, deleted data. To defragment your hard drive:

■ Choose **Start** ➤ **All Programs** ➤ **Accessories** ➤ **System Tools** ➤ **Disk Defragmenter**. The Disk Defragmenter opens as shown in **Figure 37.4**.
■ Click **Analyze**. Disk Defragmenter analyzes the condition of your drive. Click **Close** when the analysis is complete. A graphic report appears, as shown in **Figure 37.4**. The white areas of the report indicate unused areas of the hard drive. Those areas may contain old deleted files. When Disk Defragmenter runs, it moves files so that they are stored in a more contiguous manner on the hard drive, and files may be moved into those white spaces.
■ Click **Defragment** to defragment the hard drive.

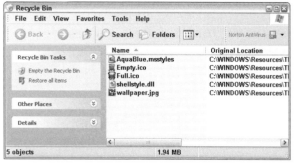

37.3

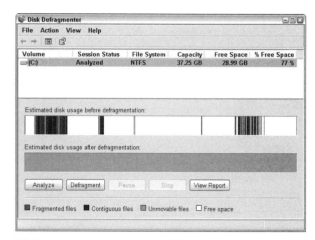

37.4

Again, keep in mind that defragmenting the hard drive isn't foolproof. Deleted files may be cleaned off the hard drive, but there is no guarantee that all of your sensitive data has been removed. For more reliable deletion, continue on to the next steps.

STEP 3: RUN A FILE DELETION UTILITY

Various utility programs are available that help you delete files completely from your hard drive. In **Figure 37.5**, I am using a freeware program called CuteShield File Shredder, which you can download from www.sys-shield.com. As the name implies, CuteShield File Shredder works as a sort of electronic

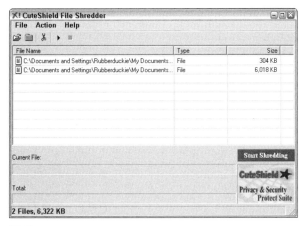

37.5

file shredder on files you want to delete. This program only works on files that haven't been deleted from Windows yet.

Software vendors usually sell file deletion utilities, or you can search the Web. Another good source of downloadable software is Tucows, at www.tucows.com. File deletion utilities can be found in the File removers category of the Windows utilities Web site at Tucows.

STEP 4: REFORMAT THE HARD DRIVE

The most complete and drastic way to clean files from your hard drive is to reformat the drive. Obviously this isn't something you want to do on a regular basis, because if you reformat the hard drive you'll need to reinstall Windows and all your other software. However, reformatting is something you should seriously consider if you plan to sell a computer that contained company secrets, customer data, or other sensitive information.

You can reformat a hard drive using the Windows XP CD-ROM. Boot from the CD and launch the Recovery Console as described in Technique 21, "Installing the Recovery Console," in Chapter 4. Run the Recovery Console and use the **FORMAT** command to format the hard drive. Do not perform a quick format, because a quick format does not necessarily destroy all data currently on the drive.

SQUASHING POP-UPS

38.1

38.2

If you're like most computer users, the Internet has changed the way you work and live over the last couple of years. It is simply the greatest information resource in history. Wonderful though the Internet is, it still presents some annoyances and aggravations. Chief among them are pop-up windows that appear when you visit some Web sites. Pop-up windows like the one shown in **Figure 38.1** usually contain advertising for products and services that you probably don't want. The most aggressive and annoying pop-up ads appear when you try to close another window, quickly spawning additional windows that appear as quickly as you can close them, if not quicker.

Pop-ups are frustrating, but they don't have to be inevitable. There are a couple of things you can do in Windows to prevent a majority of pop-ups. In **Figure 38.2**, I'm disabling a feature in Internet Explorer that allows some Web sites to open pop-ups. You can further suppress them by using third-party pop-up blocker programs. This technique shows you how.

STEP 1: DISABLE THE MESSENGER SERVICE

In November 2003, the United States Federal Trade Commission — FTC — sought and obtained a temporary restraining order against a company called D-Squared Solutions LLC. The FTC contended that the company unlawfully exploited the Messenger service that is part of the Windows XP operating system. The Messenger service — which is *not* the same as Windows Messenger, Microsoft's instant messaging program — was designed to allow network administrators to send important system messages to network users, advising them of events such as server reboots, for example. If you have a single computer or a small home or office network, you probably don't need the Messenger service.

Some Web developers have learned how to exploit the Messenger service, using it to display pop-up ads on your computer when you least expect them. The problem is certainly not limited to one company, and it seems unlikely that a government lawsuit or two can stop the practice entirely. To prevent pop-up ads that use the Messenger service, simply disable the service. As I mentioned, chances are pretty good that you don't need it anyway.

To disable the Messenger service:

- Choose **Start** ➢ **Control Panel** to open the Windows Control Panel. If your Control Panel uses Category view, click the **Performance and Maintenance** category to open it.

> **NOTE**
>
> If you work on a network administered by someone else, consult with the administrator before you disable the Messenger service. This ensures that you remain in compliance with network policies.

- Click the **Administrative Tools** icon. The Administrative Tools control panel appears.
- Click the **Services** icon. The Services control panel appears.
- Scroll down the list of services to find **Messenger**. Double-click **Messenger** to open the Messenger Properties dialog box as shown in **Figure 38.3**.
- In the **Startup type** menu, choose **Disabled**. This option ensures that Messenger doesn't start every time you restart Windows.
- Click **Stop** if the button is available. Windows XP shuts down the Messenger service.
- Click **OK** to close the Messenger Properties dialog box, and then close the Services control panel.

Web sites can no longer use your Messenger service to send unwanted advertisements and messages.

38.3

STEP 2: TURN OFF ACTIVE SCRIPTING IN INTERNET EXPLORER

The Messenger service is a potential source of annoying pop-up ads, but a more common source is the Active Scripting feature in Internet Explorer. You can disable Active Scripting, but that can cause problems when you visit some of your favorite Web sites. For example, if you frequent any sites that use pop-up windows for login screens or other features, disabling Active Scripting will probably disable those windows. So basically, you have two choices:

- **Disable Active Scripting for all Web sites.** Do this to block most pop-up windows, but it can cause problems if some of your favorite Web sites use pop-ups for log on or other functions.

- **Disable Active Scripting for specific Web sites.** Internet Explorer can apply different security settings to different Web sites through the use of security zones. You can disable Active Scripting for the Restricted Sites zone, and then add specific sites to the Restricted zone. You may want to do this if you regularly visit a site that has a lot of annoying pop-ups.

To disable Active Scripting for all sites, follow these steps:

- Open Internet Explorer, and choose **Tools ➢ Internet Options**. The Internet Options dialog box appears.
- Click the **Security** tab to bring it to the front.
- Make sure that **Internet** is the selected zone as shown in **Figure 38.4**, and click **Custom Level**. The Security Settings dialog box appears as shown in **Figure 38.5**.
- Scroll down the list of security settings to the **Active scripting** setting under **Scripting**. Choose **Disable** under **Active scripting**.
- Click **OK** to close the Security Settings dialog box. Click **Yes** in the warning dialog box that appears to confirm your changes, and then click **OK** to close the Internet Options dialog box.

38.4

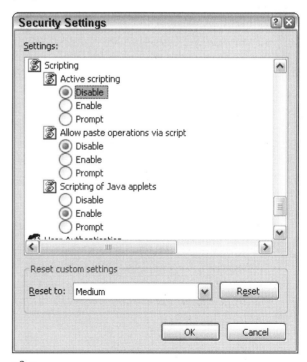

38.5

Active Scripting is disabled by default in the Restricted sites security zone. This means that if you add a Web site to the Restricted zone, Active Scripting pop-up windows on that site will not appear. To add a site to the Restricted zone:

■ Open the home page of the site that you want to restrict.

■ Click the URL in the Address bar to select it, and press **Ctrl+C** on your keyboard to copy the URL.

■ Choose **Tools** ➢ **Internet Options** to open the Internet Options dialog box.

■ Click the **Security** tab to bring it to the front, as shown in **Figure 38.6**.

■ Click the **Restricted sites** zone to select it, and then click **Sites**. The Restricted sites dialog box appears, as shown in **Figure 38.6**.

■ Click to place the cursor in the **Add this Web site to the zone** field, and press **Ctrl+V**. The Web site URL is pasted into the dialog box.

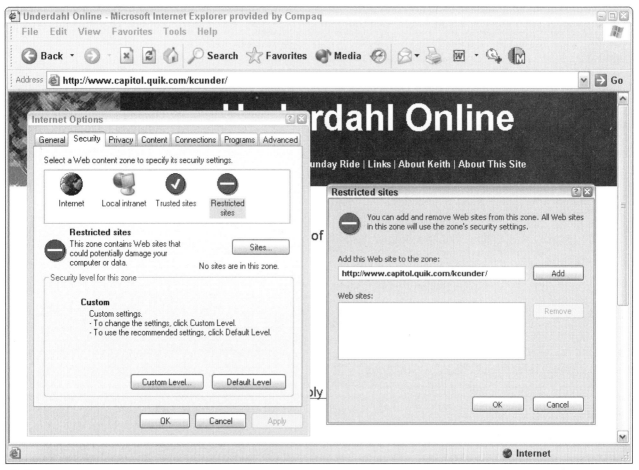

38.6

■ Click **Add**. The Web site is added to your Restricted sites zone.

■ Click **OK** to close the Restricted sites dialog box, and then click **OK** to close the Internet Options dialog box.

STEP 3: INSTALL A POP-UP BLOCKER

A third step you can take to avoid pop-up windows is to install and use a third-party pop-up blocking program. Be careful, however, because not all pop-up blockers work as advertised. Some pop-up blockers are resource intensive, or they cause errors when you try to visit your favorite sites. A few pop-up blockers are offered by the companies that are chief propagators of pop-up ads. There is something rather dubious about a company that chokes your computer with annoying pop-up ads and then offers to sell you a fix for those same pop-ups.

The only way to find an effective pop-up blocker is to conduct research online. One program that reviews well and performs reliably with Internet Explorer is PopUp Cop, available from www.popupcop.com. Tucows also offers a good selection of downloadable pop-up blockers at www.tucows.com. Click the link for Windows software, open the **Internet** category, and click the link for **Pop-up blockers** under **Web browsers and tools**.

MANAGING THE COOKIE MONSTER

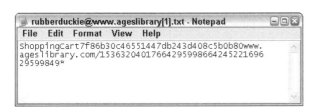

39.1   39.2

In the recent science-fiction film *Minority Report*, society members are constantly bombarded by advertisements custom-tailored to each individual. A billboard detects the identity of a person walking past and displays ads of interest to that individual. Many ads even address the passing individual by name, further personalizing the experience.

If you've been using the Internet for a while, you've probably noticed that the online world looks more and more like the science-fiction world in *Minority Report*. Web sites address you by name when you visit, and they seem to know things about you. Web sites don't identify you using DNA samples or computer chip implants — yet — but they do use simple little software tools called *cookies*. When you visit a Web site that uses cookies, a small text file is written on your hard drive containing information about your visit. You can open these text files, as shown in **Figure 39.1**, but the

203

information is usually stored in a cryptic manner only understood by Web programs. Cookies can contain many different kinds of information, including:

- **Web site log on information.** Many Web sites and forums require you to log on, but some allow you to save your log on information so that you don't have to reenter it every time you visit the site. The Web site saves your log on information in a cookie, and when you visit the site again it reads your log on data from the cookie and logs you on automatically.
- **Shopping cart contents.** If you shop online you're probably familiar with the concept of shopping carts. These are the special pages on a Web site where your order items are listed as you shop. Most shopping sites use cookies to record the contents of your shopping cart so that you can continue shopping for other items before you actually check out and make your purchase.
- **Usage data.** Some Web sites record your usage data from the site in cookies. The pages you visit, the length of time you spend at each one, and other usage data is often recorded in a cookie. Some Web sites use third-party advertisement servers that place ads on many different sites. If you visit several different Web sites that have ads from the same third-party ad server, the third-party ad server can use cookies to track your Web usage habits across all those different sites. These types of cookies raise the greatest privacy concerns.

Cookies are often misunderstood. Although they can raise privacy concerns, cookies cannot search your computer and provide additional personal data about you to a Web site. For example, if you do not provide a Web site with your e-mail address, the site can't use a cookie to search your computer and find your e-mail address. Nor can a cookie look at *other* cookies on your computer and find your address

there. A cookie can only be accessed by the Web site or server that placed it. Also, cookies can't contain viruses.

Controlling cookies is now easier than ever in Windows XP and Internet Explorer 6 or higher. You can apply different settings to different kinds of cookies, you can use custom cookie settings for different Web sites, and you can easily delete existing cookies. Privacy settings, as shown in **Figure 39.2**, let you quickly change how cookies are managed on your system.

STEP 1: CHOOSE A PRIVACY LEVEL

Open Internet Explorer, and choose **Tools ➢ Internet Options**. The Internet Options dialog box appears. Click the **Security** tab to bring it to the front. Your first step in controlling cookies is to set a basic privacy level for your **Internet** zone. Recall that Internet Explorer uses zones to manage security settings for different locations. The **Internet** zone applies to virtually all Web sites that you visit. The only Web sites that are not in the **Internet** zone are sites that you've manually added to your **Trusted sites** or **Restricted sites** zones, or pages on your local network.

Now click the **Privacy** tab to bring it to the front, as shown in **Figure 39.3**. The **Privacy** slider lets you quickly set a basic privacy level for cookies. You can choose one of six levels:

NOTE

The steps shown here apply to Internet Explorer. If you use a different Web browser some settings may vary, but you should still have similar control over cookie settings.

■ **Block All Cookies.** This setting provides the highest level of privacy. No new cookies can be created on your computer, and Web sites cannot access any cookies that are currently on your computer.

■ **High.** Cookies that don't have a privacy policy recognized by Internet Explorer are blocked, as are any cookies that contain personal information that could identify you. This privacy level blocks a majority of cookies.

■ **Medium High.** This level also blocks cookies that contain personal information, and it blocks third-party cookies that don't have a privacy

policy. Third-party cookies are cookies that come from a third-party ad server or similar source that is part of a Web site that you visit. I recommend this setting for a good balance of privacy and Web site usability.

■ **Medium.** This is the default level. If a Web site tries to create or read a first-party cookie containing personal information, a warning message appears asking whether you want to accept the cookie. This privacy level also provides a reasonable usability versus privacy balance.

■ **Low.** All first-party cookies are allowed. You are prompted to accept third-party cookies. This setting provides little privacy.

■ **Accept All Cookies.** As the name implies, this setting accepts all cookies from all sources. I recommend against using this setting because it provides an unacceptably low level of privacy.

After choosing a privacy level, click **Apply** to apply your changes.

39.3

TIP

If you begin to have problems using your favorite Web sites after changing cookie settings, try moving the privacy level down a notch to see if that improves usability. This helps you troubleshoot whether the source of the difficulties are your cookie settings or a problem on the Web site.

STEP 2: CUSTOMIZE COOKIE SETTINGS

Like most settings in Windows XP, Internet Explorer privacy settings can be fine-tuned beyond the basic settings levels described in the previous step. To customize privacy settings:

■ Open the **Privacy** tab of the Internet Options dialog box if it isn't already open, and then click **Advanced**. The Advanced Privacy Settings dialog box appears, as shown in **Figure 39.4**.

■ Place a checkmark next to **Override automatic cookie handling**. The remaining settings in the dialog box become available.

■ Choose an option for first-party cookies. You can choose to **Accept** or **Block** all first-party cookies, or you can choose **Prompt** as I have done in **Figure 39.4**. Prompt means that a warning dialog box asks if you want to accept each cookie that a Web site tries to plant on your system. Depending on the Web sites you frequent, these prompts could get tiresome after a while.

39.4

■ Choose an option for third-party cookies. I generally prefer to just block all third-party cookies, since third-party cookies are usually only used for marketing and usage tracking purposes. Third-party cookies usually don't enhance the usability of your favorite Web sites.

■ If you want to accept all session cookies, place a checkmark next to **Always allow session cookies**. Session cookies are temporary cookies that only remain active during the current Internet Explorer session. As soon as you close Internet Explorer, the session cookies disappear. Session cookies are usually harmless and are often connected to the usability of Web sites. For example, many shopping cart cookies are session cookies.

■ Click **OK** to accept your changes and return to the Internet Options dialog box.

STEP 3: BLOCK OR ALLOW A SPECIFIC WEB SITE

So far I've shown you how to control blanket cookie settings that apply to all Web sites in the Internet zone. Windows XP and Internet Explorer also allow you to block or allow cookies from specific Web sites. For example, if you set strict cookie privacy settings that cause usability problems on your favorite Web

> **NOTE**
>
> If you want to return to one of the default privacy levels, click **Default**. The privacy slider returns to Medium on the **Privacy** tab.

site — and that site is one you trust — you can specify more relaxed privacy settings just for that site. Here's how:

■ Open the **Privacy** tab of the Internet Options dialog box if it isn't open already, and then click **Edit** in Web sites area. The Per Site Privacy Actions dialog box appears, as shown in **Figure 39.5**.

■ Type the address for a Web site in the **Address of Web site** field. You can also copy and paste the address into the **Address of Web site** field.

■ If you want to block all cookies from the Web site, click **Block**. If you want to allow all cookies from the Web site, click **Allow**. Blocked and allowed Web sites are listed in the bottom of the Per Site Privacy Actions dialog box, as shown in **Figure 39.5**.

■ Click **OK** to close the Per Site Privacy Actions dialog box.

STEP 4: DELETE COOKIES (OPTIONAL)

If you are seriously concerned about what may be contained in the cookies already on your system, you can delete them. Windows XP organizes all cookies in individual cookie folders by user, so finding and deleting them is easy. Follow these steps:

■ Choose **Start** ➤ **My Computer** to open My Computer, and then click the icon for your hard drive. If you have more than one hard drive or partition, open the drive that contains your Windows XP installation.

■ Open the **Documents and Settings** folder.

■ Open the folder for your user account, and then open the **Cookies** folder. You see a list of cookies similar to **Figure 39.6**.

■ To delete all cookies, choose **Edit** ➤ **Select All**, and then press the **Delete** key on your keyboard. Your cookies are sent to the Windows Recycle Bin.

39.5

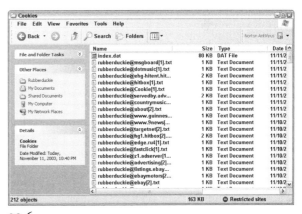

39.6

FINDING AND DESTROYING SPYWARE

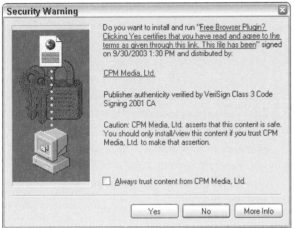

40.1

40.2

ABOUT THE FEATURE

Spyware programs degrade your computer's performance, display annoying ads, and in some cases violate your privacy. Finding and getting rid of spyware is challenging, but not impossible.

C ookies — described in the previous technique — were originally designed to make your Web browsing experience easier and more personalized. It didn't take online marketers long to figure out how to exploit cookies, but as I show in the previous technique, cookies are easy to control and they offer only limited power and information to marketers.

To address the shortcomings of cookies, programmers invented little programs that reside on your computer. These programs — often called *adware* or *spyware* — monitor your Web usage, displaying ads based on your usage. Some spyware programs replace banner ads on Web pages with different banner ads from the company that created the spyware. Others change your Web browser settings, switching your home page to a different Web site or adding unwanted toolbars to the browser window. In some rare cases, spyware programs can even collect personal information about you from e-mail and instant messaging programs.

Most spyware programs don't violate your privacy, but virtually all of them degrade the performance of your computer. When installed, spyware programs usually launch and run in the background every time you start Windows. This means that spyware eats some processor and memory resources, and in some cases spyware can cause system crashes.

Despite the scary-sounding name, spyware is usually legal. It can get on your system through a variety of techniques:

- Some Web sites are programmed to try to install spyware programs on your computer. When you visit a Web site and see a window like the one shown in **Figure 40.1**, it usually means that the site is trying to install a spyware program.
- Sometimes spyware programs are installed along with other programs such as e-mail programs, online file sharing programs, or instant message programs.
- In rare cases, spyware programs are installed by pop-up windows from some Web sites. This can happen with little or no visual indication that a new program is being installed on your computer.

Unlike cookies, spyware offers you no real redeeming value, unless, of course, you like to view random advertisements that slow down your computer. Combating spyware is a three-step process: Avoid, identify, and remove. Programs like Ad-Aware, shown in **Figure 40.2**, help you combat spyware on your computer.

STEP 1: AVOID SPYWARE

Believe it or not, most spyware programs only install on your computer after you agree to install them. If the spyware accompanies another program, information about the spyware was probably contained in the ten-page license agreement that you accepted. Stand-alone spyware programs often disguise themselves as pseudo-useful programs such as the one in **Figure 40.3**,

> **NOTE**
>
> In some cases, adware is built into a free version of a program. You may decide that viewing a few ads is a small price to pay for the free use of some valuable software, but you should do some research first to make sure the built-in adware doesn't cause problems for other people. Perform a Web search on the name of the program, or visit a related support forum and see if a lot of people complain about system instability or poor performance when the adware runs.

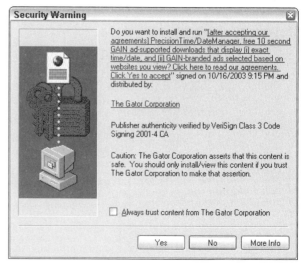

40.3

which is an ad-supported time and calendar program. When you see windows like this, you need to ask yourself if you really need a free browser plug-in or an "online wallet," and why is the Web site so eager to provide it?

Generally speaking, if you see a window similar to **Figure 40.3** you should click **No**. Instruct anyone else who uses your computer to click **No** as well. This helps you avoid the vast majority of spyware programs.

You should also be spyware-savvy when you install a new program. For starters, read the whole license agreement before you accept it, regardless of how long it is. Be wary of any program for which the license agreement grants the software provider or any other third party the right to collect personal information about you or your usage habits.

STEP 2: IDENTIFY SPYWARE

The best way to combat spyware is to keep it off your computer in the first place. Unfortunately, that is often easier said than done. Your computer may have spyware running on it right now. Perhaps you or another user inadvertently allowed the spyware program to install. Maybe a Web site's pop-up window installed the spyware without your knowledge. Or perhaps an adware program was installed when you installed some other program. The point is, despite your best efforts, spyware and adware can get on your computer.

> **NOTE**
>
> Make sure you read and comply with the license agreements for all your programs. The licenses for some programs may require you to keep adware programs on your system in order to use the software.

Most spyware programs provide some clues that they are installed. Clues can include:

- **System tray icons.** The system tray is the area in the lower-right corner of the Windows screen, next to the clock. Some spyware and adware programs install an icon in the system tray. You can use these icons to temporarily disable the spyware, but as soon as you restart your computer the spyware is back.
- **Pop-up windows.** Pop-up advertisements sometimes indicate an installed spyware program. In some rare cases, pop-up windows appear even when you aren't browsing the Web.
- **Audible indicators.** When you click a Web link, Internet Explorer makes a clicking sound. If you hear this clicking sound even when you haven't clicked any links for a long time, this may suggest that a spyware program is replacing banner ads on the current Web site with different ads.

These clues suggest that spyware may be installed, but a more reliable way to check is to use a spyware cleaner program such as Ad-Aware. You can download a free version of Ad-Aware for noncommercial use from www.lavasoft.de. Lavasoft also offers affordable licensing solutions for business use.

Spyware cleaners are often misunderstood because new spyware programs can appear on your system even after you install the cleaner program. Unlike antivirus programs, spyware cleaners usually don't run constantly and provide a continuous anti-spyware scan. Instead, you must periodically scan for spyware. Follow these steps:

- Install a spyware cleaner. In this example, I'm using Ad-Aware. Launch the spyware cleaner program after it's installed.
- In Ad-Aware, click **Scan Now**.
- Choose **Perform smart system-scan**, and click **Next**. The scan process begins. The scan takes a few minutes. When the scan is complete, a report

appears, as shown in **Figure 40.4**. As you can see in the figure, 46 possible spyware-related objects have been identified. These objects may be registry entries or program files that are possibly related to spyware programs.

■ Click **Next**. A summary of results appears as shown in **Figure 40.5**. Most of the objects shown in **Figure 40.5** are tracking cookies. For more details on each recognized object, click **Show logfile**.

STEP 3: REMOVE SPYWARE

Virtually any object identified by Ad-Aware or a similar spyware cleaner is related to a spyware or adware

program, and you can safely remove those objects. You should, however, carefully review the list and identify each object. If you want to keep any item in the summary list — see **Figure 40.5** — remove the checkmark next to it.

To remove spyware and adware objects, click **Next**. Ad-Aware asks you to confirm removal of the selected objects. Click **OK** to remove the objects.

If you don't want to use a spyware cleaner like Ad-Aware, you can sometimes remove spyware manually. To manually remove spyware:

■ Use **msconfig** to remove suspected spyware programs from your list of programs that launch whenever Windows XP starts. See Technique 2, "Controlling Startup Items," in Chapter 1 for more on using **msconfig**.

■ Check the registry keys **HKEY_CURRENT_USER\Software\Microsoft\Windows\CurrentVersion\Run** and **HKEY_LOCAL_MACHINE\Software\Microsoft\Windows\CurrentVersion\Run** for spyware programs. Technique 2, "Controlling Startup Items," in Chapter 1 also shows you how to review and edit the registry.

■ Disable and delete cookies as described in Technique 39, "Managing the Cookie Monster," in this chapter.

40.4

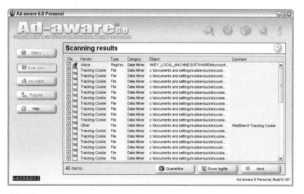

40.5

WARNING

Do not delete any registry key or disable any startup item unless you can positively identify it as spyware. If you're not sure about an object, perform a Web search on the filename. Countless Web sites can help you identify programs and files on your computer and determine whether they are spyware or serve a legitimate system function. If you remove something important, your computer or parts of it could cease to function properly.

SAFEGUARDING E-MAIL
IN OUTLOOK EXPRESS

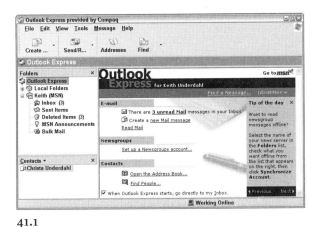

41.1

41.2

E-mail has become one of the most important things that people do with their computers. Microsoft includes a pretty good e-mail program with Windows XP called Outlook Express, shown in **Figure 41.1**. Just as e-mail is one of the most common uses for a computer, e-mail is also the most common method used for modern virus infection. E-mail viruses have proliferated in recent years, and Outlook Express is one of the most commonly targeted e-mail programs.

Outlook Express isn't inherently susceptible to viruses. It's often targeted by e-mail viruses simply because so many people use Outlook Express, as well as Microsoft's other e-mail program, Outlook. A common attack occurs when an e-mail virus infects the Outlook Express address book. The virus replicates itself and automatically sends itself to other people in your address book.

Some people advise against using Outlook Express because e-mail viruses so often target it. You can use Outlook Express safely, but there are some measures you should take to safeguard yourself from the most common infection methods. Start with antivirus software that reviews and disinfects incoming mail. You should also review security settings in Outlook Express, as shown in **Figure 41.2**. If you use Outlook Express, this technique shows you how to use it safely.

STEP 1: DISABLE THE PREVIEW PANE

By default, the Outlook Express Inbox displays messages in a preview pane, as shown in **Figure 41.3**. When you click a message in the list of messages, a preview appears in the preview pane below. In **Figure 41.3**, the preview pane shows a message I received from MSN Member Services.

When a message appears in the preview pane, that message is actually being opened. Some e-mail viruses infect your computer as soon as the message is opened. This means that if you receive one e-mail message and it's infected with a virus, the preview pane immediately opens the message and infects your computer. To prevent this problem you should disable the preview pane. This gives you a chance to

review the list of new e-mail messages and inspect or delete suspicious ones before they infect your system.

To disable the Outlook Express preview pane, choose **View ➤ Layout**. The Window Layout Properties dialog box appears. Remove the checkmark next to **Show preview pane** as shown in **Figure 41.4**. Click **OK** to close the Window Layout Properties dialog box. The preview pane is gone.

STEP 2: REVIEW SECURITY SETTINGS

Outlook Express has some important security settings that you should review. Choose **Tools ➤ Options** to open the Outlook Express Options dialog box as shown in **Figure 41.5**. Check the following settings:

- Choose **Restricted sites zone**. E-mail messages can include HTML and other content usually found on Web pages. This content can include

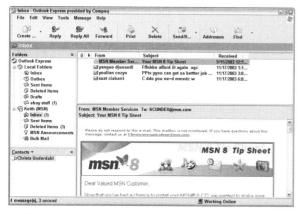

41.3

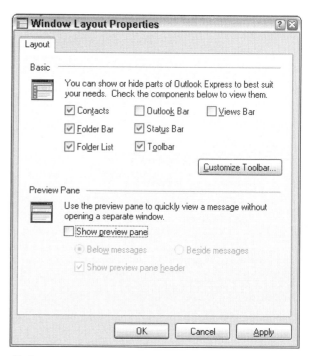

41.4

malicious code that can damage your computer or violate your privacy. Internet Explorer uses security zones to isolate this malicious code. A security zone is actually a group of settings, and the **Restricted sites zone** offers a more secure group of settings. This higher security level is advisable for Outlook Express because e-mail messages should not contain any code beyond basic HTML. This setting ensures that most types of malicious code are isolated in e-mail messages.

■ Make sure that the **Warn me when other applications try to send mail as me** option is checked. Many e-mail viruses send messages to others while putting your identity on the message to fool recipients into thinking the messages are legitimate.

■ Check the **Do not allow attachments to be saved or opened** option.

41.5

STEP 3: ANALYZE SUSPICIOUS MESSAGES

If you have a good antivirus program installed, it should identify and warn you about incoming messages that are infected with viruses. Some infected messages can slip through, however. You should carefully review your list of new messages before you open any of them. Several clues can indicate an infected message:

■ **Attachments.** A paper clip icon means that the message has an attachment. The message from Keith Underdahl named Wicked Screensaver shown in **Figure 41.6** has an attachment. Any message with an attachment should be greeted with suspicion.

■ **Sender.** If an e-mail contains an attachment and is from an unknown sender, it's almost certainly an e-mail you want to avoid. However, just because you recognize the sender doesn't mean it is a legitimate message. As mentioned earlier, some e-mail viruses send themselves from an infected account without the knowledge of the computer's owner.

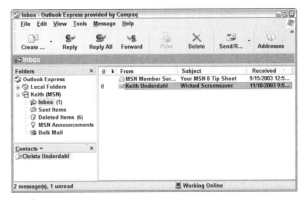

41.6

■ **Subject.** Subject lines can help you identify a message. Some common e-mail viruses have identifying subject lines. For example, Wicked Screensaver is a subject line associated with the virus WORM_SOBIG.F.

If you are suspicious of any e-mail message, you can get more information about what is contained in the message without actually opening it. Right-click the suspicious message in your Inbox and choose **Properties** from the context menu that appears. A properties dialog box for the message appears. Click the **Details** tab. This tab provides detailed information about the source of the message. Now click the **Message Source** button. This opens a text window that displays every bit of data in the message in ASCII text format. Viewed in this manner, any virus contained in the e-mail is harmless. As you can see in **Figure 41.7**, most of what you see in this window is pretty cryptic, but you can search through the contents for any text that may be useful and helps you identify the message. If you still can't identify the message after viewing the source, close the text window and the Properties dialog box, and delete the message without opening it.

STEP 4: FORCE PLAIN TEXT (OPTIONAL)

If you're really paranoid about e-mails that contain HTML formatting, you can force Outlook Express to display all messages in plain text format, regardless of the format that the sender used. Follow these steps:

■ In Outlook Express, choose **Tools** ➢ **Options**. The Options dialog box appears.

■ Click the **Read** tab to bring it to the front.

■ Place a checkmark next to **Read all messages in plain text** and click **OK** to close the Options dialog box.

Now, when you open an e-mail message, it displays in plain text. A warning message appears at the top of the message window advising you of any changes that were made to the message. Usually it says something like, "OE removed access to the following unsafe attachments in your mail: ATT00031.htm."

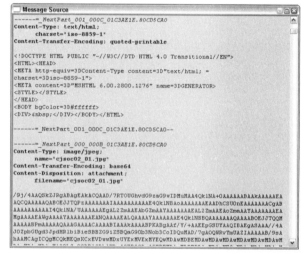

41.7

CHAPTER **7**

MASTERING DIGITAL MEDIA

S ince the multimedia Windows PC concept appeared more than a decade ago,
each new version of Windows has incor-
porated better, more-advanced multimedia capabilities. Windows has come a
long way since the days when a typical Windows 95
computer could barely play stuttering, postage
stamp–sized videos. Today, a typical Windows XP
computer can play full-screen DVD movies, store and
play thousands of MP3 or Windows Media songs,
and even edit and record DVDs of your own.

The techniques in this chapter show you how to
make the most of some of Windows XP's multimedia
features. I show you how to use Windows Media
Player to manage your music jukebox or play DVD
movies. I show you how to edit movies using
Windows Movie Maker, work with digital photos, and
build a home media server based on Windows XP.

Managing Your Music Jukebox

Creating Home Movies

Working with Digital Photographs

Turning Windows Media Player into a DVD Player

STOCKING AND MANAGING YOUR MUSIC JUKEBOX

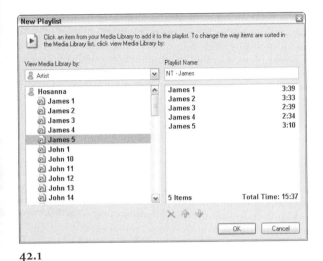

42.1

42.2

Personal computers have become much more than business workstations, game machines, or home Internet portals. PCs are now also multimedia-rich entertainment centers. Windows Media Player is a key component of Windows XP's multimedia capabilities. With Windows Media Player you can:

- Play music CDs
- Play movie DVDs (with the right plug-in software)
- Copy music from CDs to your hard drive
- Organize music on your hard drive
- Create custom playlists, as shown in **Figure 42.1**
- Record music onto portable music players or recordable CDs, as shown in **Figure 42.2**

This technique focuses on Windows Media Player's music capabilities, which allow you to turn your computer into a personal jukebox.

STEP 1: COPY MUSIC FROM A CD-ROM

Windows Media Player can quickly and easily copy music from audio CDs to your hard drive. This has many advantages, not the least of which is the fact that you don't have to constantly swap CDs when you want to listen to music from different discs. When a song is copied to your hard drive you can listen to it at any time using Windows Media Player.

By default, Windows Media Player copies music in Windows Media Audio — WMA — format. Plug-ins for Windows Media Player also allow you to copy music in MP3 format, but WMA offers superior quality with smaller file sizes. You can copy an entire disc at CD quality to your hard drive and use only about 42MB of hard drive space. By comparison, the same amount of CD-quality audio in MP3 format would use about 72MB of free space.

The only real problem with WMA is that it isn't as widely supported in consumer audio hardware as MP3. Whereas many car and portable audio players can play MP3 files, only a few can play WMA files. Nevertheless, if all you want to do is build a music library on your computer, WMA is a great format to use. You can adjust the data rate for the audio you copy in WMA format. If storage space is at a premium, reduce the data rate to reduce quality and file size. If you have plenty of storage space, increase the

---

TIP

Windows Media Player is probably already installed on your computer, but you should check to make sure that you have the latest version. Choose **Help ➢ Check for Player Updates**. Windows Media Player checks the Microsoft Web site for updates and provides instructions to download and install any updates that are available. This technique assumes you have Windows Media Player 9 or better.

---

data rate to create larger, higher quality files. To adjust the data rate for copied audio, open Windows Media Player, choose **Tools ➢ Options**, and click the **Copy Music** tab to bring it to the front, as shown in **Figure 42.3**. Choose **Windows Media Audio** in the **Format** menu, and move the **Audio quality** slider to change the data rate. A data rate of 96 Kbps or better is considered CD quality for WMA-format audio.

Copying music using Windows Media Player is easy. Follow these steps:

- Open Windows Media Player, and then place an audio CD in your CD-ROM drive.
- Click **Copy from CD** on the left side of the Windows Media Player window. A list of tracks on the audio CD appears. If your computer is connected to the Internet, Windows Media Player tries to obtain information about the CD from online databases. If Media Player can identify the

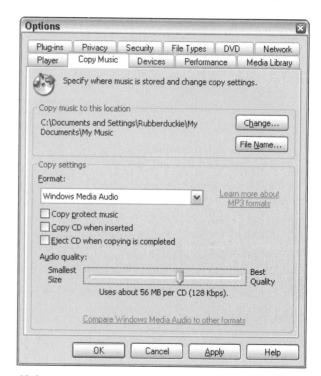

42.3

CD, it fills in the names of tracks, artists, composers, and other information automatically.

■ If track information doesn't appear automatically, enter your own track information for tracks you want to copy. At the very least you should enter the song title and artist name as I've done for the first track in **Figure 42.4**. This helps you identify and organize the songs later in your Windows Media Player library. To modify track information, click once on the piece of information you want to change — such as the title — wait a second, and then click it again. The cursor appears and you can type new information about the track into the field. Press **Tab** to quickly move to the next information field.

■ Remove checkmarks next to songs that you don't want to copy. In **Figure 42.4**, I am only going to copy the first song.

■ Click **Copy Music** at the top of the Windows Media Player window. Progress bars show you the progress of the copying process. When copying is complete, the song is added to your Windows Media Player library.

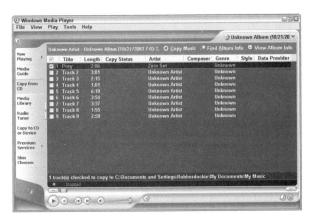

42.4

STEP 2: IMPORT MUSIC FILES

If you already have some music files on your computer in MP3 or another format, you can import those files into Windows Media Player so that those files can be organized with the rest of your music. You can add files to your Media Player using one of several different methods:

■ Make Windows Media Player search your computer for media files. To perform the search, choose **Tools ➢ Search for Media Files** and follow the instructions on-screen to search your computer.

■ Choose **File ➢ Add to Media Library ➢ Add File or Playlist** to add a single file to your library.

■ Choose **File ➢ Add to Media Library ➢ Add Folder** to add all of the files in a given folder to your library.

Remember, you can organize files by artist, album, or genre in Windows Media Player. To effectively manage your media library you need to know what each file contains, so make sure that all newly imported files have a title, artist, and genre listed.

STEP 3: CREATE A PLAYLIST

Radio stations use playlists to plan which songs they play during the day. You can use playlists to plan which music you want Windows Media Player to play. You can add any song from your Windows Media Player library to a playlist, specifying which songs play and in what order. To create a playlist in Windows Media Player:

■ Click the **Media Library** button to open the Media Library, and then click the **Playlists** button near the top of the Windows Media Player window, and choose **New Playlist** from the submenu that appears. Alternatively, choose **File ➤ New Playlist**. The New Playlist dialog box appears, as shown in **Figure 42.5**.

■ Enter a descriptive name for your playlist in the **Playlist Name** field.

■ Choose a selection criterion in the **View Media Library by** field. In **Figure 42.5** I've chosen **Artist**, which means that a list of artists appears below. I can click an artist's name to view all songs by that artist.

■ Click a song on the left to add it to the playlist on the right. Use the arrow buttons under the playlist to move a song up or down in the playlist, thereby changing the order of play.

■ Click **OK** to close the New Playlist dialog box.

Your new playlist now appears in the list of Windows Media Player's playlists as shown in **Figure 42.6**. You can click and drag additional songs to add them to the playlist if you want.

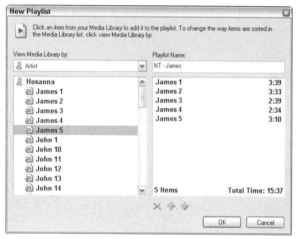

42.5

42.6

STEP 4: RECORD A MIX CD

Another cool feature of Windows Media Player is the ability to record songs directly from your media library to recordable CDs. If your computer has a CD-R or CD-RW drive, you can use Windows Media Player to directly assemble and record audio CDs. This comes in handy if you want to record a CD of songs that suit a special occasion. For example, you may want to record a disc of your favorite rock songs to listen to when you jog or exercise, or a disc of romantic songs for a quiet evening with that special someone. To record a CD using Windows Media Player:

■ Create a playlist as described in the previous step. The playlist should include all of the songs you want to record on the CD, in order. Keep an eye on the **Total Time** listed at the bottom of the screen for the playlist to make sure the total doesn't exceed 72 minutes, or 80 minutes if you have 700MB recordable CDs.

■ Place a blank recordable CD in your CD-R drive. If Windows XP detects the blank disc and shows a dialog box asking what you want to do, click **Cancel**.

■ Click **Copy to CD or Device** on the left side of the Windows Media Player window.

■ In the pull-down menu above the left side of the screen, choose the playlist that you created for the CD. The list of songs from the playlist appears in the left window. In **Figure 42.7**, I have chosen a playlist called **NT - James**. If you want to leave one or two songs from the playlist off the CD, remove the checkmark next to the unwanted songs.

■ Click **Copy** in the upper-right corner of the Windows Media Player window. Media Player inspects each song and converts them to CD audio format. This means that you can play the disc in almost any music CD player.

42.7

CREATING HOME MOVIES

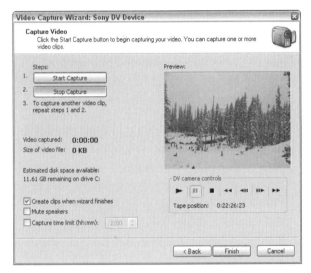

43.1

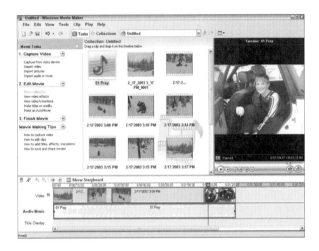

43.2

ABOUT THE FEATURE

Moviemaking was at one time a complex and wildly expensive proposition, but modern computers bring this art within reach of almost anyone. With a digital camcorder and the right software you can edit video, add special effects, and quickly publish your finished movies on tape, DVD, or the Internet.

The art of moviemaking has been refined and advanced for more than a century, but until recently this art form was out of reach for most of us. Unless you had access to Hollywood or broadcast-style video production facilities with equipment costing millions of dollars, your home movies probably consisted entirely of raw, unedited footage.

But times have changed for the better, and if you have a fairly modern computer and a camcorder, you can easily and cheaply perform movie magic that was unheard of just a few years ago. With editing software on your computer, you can pick and choose scenes, trim out the unwanted parts, and add some special effects. And now, thanks to broadband Internet access and affordable DVD burners, sharing your finished movies has never been easier.

Before you can make movie magic, you need to make sure that you have the right gear. Things you need include:

- **Camcorder.** A digital camcorder provides better quality and is easier to work with. Common digital camcorder tape formats include MiniDV, Digital8, and MicroMV. However, if you have an analog camcorder — for example, Hi8 or VHS-C — you can still use it to make movies. If you're shopping for a new camcorder, I recommend a digital camcorder that uses the MiniDV tape format.

- **Computer.** Almost any computer that can run Windows XP should also be able to make movies. Ideally your computer should have a 1GHz or faster processor and 512MB of RAM. You can get by with only 256MB of RAM, but you'll find that editing tasks happen much more slowly. Your computer should also have the biggest hard drive you can afford because video files take up lots of space. An 80GB or larger drive should provide adequate working space.

- **Capture device.** This is what gets video from the camcorder into your computer. Digital camcorders use the IEEE-1394 — also called FireWire — interface for video capture. If your computer doesn't already have an IEEE-1394 port, you need to add one. IEEE-1394 cards are often sold as *digital video capture cards*. In **Figure 43.1**, I am capturing video from a digital camcorder attached to an IEEE-1394 port. If you want to capture video from an analog camcorder or VCR, you need a special analog capture device. Products like Pinnacle Studio AV or InterVideo WinDVD Creator AVDV

> **NOTE**
>
> If you buy a new hard drive, make sure its speed is at least 7200rpm. Also, do not use external hard drives for video editing; they usually aren't fast enough.

are available for less than $150 and include both analog capture cards and versatile editing software.

- **Software.** Video-editing software is what turns your computer into a personal movie studio. Many video capture cards come with editing software, and Microsoft offers Windows Movie Maker — shown in **Figure 43.2** — free for Windows XP users. If you don't already have Windows Movie Maker 2 or higher, visit Microsoft at www. microsoft.com/downloads/ and download the latest version. Version 2 offers many important improvements over the first version of Windows Movie Maker. Windows Movie Maker 2 makes it easy to edit your movies and distribute them online or on video tape, but if you want to record DVDs you need a third-party program, such as Pinnacle Studio or InterVideo WinDVD Creator, that supports DVD creation.

- **DVD burner (optional).** If you want to put your movies on DVD, you need to install a DVD burner. I recommend a DVD burner that lists support for both the DVD-R and DVD+R media formats. This ensures that you do not accidentally buy the wrong kind of blank DVDs.

STEP 1: PREPARE YOUR COMPUTER

After you install video capture hardware and editing software on your computer, you're almost ready to start making movies. Video editing is very resource intensive, and if your computer runs low on resources while you are capturing, editing, or exporting video, serious quality problems result. Before you work with video:

- Close all other applications, including e-mail programs, Web browsers, and media players.
- Temporarily disable as many memory-resident programs as possible, including antivirus programs. Memory-resident programs can usually be disabled by right-clicking their respective icons in the Windows system tray, in the lower-right

corner next to the clock, and choosing a close or disable option from the menu that appears.

■ Defragment your hard drive by choosing **Start ➢ All Programs ➢ Accessories ➢ System Tools ➢ Disk Defragmenter**. Many computer experts believe that hard drive defragmentation is no longer important with Windows XP, and in most cases they're right. However, video editing is one of the few tasks that still benefits from a freshly defragmented hard drive.

■ Make sure you have plenty of free hard drive space. One minute of digital video usually consumes about 200MB of storage space. Editing tasks require even more space. Figure that you'll actually need about 600MB of free space for every minute of video.

■ Temporarily disable screen savers from the Display icon in the Windows Control Panel as shown in **Figure 43.3**. Temporarily disable power management settings in the Control Panel's Power Options icon as shown in **Figure 43.4**. This is

especially important if you plan to record your movie onto DVD, because the DVD creation process can take hours even with a fast computer. If you use a laptop, plug it in to wall power rather than worry about battery life.

STEP 2: CAPTURE VIDEO

Capturing is the process of transferring video from the camcorder tape to your computer's hard drive. If you use an analog capture card to capture video from an analog camcorder, you probably need to use the software that came with the card. If you capture video from a digital camcorder, you can use Windows Movie Maker.

■ Connect your digital camcorder to the computer's IEEE-1394 port. If you don't already have the right cable, buy a 6-pin to 4-pin IEEE-1394 cable, available at most electronics retailers.

■ Turn the camcorder on to VTR or Player mode.

43.3

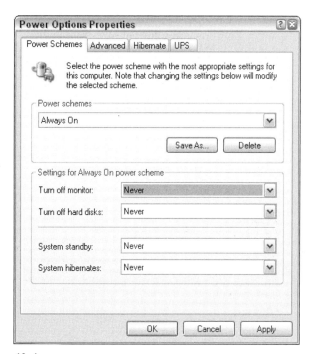

43.4

- Launch Windows Movie Maker from the **All Programs** menu.
- In Movie Maker, choose **File ➢ Capture Video**. In the Video Capture Wizard that appears, enter a name for your capture and click **Next**.
- Choose a video quality setting. If you plan to export the movie back to tape for viewing on TVs, choose **Digital Device Format (DV-AVI)**. Otherwise, choose the **Best Quality** option. The **Best Quality** option makes more efficient use of hard drive space, and offers adequate quality if you only plan to share your movies online. Click **Next** again.
- Choose a Capture Method. Most of the time you want to choose **Capture parts of the tape manually**, because the tape probably contains portions of video that you don't want to capture. Click **Next**.
- Use the DV camera controls (**Figure 43.5**) to identify video that you want to capture. If you are capturing from a digital camcorder connected to an IEEE-1394 port, the playback controls in the Capture Wizard should automatically control the camcorder. Use the **Start Capture** and **Stop Capture** buttons to start and stop video capture. When you're done capturing, click **Finish**.

STEP 3: ARRANGE SCENES

Captured video clips appear as icons in Windows Movie Maker. Each clip represents a different scene, and arranging those scenes into a movie is easy.

> **TIP**
>
> If your computer has less than 512MB of RAM, disable the **Show Preview During Capture** option. This helps prevent quality problems if your computer runs low on resources. You should still be able to preview the video on your camcorder's viewfinder or LCD screen.

- Click and drag scenes to the Storyboard, as shown in **Figure 43.6**. Place scenes in the order in which you want them to appear in the movie.
- To fine-tune your edits, click **Show Timeline** above the Storyboard to reveal the Timeline (**Figure 43.7**). Click and drag left or right on the edges of clips to trim off portions that you don't want to use.

STEP 4: ADD TRANSITIONS AND EFFECTS

Transitions can provide interesting visual breaks between scenes, and effects can modify the appearance of a clip. Like most editing programs, Windows Movie Maker includes a diverse set of transitions and effects.

- Choose **Tools ➢ Video Transitions** to reveal a collection of transitions. Select a transition and click the **Play** button on the right side of the screen to preview it. Click and drag a transition between scenes in the Storyboard or Timeline to add it to your movie. Use transitions sparingly; often, the best transition is no transition at all.

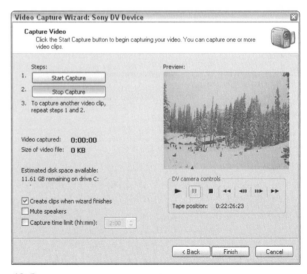

43.5

■ Choose **Tools ➢ Video Effects** to view a list of effects in Windows Movie Maker. Like transitions, effects can be previewed on the right side of the screen. Click and drag an effect you want to use to a clip in the Timeline or Storyboard. You can use the **Film Age** effects, for example, to give a clip an old-fashioned appearance.

STEP 5: ADD A SOUNDTRACK

The right music can profoundly influence the emotions and perceptions of your movie viewers. Windows Movie Maker can import music in WAV, MP3, and WMA formats among others, which means that songs you copy to your hard drive using Windows Media Player can be imported directly into Windows Movie Maker.

■ In Windows Movie Maker choose **File ➢ Import Into Collections** and locate an audio file that you want to use in your movie.

■ Click and drag an imported audio file to the **Audio/Music** track in the Timeline, as shown in **Figure 43.8**. Click and drag the edges of the audio clip in the Timeline to trim it.

■ Right-click the audio clip in the Timeline and choose **Volume** from the context menu that appears. Adjust the volume slider to fine-tune the volume of the clip.

43.6

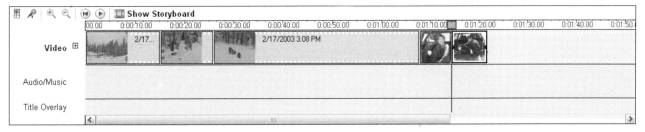

43.7

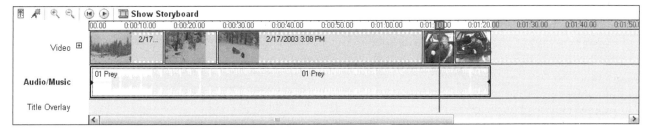

43.8

STEP 6: EXPORT YOUR MOVIE

Perhaps the most difficult part of moviemaking is deciding when the project is finished. It seems like there is always some little detail that could be better, but at some point you need to wrap up your movie and call it done.

- Choose **File ➢ Save Movie File**. The Save Movie Wizard begins.
- Select a medium to which you want to save your movie. If you're not sure what to choose, click **My Computer** and then **Next**.
- Type a filename for the movie, and click **Next** again.

> **NOTE**
>
> Make sure you check with friends and associates before sending large movie files in e-mail. Try to keep any e-mailed movie under 2MB, because many e-mail servers reject file attachments that are larger than 2MB. If you plan to put your movie on a Web page, keep in mind that over half of all Internet users still have slow dial-up connections. The larger your movie file, the less likely it is that dial-up users will view it.

- Review the details in the Movie Setting screen. Pay special attention to the **Estimate Space Required** field. In **Figure 43.9**, the estimated size of my movie is 4.10MB. If I want to e-mail my movie to friends, that is probably too big. If the file size seems too large, click **Show More Choices**. Choose **Best Fit to File Size**, and choose a preferred file size.
- Click **Next** to save the movie.

43.9

WORKING WITH DIGITAL PHOTOGRAPHS

44.1

44.2

ABOUT THE FEATURE

If you have a digital camera, Windows XP includes tools to help you organize and even modify your pictures.

Depending on whom you ask, digital camera sales are either about to or already have overtaken film camera sales. If you're reading this, chances are you are already in that group of people who already owns a digital camera. One of the most important advantages of a digital camera is the ability to transfer images directly from the camera to your computer. Digital images that are saved on your hard drive can be retouched to improve their appearance, or shared through e-mail and on the Web.

Windows XP includes tools that you can use to work with digital images whether they are produced by a digital camera or scanned using a scanner. Windows XP helps you organize and preview your photos as shown in **Figure 44.1**, and Windows Paint helps you prepare images for online use as shown in **Figure 44.2**.

STEP 1: ORGANIZE AND PREVIEW PHOTOS

The **My Documents** folder in Windows XP includes a subfolder called **My Pictures**. This is a good place to store your image files, and you can create subfolders in the **My Pictures** folder to further organize your images. If you want to share images with other people who use your computer or other network users, place pictures in the **Shared Pictures** folder within the **Shared Documents** folder.

Windows XP provides several options to help you preview your images. Open a folder containing images, and use one of these methods to preview pictures:

■ Choose **View ➤ Thumbnails**. The folder view changes so that small thumbnails of each image file appear as shown in **Figure 44.3**.

■ For a larger preview of individual images, choose **View ➤ Filmstrip**. Images now appear in

> **TIP**
>
> To open an image in the default image-editing program, simply double-click the file.

a single horizontal row as shown in **Figure 44.4**. Click an image to see a larger preview above the filmstrip of thumbnails.

■ To get an even larger preview, right-click an image and choose **Open With ➤ Windows Picture and Fax Viewer** from the context menu. A larger preview appears as shown in **Figure 44.5**.

44.4

44.3

44.5

STEP 2: CROP PICTURES USING PAINT

Microsoft Paint isn't the most advanced image-editing program, but if you don't have another program, you can use Paint for basic tasks. One of the most basic tasks is cropping, where you remove unwanted portions of an image near the edges of the picture. To crop an image using Paint:

- Choose **Start** ➤ **All Programs** ➤ **Accessories** ➤ **Paint**. Paint opens.
- In Paint, choose **File** ➤ **Open** and browse to the image you want to edit. Open the image.
- Click the **Select** tool at the top of the right-hand column on the Paint toolbar, and click and drag a box around the portion of the image that you want to keep, as shown in **Figure 44.6**.

- Choose **Edit** ➤ **Copy** to copy the selection.
- Choose **File** ➤ **New** to create a new image file. If you are asked to save changes to the previous file, click **No**.
- Choose **Edit** ➤ **Paste**. The selection is pasted into the new image, as shown in **Figure 44.7**. If necessary, click and drag the selection handles at the edges of the white background area to eliminate it.

STEP 3: CHOOSE AN IMAGE FORMAT

If you plan to use your image on the Internet, you should choose the image's file format carefully. When

44.6

44.7

you're done making changes to the image in Paint, choose **File ➤ Save**. The Save As dialog box appears, as shown in **Figure 44.8**. Type a name for the image file, and then choose a format from the **Save as type** menu. The format you choose depends on the type of image you are saving. Microsoft Paint offers three Web-friendly formats:

- **GIF.** This format offers excellent compression for images with less color variety. GIF is a good format to use for buttons, line art, and other Web graphics, but it is not well suited for photographs and images with many different colors.
- **JPEG.** This is the ubiquitous format for sharing digital photos online.
- **PNG.** This alternative to GIF offers superior compression, which means smaller file sizes. Unfortunately PNG is not as widely supported as GIF or JPEG.

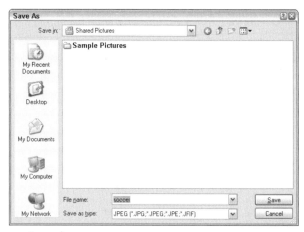

44.8

45

TURNING WINDOWS MEDIA PLAYER INTO A DVD PLAYER

45.1

45.2

DVD-ROM drives have become virtually ubiquitous in modern personal computers. But users are often surprised to find that even though their new computer has a DVD drive, it cannot play DVD movies. In order to play DVD movies in Windows XP, you must have a DVD decoder installed on your system. A decoder is a software tool that allows Windows to use your DVD-ROM drive to play movies.

If you recently bought a new computer with a DVD-ROM drive, chances are you already have a DVD decoder. If you're not sure, place a movie DVD in the DVD-ROM drive. Does the movie play? If so, you already have a DVD decoder, and you don't need to install another one. But if the movie doesn't play, then you probably need a decoder. Some new computers don't include DVD decoders even if a DVD-ROM drive is installed. And of course, if you added a DVD-ROM drive to your existing computer, there's a chance that the drive's installation software did not include a DVD decoder.

If you need a decoder, an easy and affordable way to get one is to purchase a decoder that works as a plug-in to Windows Media Player. When a DVD decoder plug-in is installed, you can play DVD movies directly in Windows Media Player, as shown in **Figure 45.1**. Windows Media Player even offers a full-screen viewing mode, as shown in **Figure 45.2**, which turns your computer monitor into a high-quality, clutter-free TV screen. This technique shows you how to find, install, and use DVD player plug-ins for Windows Media Player.

STEP 1: FIND A PLUG-IN

Several companies offer affordable DVD decoder plug-ins for Windows Media Player. Microsoft makes it easy to find and obtain these plug-ins. In Windows Media Player, choose **Tools** ➢ **Download** ➢ **Plug-ins**. Your Web browser opens to a Microsoft Web page listing various plug-ins available for Windows Media Player. Three DVD decoder plug-ins that likely appear on the page include:

- CyberLink PowerDVD SE
- InterVideo DVD Xpack
- Sonic CinePlayer DVD Decoder

TIP

If you're thinking about buying a portable DVD player, consider buying a low-cost DVD-equipped laptop instead. If you shop around you should be able to find a suitable laptop for only a couple hundred dollars more than the price of a typical portable DVD player, and the laptop — besides being useful for many different things — will almost certainly have a larger display screen.

Each of these DVD decoders retails for about $15. If you are willing to spend an extra $5, each company will also throw in a plug-in that allows you to encode audio in MP3 format directly in Windows Media Player.

The Microsoft Web site featuring these plug-ins includes links to purchase and download whichever plug-in you choose. Make sure that the plug-in you choose is compatible with your version of Windows Media Player. For example, a plug-in designed for Windows Media Player 9 may not work if you still have Windows Media Player 8. If you're not sure which version of Media Player you have, choose **Help** ➢ **About Windows Media Player**. A dialog box listing the version number appears. Choose **Help** ➢ **Check for Player Updates** to update your version of Windows Media Player.

STEP 2: INSTALL THE PLUG-IN

Follow the instructions provided by the software vendor to install your DVD decoder plug-in. Usually you just double-click the downloaded installer file and follow the instructions on-screen to complete setup. Make sure Windows Media Player is closed when you run the installer. When the plug-in is installed, follow these steps to review and adjust settings for the decoder:

- Open Windows Media Player and choose **Tools** ➢ **Options**. The Options dialog box appears.
- Click the **DVD** tab to bring it to the front as shown in **Figure 45.3**.
- To activate parental controls, place a checkmark next to **Parental controls**, and choose a rating level from the **Select a rating** menu. If you set a maximum rating, anyone who logs on to Windows with a restricted access user account cannot view movies that have a higher rating. For example, if you set the rating at **PG-13**, restricted

account users — such as your kids — cannot watch movies that are rated R, NC-17, or are unrated.

■ Click **Defaults** under Language settings. Choose default languages for DVD audio, captions and subtitles, and menus as shown in **Figure 45.4**. If you just want to use whatever language is the default for each DVD you watch, choose (**Title Default**) from the top of each pull-down menu. Click **OK** to close the Default Language Settings dialog box.

■ Click **Advanced** to set advanced decoder options. Available options vary depending on which decoder you have installed. The default settings are usually acceptable, but if you want to use advanced settings, consult the plug-in's documentation for details. Click OK to close the advanced settings dialog box.

■ In the Options dialog box, click the **File Types** tab.

■ Make sure that a checkmark appears next to **DVD Video**. This makes Windows Media Player the default DVD movie player on your computer.

■ Click **OK** to close the Options dialog box.

STEP 3: PLAY A DVD

When you place a DVD movie in your computer's DVD-ROM drive, one of several things may happen:

■ Windows XP detects the DVD movie and automatically plays it in Windows Media Player.

■ Windows XP detects the DVD movie and asks you what you want to do. Choose **Play DVD in Windows Media Player** from the dialog box that appears, and click **OK**.

■ A message window appears asking if you want to install player software from the DVD. Some newer movie DVDs include decoder software on the disc that automatically tries to install when you place the disc in your DVD-ROM drive. If you have a DVD decoder plug-in for Windows Media Player you don't need additional DVD decoder software, so you can safely cancel the installation process.

■ Nothing seems to happen.

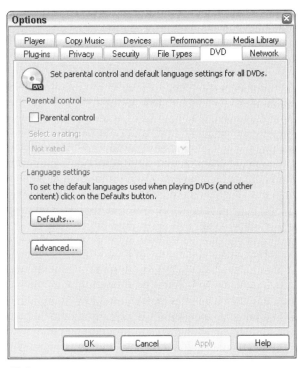

45·3

45·4

If nothing happens, or if you have to cancel installation of some other software, open Windows Media Player and choose **Play ➢ DVD, VCD, or CD Audio**. The DVD movie plays, as shown in **Figure 45.5**. Use the playback controls at the bottom of the Windows Media Player window to control playback, or click DVD menu items using the mouse pointer. To return to the DVD's menu, right-click the video image at

any time and choose **DVD Features ➢ Root Menu** from the context menu. If you want the movie to fill the whole computer screen, as shown in **Figure 45.6**, maximize the Windows Media Player window, and then press **Alt+Enter** on your keyboard. Press **Alt+Enter** again to restore the view to normal.

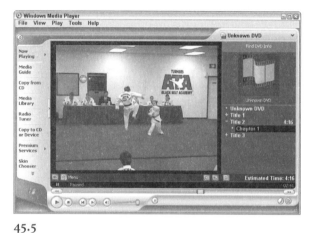

45.5

45.6

BUILDING A HOME MEDIA SERVER

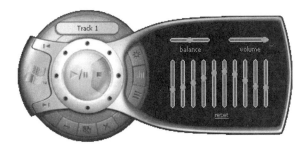

46.1

46.2

ABOUT THE FEATURE

Thanks to powerful multimedia capabilities, a computer running Windows XP can replace traditional audio and video equipment in your home entertainment system.

As you have seen in this chapter and throughout your user experience, Windows XP offers powerful multimedia features. With the right hardware, a computer running Windows XP can store and play thousands of CD-quality songs, play DVD movies, and more. Because of Windows XP's multimedia capabilities, many people are choosing to replace the traditional audio and video components in their home entertainment and theater systems with computers running Windows XP. A Windows XP computer can serve virtually all home-theater functions:

■ **CD player.** Windows computers have been able to play music CDs for years, as shown in **Figure 46.1**. With Windows Media Player you can copy CDs to your hard drive in WMA format, allowing you to quickly access your entire music library without constantly switching discs.

■ **DVD player.** With a DVD-ROM drive and DVD decoder software, Windows XP plays DVD movies at full quality, as shown in **Figure 46.2**.

- **TV player.** Watch TV on your computer using a TV tuner card.
- **Digital video recorder.** A popular accessory in modern home entertainment systems are devices that digitally record video. Many systems rely on subscription-based services like TiVo and Replay TV, but with the right software and a big enough hard drive you can turn your media center computer into a digital video recorder as well. When your media center computer is set up as a digital video recorder, you can pause live TV or watch your favorite shows later, just like with a subscription-based recorder.

This technique helps you choose or build a Windows XP–based home media server.

STEP 1: CHOOSE A PREBUILT SYSTEM

Many computer vendors offer computer systems specifically designed as home media servers. In fact, Microsoft offers a special version of Windows called Windows XP — Media Center Edition. This edition of Windows is only available preinstalled on new PCs, and any new computer running Media Center Edition should make an excellent basis for your media server PC. Purchasing a computer that already includes all of the features you want is by far the easiest way to go. Features you should look for include:

- **Display adapter.** The computer should have a high-quality display adapter. I recommend an AGP display adapter with no less than 128MB of

> **NOTE**
>
> Building or upgrading a computer is a complex process that should only be undertaken if you are experienced with upgrading and configuring PC hardware. Full instructions for building a PC are beyond the scope of this book.

video memory. Ideally the display adapter should not share system RAM, and it should also include video outputs that are compatible with a high-quality TV or video monitor. A composite video output is compatible with more TVs, but a component or S-video output gives better quality.
- **Sound card.** Make sure the sound card is compatible with 5.1 channel surround-sound audio.
- **Hard drive.** The bigger the hard drive, the better. A large hard drive allows you to store more songs as well as record more digital video. With modern hard drive prices, there's no reason to get a media center computer with less than a 200GB hard drive.
- **Processor and RAM.** Almost any new computer will have a processor that is powerful enough for your media center. I recommend a 3GHz or better Intel Pentium 4 or AMD Athlon XP processor. Your media center PC should also have at least 512MB of DDR RAM.
- **TV tuner.** If the computer has a built-in TV tuner card you can connect the cable for your TV signal directly to the computer.
- **Radio tuner.** Some computers include radio tuners that receive broadcast radio signals. A radio tuner card allows you to listen to your favorite local radio stations on your media center PC.
- **Remote control.** A modern entertainment center isn't complete without a remote control. Try to choose a media center PC that includes an easy-to-use remote control.
- **Software.** Look for a media center PC that includes software for multimedia functions such as digital video recording and remote control. A computer you plan to use as a media center PC should run Windows XP Media Center Edition.

STEP 2: BUILD YOUR OWN SYSTEM

If you have a lot of experience building your own PCs and you plan to build your own media center computer, try to follow the specs listed in the previous step for choosing a prebuilt system. Some special considerations when building your own media center PC include:

- **Windows XP.** Microsoft does not offer Media Center Edition as a stand-alone product; it is only available with a new PC. Fortunately, this isn't a big problem, because you can run a media center PC just fine with Windows XP Home or Windows XP Professional.
- **Motherboard.** Avoid a motherboard that includes an integrated display adapter that shares system RAM with video memory. Choose a motherboard that includes a separate AGP slot to accept an AGP video card.
- **Video card.** If possible, choose an AGP video card that also incorporates TV inputs and outputs such as the ATI *All in Wonder* cards. Some video cards — those designed specifically for media center PCs — include remote controls as well. While you're at it, look for a video card that includes a remote control.
- **Hard drive.** Buy the biggest hard drive you can afford. I recommend a 7200rpm EIDE drive.
- **IEEE-1394 adapter.** Add an IEEE-1394 adapter — also called a FireWire port — so that you can easily connect your digital camcorder to your media center PC.

STEP 3: ADD A REMOTE CONTROL

No home entertainment center is complete without a remote control. You can easily add a wireless remote control to your media center PC if it doesn't already

have a remote. Add-on remotes usually have a receiver that connects to your computer's USB or serial port. A couple of commercially available multimedia remotes include:

- ATI Remote Wonder — www.ati.com/products/remotewonder/
- Harmony SST-series remotes — www.harmonyremote.com

Another option is to control your media center PC using a Pocket PC. If you have a Pocket PC with wireless networking capability, you can use the Pocket PC to remotely control your media center computer. Programs are available that allow you to control your media server with a Pocket PC or virtually any other network PC. Two such programs include:

- NetOp Remote Control — www.netop.com
- Griffin Technology Total Remote — www.griffintechnology.com/griffinmobile/

STEP 4: CONFIGURE WINDOWS XP

Windows XP doesn't require much in the way of configuration as you turn the computer into a media server. However, I do have some general recommendations:

- Don't install any programs on the media server that aren't directly related to media playback and management. This saves computer resources for music storage and other media-related tasks.
- Minimize the number of startup programs that run on the media server. Although you should still run antivirus software on your media server, other startup programs simply eat up memory that is better devoted to movie playback. See Technique 2, "Controlling Startup Items" in Chapter 1 for more on taking command of startup items on your computer.
- Use a screen saver. Screen savers were originally invented to prevent screen burn caused by images that remained static for long periods of time. Modern computer monitors are resistant to screen

> **NOTE**
>
> Remember, if you're building a new PC from scratch, you need to buy a full version of Windows XP, not an upgrade version.

burn, but some TVs are still easily damaged if you leave a single, unchanging picture on-screen for long periods of time. A screen saver doesn't interfere with DVD playback because Windows XP does not activate screen savers while movies play.

■ Set up your display for across-the-room visibility. Windows XP Media Center Edition incorporates an interface that you can easily see and use while sitting on a sofa across a room. You can adjust the display for any version of Windows XP so that you can see it better as well. Right-click an empty area of the Windows desktop, and choose **Properties**. On the **Settings** tab, choose a smaller screen resolution such as 800 × 600 as shown in **Figure 46.3**. On the **Appearance** tab, choose **Extra Large Fonts** from the **Font size** menu. If you still find that screen elements are too small to see easily, see Technique 9, "Making Windows XP Accessible," in Chapter 2 for more on making the Windows interface more visible.

■ Choose **Start ➢ Set Program Access and Defaults**, and specify your default media player. In the Add or Remove Programs window that appears, choose the **Custom** configuration mode, and then specify which program you want to be the default media player. In **Figure 46.4** I've chosen Windows Media Player as the default player, and I've disabled the **Enable access to this program** option for other media players on the computer. This ensures that my default media player settings don't get hijacked the next time I try to play a DVD movie.

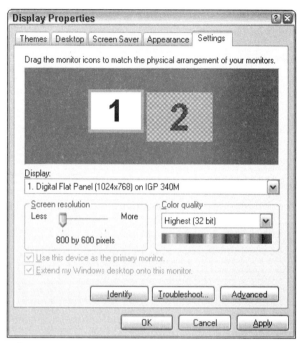

46.3

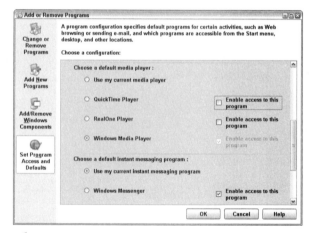

46.4

CHAPTER 8

USING WINDOWS XP ADD-ONS

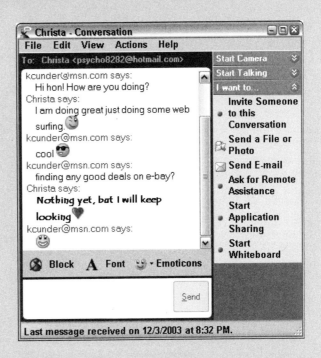

Microsoft offers more than just the Windows XP software. Microsoft also offers a variety of add-ons and accessories that help you get more out of Windows XP. Some of these accessories are free, while others are available for purchase.

I show you several useful Microsoft add-ons for Windows XP in this chapter. First, I show you how to communicate with others in real time using Windows Messenger, a free instant messaging program. Next, I show you how to use some of Microsoft's more advanced tools, which are collectively called PowerToys. Windows XP PowerToys give you advanced command and control over various aspects of the Windows interface. I also show you how to use Windows fun packs, free downloadables that help you explore your creativity. Finally, I show you how to use Microsoft Plus!, a Windows accessory available for purchase at most computer retailers or directly from Microsoft.

Using Power Toys for Windows XP

Using Microsoft Plus!

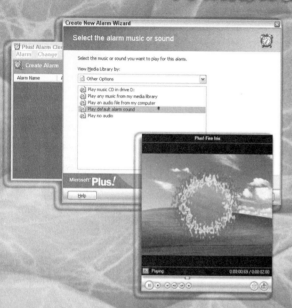

Using Windows Fun Packs

Communicating with Windows Messenger

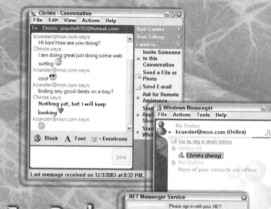

COMMUNICATING WITH WINDOWS MESSENGER

47.1

47.2

ABOUT THE FEATURE

Windows Messenger is a free instant messaging program that you can use to quickly and privately chat with others across the Internet.

In my day job, I telecommute about 2,000 miles across the United States every day. My co-workers and I have several means of communication that we can use as we conduct our work. We can call each other on the phone, but long-distance phone bills add up quickly. We send e-mail to each other, but it's hard to hold a real conversation using e-mail, especially if mail servers take a few minutes to deliver our messages. To address these issues we have increasingly turned to instant messaging programs as our preferred method of workday communication. Instant messaging programs are similar to Internet chat programs, but they allow private conversations between two individuals.

Of course, instant messaging programs are also a great way to keep in touch with friends and family. Microsoft offers a free instant messaging program called Windows Messenger — shown in **Figure 47.1** — that allows you to chat with others who use Windows Messenger or MSN Messenger. In **Figure 47.2**, I'm holding an online conversation with Christa. Versions of MSN Messenger are available for Windows 95 and better, Pocket PCs, Macs, Microsoft TV set-top boxes, and Smartphones. This means you can use Windows Messenger to communicate with virtually anyone with a semi-modern computer, so long as the other user downloads and installs the software, too. This technique shows you how to install, configure, and use Windows Messenger.

STEP 1: DOWNLOAD WINDOWS MESSENGER

Windows Messenger is preinstalled on many new computers that run Windows XP. If Windows Messenger isn't already installed on your computer, you can download it from: www.microsoft.com/windows/messenger/.

The version of Windows Messenger available at this Web site is only for Windows XP computers. Users of other types of computers, such as Macs or Windows 98 PCs can download MSN Messenger from: http://messenger.msn.com/.

> **NOTE**
>
> Windows Messenger is similar to but not exactly the same as MSN Messenger. This technique shows you how to use Windows Messenger in Windows XP. If you want to use MSN Messenger instead, I recommend that you first uninstall Windows Messenger on your Windows XP computer to avoid potential conflicts between the two programs.

STEP 2: INSTALL MESSENGER

Installing Windows Messenger is incredibly simple. After the installation file is downloaded, open it and follow the simple on-screen instructions to install the program. Installation takes only a few seconds. To launch Windows Messenger, double-click the **Windows Messenger** icon in the Windows system tray next to the clock, or choose **Start ➢ All Programs ➢ Windows Messenger**.

STEP 3: SIGN IN

Before you can actually use Windows Messenger you must have a Microsoft .NET Passport. This is a free service that allows you to create a free online identity that includes access to Windows Messenger service as well as a free Hotmail e-mail account. In Windows Messenger, choose **File ➢ Sign In**. A .NET Messenger Service sign-in dialog box appears, as shown in **Figure 47.3**. If you already have a .NET Passport, enter the e-mail address and password for your Passport.

If you don't have a .NET Passport, click **Get a .NET Passport**. A wizard appears to guide you through the

47.3

process. The sign-up process is simple and requires you to provide a minimum of personal information. When you're done creating your Passport, sign in to Messenger using the e-mail address and password for your .NET Password. When you're signed in, your Windows Messenger window resembles **Figure 47.4**.

STEP 4: ADD CONTACTS

Windows Messenger maintains a list of your contacts, making it easier to keep in contact with your friends, family, and co-workers. In **Figure 47.1**, my contacts list includes "Christa." You can add contacts in two ways:

■ If someone else adds you to his or her contacts list, a message appears on your computer like the

one shown in **Figure 47.5**. When you see this message, choose whether or not you want to allow the user to see whether or not you are online. To automatically add this person to your contacts list, place a checkmark next to **Add this person to my contact list**. Click **OK** to close the dialog box.

■ To add someone to your contacts list, choose **Tools ➢ Add a Contact**. A wizard appears to help you add someone to your contacts list. Adding a contact is easiest if you already know the e-mail address or sign-in name that the person uses for his or her .NET Passport, but you can search the .NET user database as well. Remember, you can only add users who already have a .NET Passport.

STEP 5: COMMUNICATE

To communicate with one of your contacts using Windows Messenger, simply double-click the name in your contacts list. A Conversation window appears, as

> **TIP**
>
> Place a checkmark next to Sign me in automatically if you don't want to reenter your Passport information each time you sign in to Messenger, and you aren't worried about other users accessing your user account.

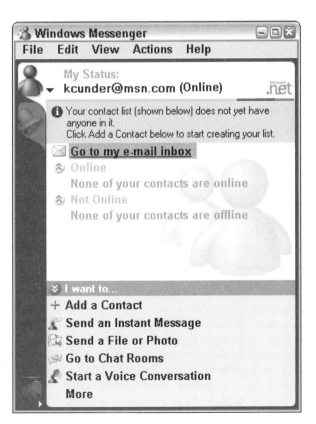

47·4

47·5

shown in **Figure 47.6**. Type a message in the bottom of the window and click **Send**. A Conversation window automatically appears on the other person's computer. A record of your conversation appears in the upper portion of the window. As you can see in **Figure 47.6**, I've used a few emoticons in my conversation. You can access smiley faces and other cute graphics by clicking **Emoticons** in the Conversation window.

STEP 6: CONTROL YOUR STATUS

Windows Messenger displays your status to other users. The default status is **Online**, but if your computer is inactive for ten minutes Messenger automatically sets your status to **Away**. In **Figure 47.1**, Christa's status is **Away**. You can manually change your status by clicking your e-mail address, as shown in **Figure 47.7**. Choose a status from the submenu that appears.

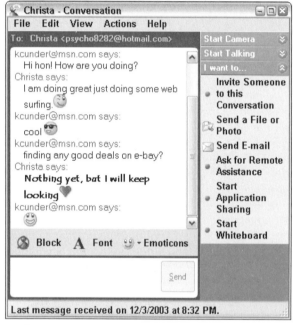

47.6

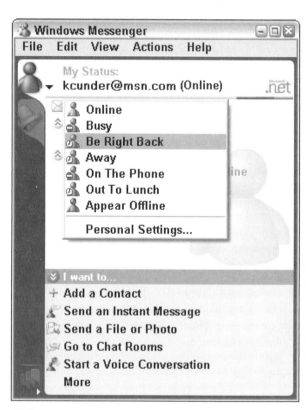

47.7

USING POWERTOYS FOR WINDOWS XP

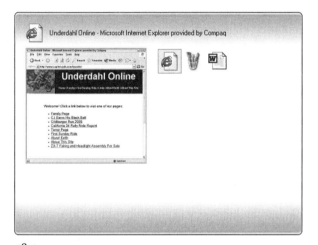

48.1

48.2

ABOUT THE FEATURE

Microsoft's PowerToys for Windows XP add advanced control and features to your computer.

Programmers enjoy their work. Developing new software is like solving a puzzle, and programmers are always looking for new puzzles to solve. The programmers at Microsoft are no different, as evidenced by the many extras and add-ons they've developed for Windows over the years. Some of the most useful add-ons are part of the PowerToys collection. PowerToys add advanced interface controls and customizations to Windows XP, such as Alt-Tab Replacement, shown in **Figure 48.1** and Image Resizer, shown in **Figure 48.2**.

You can download PowerToys free from the Microsoft Web site. Keep in mind, however, that Microsoft does not offer support for PowerToys. Technical problems are unlikely, but if you do encounter a problem, don't expect Microsoft's support staff to bail you out. This technique introduces you to some of the PowerToys offered for Windows XP and shows you how to use some of them. I don't have room to detail every PowerToy, but I can show you some of my favorites.

STEP 1: DOWNLOAD POWERTOYS

You can download PowerToys free from Microsoft's Web site. To begin downloading PowerToys, visit www.microsoft.com/windowsxp/downloads/.

Click the link for downloads for your version of Windows, and then locate and click the **Microsoft PowerToys for Windows XP** link. The PowerToys Web page opens with information and download links for each available PowerToy. Although the available PowerToys may vary, the PowerToys available as of this writing are:

- **Open Command Window Here.** If you use the Command Prompt window very often, this PowerToy may come in handy. When this PowerToy is installed, you can right-click system folders and choose **Open Command Windows Here** from the context menu. A Command Prompt window opens, and the active folder is the folder on which you right-clicked.
- **Alt-Tab Replacement.** The **Alt+Tab** key combination is a quick way to switch between programs. This PowerToy adds thumbnail previews to the pop-up window that appears when you press **Alt+Tab**.
- **Tweak UI.** This PowerToy gives you advanced control over the finer points of the Windows XP interface. This PowerToy is so powerful that I devote an entire technique in this book to it. See Technique 10, "Tweaking Your Interface with Tweak UI," in Chapter 2 for more on using Tweak UI.
- **Power Calculator.** If you need an advanced graphing calculator, download and install this PowerToy.
- **Image Resizer.** Don't like opening images in a graphics program to resize them? Install this PowerToy, and you can quickly resize images by simply right-clicking them and choosing a new size from the context menu.
- **CD Slide Show Generator.** This PowerToy generates a slide show for images stored on a CD-ROM. This greatly simplifies the process of archiving and viewing your digital photos.
- **Virtual Desktop Manager.** Use this PowerToy to remotely manage desktops on your network from a single computer.
- **Taskbar Magnifier.** Do you find that you frequently need to squint or grab your reading glasses to view tiny items on-screen? This PowerToy adds a handy magnifying glass to the Windows XP taskbar.
- **HTML Slide Show Wizard.** If you like to share your pictures online but don't like to spend a lot of time making Web pages so that your audience can easily view the pictures, use this PowerToy to quickly generate HTML slide slows for your photos.
- **Webcam Timershot.** If you have a camera attached to your computer, you can use this PowerToy to automatically snap photos at regular intervals and store the pictures on your hard drive.

Follow the instructions on the Microsoft Web site to download and install a PowerToy. The following steps show you how to use select PowerToys for Windows XP.

STEP 2: ENHANCE THE ALT+TAB COMMAND

Windows XP is a multitasking operating system, which means you can have many open programs at the same time. For example, as you work in a word processor or spreadsheet program, you may have an e-mail program and media player open in the background. To quickly switch between open programs, hold down the **Alt** key and press **Tab**. A pop-up window appears with an icon for each program that is currently open on your computer. Press **Tab** repeatedly until the program you want to use is selected, and then release the **Alt** key.

The Alt-Tab Replacement PowerToy improves the beloved **Alt+Tab** key combination by adding a preview of each program to the pop-up window. Install the Alt-Tab Replacement PowerToy, and then press **Alt+Tab**. A preview of the selected program window appears on the left side of the pop-up window, as shown in **Figure 48.3**.

STEP 3: USE THE IMAGE RESIZER

Another PowerToy that I find useful is the Image Resizer. With this PowerToy you can quickly resize digital images without having to open them in a graphics program. After you install the Image Resizer, use Windows Explorer or My Computer to locate an image you want to resize. Right-click the image, and choose **Resize Pictures** from the context menu. The Resize Pictures dialog box appears. Click Advanced to reveal the additional options shown in **Figure 48.4**. Options in the Resize Pictures dialog box include:

■ Choose a predetermined size by clicking one of the image size radio buttons.

■ To use a custom size, choose the **Custom** radio button, and enter a custom size. Don't worry about getting the height-to-width ratio exactly right. The Image Resizer PowerToy automatically adjusts the image to the same ratio as the original,

thus avoiding the image distortion that may result from an improper size ratio.

■ Place a checkmark next to **Make pictures smaller but not larger** if you only want to make pictures smaller than the original size and not larger. If you make pictures larger, they may appear pixelated and distorted.

■ If you want to resize the original image, place a checkmark next to **Resize the original pictures**. If you leave this option unchecked — and I recommend that you leave it unchecked — Windows creates a resized copy of the image rather than resizing the original.

Click **OK** to close the Resize Pictures dialog box and create a resized copy of your image.

STEP 4: MAGNIFY YOUR DESKTOP

In an effort to make more efficient use of screen space, software and Web site developers use ever-smaller text sizes and icons for various screen elements. If you often find yourself squinting at tiny words or items on-screen, use the Taskbar Magnifier as a simple magnification glass on your computer. After you install the Taskbar Magnifier, activate it by right-clicking the Windows XP taskbar, and choose

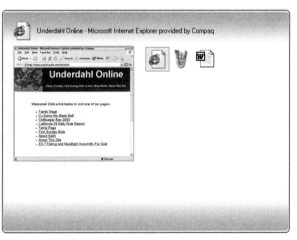

48.3

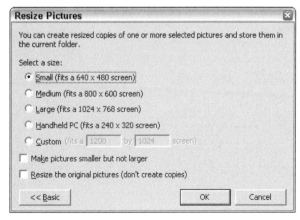

48.4

Toolbars ➤ Taskbar Magnifier. The Taskbar Magnifier toolbar is added to the Windows XP taskbar, as shown in **Figure 48.5**. A magnified image of the current mouse pointer position appears on the Taskbar Magnifier toolbar, as shown in **Figure 48.5**.

STEP 5: UNINSTALL A POWERTOY

Most PowerToys are pretty useful, but after you install a PowerToy you may find that you don't like it as much as you hoped you would. To uninstall a PowerToy, choose **Start ➤ Control Panel** to open the Windows Control Panel. Click the **Add/Remove Programs** icon, locate the unwanted PowerToy in the list of currently installed programs, and click **Remove** to uninstall the PowerToy.

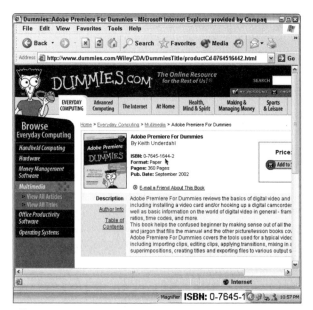

48.5

USING WINDOWS FUN PACKS

49.1

49.2

I've never considered myself to be artistically talented, yet many of the key duties at my job involve graphic arts. Computer programs allow me to be creative in ways that I would find difficult using a traditional brush and canvas. You may find that tools on your computer help you be creative as well.

Microsoft occasionally offers free fun packs that you can download to boost your creativity. The available fun packs vary with the seasons. For example, as I write this it is December, and as shown in **Figure 49.1**, Microsoft's site offers Winter Fun Packs that add snow-and-ice-themed skins and visualizations to Windows Media Player; Windows Movie Maker tools that add a winter ambience to home movies; and templates to help turn digital photos into holiday greeting cards as shown in **Figure 49.2**. In this technique, I show you general steps to obtain, install, and use fun packs from Microsoft. Again, fun packs vary throughout the year so the fun packs available as you read this may be different, but you should be able to use these steps to get started and explore your creative side.

253

STEP 1: DOWNLOAD AND INSTALL FUN PACKS

Fun packs can be downloaded for free from Microsoft's Web site. Start by visiting www.microsoft.com/windowsxp/.

This page often has a fun packs link right at the top. If not, look for a link to fun packs under Top Downloads. Follow the instructions on the Microsoft Web site to download and install the fun packs. Fun packs are usually Microsoft Installer packages with the .msi file extension. Double-click the MSI file, and follow the on-screen instructions to complete installation as shown in **Figure 49.3**.

STEP 2: USE WINDOWS MEDIA FUN PACKS

Windows Media Player fun packs usually include skins to give custom appearances to Media Player.

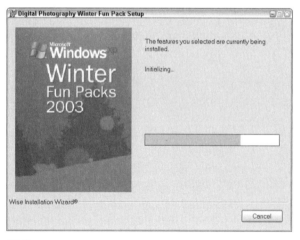

49.3

After you install the Media Player fun pack, open Windows Media Player and click **Skins** on the left side of the window. Alternatively, choose **View ➢ Go To ➢ Skin Chooser**. Select a skin from the list, and click **Apply Skin**. In **Figure 49.4** I've applied a skin that looks like a gingerbread man. This skin came with the Windows Media Player Winter fun pack that I downloaded.

Figure 49.4 also shows a winter-themed visualization that came with the Winter Fun Pack. This visualization is called **Winter: Ice Storm**. Click the **Show Visualizations** button on the Media Player controls to reveal the visualizations window, and click the arrows above the window to choose different visualizations.

STEP 3: ENHANCE YOUR VIDEOS WITH MOVIE MAKER FUN PACKS

Microsoft also frequently offers fun packs for Windows Movie Maker. Movie Maker fun packs require version 2 or better of the Windows Movie Maker program. The exact features in each fun pack vary, but most

49.4

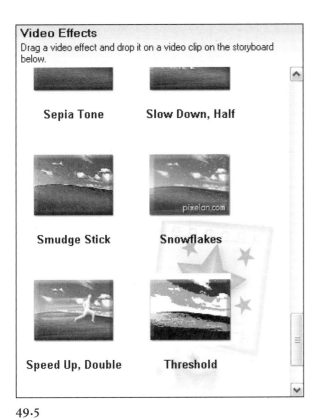

49.5

Movie Maker fun packs include special video effects and transitions. I've applied a video effect called Snowflake to one of my video clips. I simply click and drag the Snowflake effect from the Video Effects window (**Figure 49.5**) to a video clip in the storyboard (**Figure 49.6**).

STEP 4: USE DIGITAL PHOTOGRAPHY FUN PACKS

Microsoft also offers digital photography fun packs. These often include stunning photographs that you can use as desktop wallpaper, as well as templates that you can use to enhance your own digital photos. When you install a digital photography fun pack, wallpaper images are stored in the folder **My Documents\ My Pictures\Windows XP Fun Pack**.

This folder likely contains a subfolder named for the fun pack you downloaded, and within that is another subfolder called **Wallpaper**. To set a picture as your desktop wallpaper, select it, as shown in

49.6

Figure 49.7, and click **Set as desktop background** under **Picture Tasks**.

Photography fun packs usually come with other treats as well. The Winter Fun Pack I downloaded included templates for holiday greeting cards. To make a greeting card, I first open one of my own images in a graphics program, as shown in **Figure 49.8**. I use the Select tool to select a portion of the image, and then choose **Edit ➢ Copy**. Then I open one of the greeting card templates and choose **Edit ➢ Paste** to paste the image as shown in **Figure 49.9**. After pasting the image using Paint, click and drag the pasted image to position it in the image.

49.8

49.7

49.9

USING MICROSOFT PLUS!

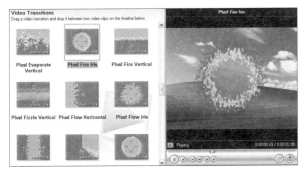

50.1

50.2

Since Microsoft released Windows 95 in 1995, it has also offered Plus!, a Windows accessory program that adds various features to your Windows PC. Early versions of Plus! included utilities and interface enhancements that allowed users to take advantage of newer, more powerful computers. Microsoft continues that tradition with Plus! for Windows XP. The Microsoft Web site for Plus! is www.microsoft.com/Windows/Plus/.

Microsoft offers Plus! for XP in two flavors. There is the standard version of Plus!, as well as a new Digital Media Edition tailored to the powerful multimedia capabilities of the latest PCs. Features in the standard version of Plus! include:

■ **Desktop themes and screen savers.** Several enhanced desktop themes give Windows XP a new, exotic look. Plus! for XP includes Aquarium, Space, Nature, and da Vinci themes that add graphics to the desktop, reskin Windows Media Player, and customize your icons. Screen savers follow these four themes, and additional 3D screen savers include a Robot Circus, Sand Pendulum, and a Mercury Pool.

■ **Games.** If you like to have some entertaining distractions throughout the day, you may enjoy some of the games that come with Plus! for XP. Games include a bowling game called HyperBowl, a Tetris-style color matching game called Russian Square, and a Labyrinth game where you tilt the playing field to move a ball through a maze while avoiding pits along the way.

■ **MP3-to-WMA converter.** As I describe in Technique 42, "Stocking and Managing Your Music Jukebox," in Chapter 7, the WMA audio format offers superior quality and smaller file size than the MP3 format. If you have a lot of MP3 files, Plus! includes a tool that scans your hard drive and converts MP3s to WMA files, thus saving you storage space.

■ **CD Label Maker.** Use this tool to make and print attractive CD labels.

■ **Windows Media Player tools.** Enhancements for Media Player include custom skins, fancy 3D visualizations, and advanced playlist creation and control tools. Plus! also includes a voice command tool that lets you control Windows Media Player simply by speaking commands.

Microsoft also offers a special Digital Media Edition of Plus!. Features in the Digital Media Edition include:

■ **Photo Story.** This program lets you turn your pictures into spectacular multimedia slide shows. Arrange your pictures along a timeline, pan across or zoom in on your pictures, add narration or background music, and insert some subtitles or credits. You can then share your slide show online as a WMV movie or burn it to a video CD that can be played in most DVD players.

■ **Windows Media Player enhancements.** A playlist enhancement called Party Mode turns your computer into a music jukebox, and a privacy feature allows others to access your

music selection while keeping your personal files and other computer features private. Plus! Digital Media Edition also includes a selection of new, intriguing skins for Media Player. Plus! Dancers add lifelike dancers to your collection of visualizations.

■ **MP3-to-WMA converter.** As I describe in Technique 42, "Stocking and Managing Your Music Jukebox" in Chapter 7, the WMA audio format offers superior quality and smaller file size than the MP3 format. If you have a lot of MP3 files, Plus! includes a tool that scans your hard drive and converts MP3s to WMA files, thus saving you storage space.

■ **CD Label Maker.** Use this tool to make and print attractive CD labels.

■ **Analog audio recorder.** Easily record audio from vinyl LP records, tapes, and other analog sources into digital format with the Plus! analog audio recorder.

■ **Alarm clock and sleep timer.** Do you like to listen to music or Internet radio as you fall asleep? Plus! Digital Media Edition includes a sleep timer that automatically turns off the music after a specific period of time. An alarm clock tool, shown in **Figure 50.2**, helps you wake up in the morning.

■ **Windows Movie Maker effects and transitions.** Plus! Digital Media Edition adds 25 video effects and 25 transitions to Windows Movie Maker 2, as shown in **Figure 50.1**.

■ **Sync & Go for Pocket PC.** If you have a Pocket PC, this tool helps you share music and videos between your desktop and your Pocket PC.

Of the two available versions of Plus!, I believe that the Digital Media Edition offers better value for most users. The Digital Media Edition includes some of the most useful tools from the standard edition of Plus!, as well as some useful multimedia tools that are only found in the Digital Media Edition. On top of that, the Digital Media Edition is more affordable, retailing for $19.95 versus $29.95 for the Plus! standard edition. In this technique I show you how to use some of the features in Plus! Digital Media Edition.

STEP 1: INSTALL PLUS!

The setup program for Plus! probably starts automatically when you place the disc in your CD-ROM drive. If not, use My Computer to open the CD-ROM drive, and double-click the **Setup** icon. The setup program makes installation easy. You can choose either the **Express** installation mode to quickly install all components, or choose **Custom** installation to pick and choose features that you want to install. For example, if you don't have a Pocket PC you probably don't need to install Plus! Sync & Go. To disable a component, click the box next to the component and choose **This feature will not be available** as shown in **Figure 50.3**.

STEP 2: CONVERT MP3s TO WMA

Both versions of Microsoft Plus! include a tool to help you convert MP3 files to WMA format with the click of a mouse button. WMA — short for Windows Media Audio — is superior to the MP3 format because it offers superior quality for a given file size.

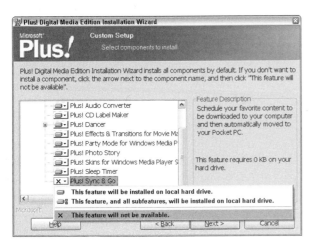

50.3

As I describe in Technique 42, "Stocking and Managing Your Music Jukebox" in Chapter 7, a CD-quality album uses about 42MB of space. That same CD-quality album in MP3 format uses 72MB of space. The advantage of the WMA format is clear, especially when you consider the limited storage capacity of many portable media players today. Many of those media players are WMA-compatible, and if you have a media player that can play WMA files, or if you just want to save space on your computer's hard drive, converting MP3s to WMA makes a lot of sense.

To convert MP3 files on your hard drive to WMA, follow these steps:

■ Open Windows Media Player and choose **Tools** ➤ **Plug-ins** ➤ **Plus! Audio Converter**. The Plus! Audio Converter window appears.

■ Choose whether you want to convert all files in a folder, or just specific audio files, and click **Next**.

■ If you chose to select specific audio files, click **Add File** in the next window and select files, and then click **Next** when you're done selecting files.

■ If you chose to convert all files in a folder, click **Browse** in the next window and select the folder containing the files you want to convert. Under **Advanced options**, choose the file types you want to search for and convert. You can choose to skip files under 100KB, because the file size savings for files smaller than that are minimal. Click **Next** when you're done choosing options. In the next window, confirm the files you want to convert, and click **Next** again.

> **NOTE**
>
> Microsoft Plus! must be activated online with Microsoft. When installation is complete, a window appears asking you to enter your product key. You can find this key on the back of the Plus! CD-ROM case. Your computer must be connected to the Internet for activation to complete.

■ Choose the file format to which you want to convert the audio files. I recommend **Windows Media Audio** as shown in **Figure 50.4**.

■ Choose a quality level with the **Quality** slider. Ninety-six Kbps is considered CD quality in the WMA format. Select output options under **Output folder**, and click **Next**.

■ Click **Start Conversion** to begin converting files. The conversion process may take a few minutes, depending on how many files you are converting.

STEP 3: ACCESS EFFECTS AND TRANSITIONS IN MOVIE MAKER

Plus! Digital Media Edition comes with 25 additional video effects and 25 new transitions for Windows

Movie Maker 2. Accessing and using these effects and transitions is easy. They appear in the regular lists of effects and transitions, as shown in **Figure 50.5**. In **Figure 50.6**, I'm previewing the Plus! Fire Iris transition, which causes the outgoing clip to appear to burn away from the center of the image to reveal the underlying incoming clip.

A number of interesting video effects are also included with Plus! Digital Media Edition. Sometimes, subtle effects are the most effective. In **Figure 50.7** I've added the Plus! Noise White effect to a snowy scene. This adds the appearance of heavy snowfall to the scene as shown in **Figure 50.8**.

50.4

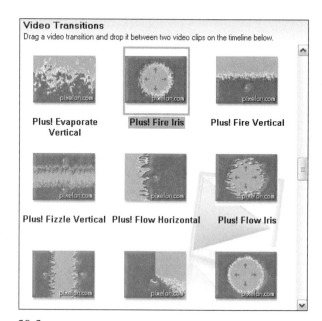

50.5

STEP 4: SET YOUR ALARM CLOCK

Another cool feature of Plus! Digital Media Edition is an alarm clock. To set up your alarm clock, choose **Start ➤ All Programs ➤ Microsoft Plus! Digital Media Edition ➤ Plus! Alarm Clock**. If you see a

welcome screen for the Plus! Alarm Clock, click **OK** to close it. Then follow these steps:

- Click **Create Alarm**. The Create New Alarm Wizard appears.
- Give the alarm a name, if you want.
- Choose how often you want the alarm to sound under **Set this alarm to occur**.

50.6

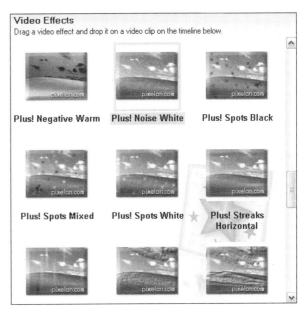

50.7

- Set a start time and date for the alarm, and then click **Next**.
- Choose a song or sound that you want to use for the alarm sound. In **Figure 50.9** I've chosen **Other Options** in the menu and **Play default alarm sound** underneath. Click **Next**.
- Review the alarm settings, and click **Finish**.

Your alarm appears in the Plus! Alarm Clock window as shown in **Figure 50.10**. Right-click an alarm

to change it. When enabled, the Plus! Alarm Clock places an icon in the Windows system tray. Double-click this icon to control the Plus! Alarm Clock.

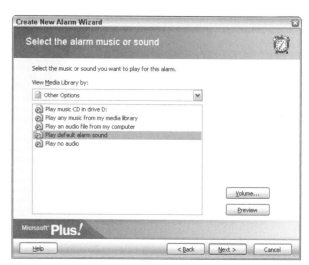

50.9

50.8

50.10

APPENDIX A
WINDOWS XP KEYBOARD COMMANDS

The term *revolutionary* is often used to describe new computer technology, but seldom is the word more apt than when speaking of the computer mouse. The mouse, invented in the 1960s by Douglas Engelbart, has truly revolutionized the way we use computers. We use it and its technological offspring, the trackball and touch pad, to execute commands and manage many computer operations.

As in previous versions of Windows and most other modern operating systems, Windows XP is designed on the assumption that you will use a mouse to control the interface. You use a mouse to choose menu commands, move and resize windows, select objects, click hyperlinks, and more. But what if you don't currently have access to a mouse, or what if you prefer to keep your hands at the keyboard? Believe it or not, almost every aspect of Windows can still be controlled using the keyboard instead of the mouse. Keyboard commands become especially useful if your mouse just failed, or if you had to boot Windows XP in Safe Mode and your USB mouse doesn't work while running in Safe Mode. This appendix provides a quick reference to keyboard commands that are available in Windows XP.

To use the mouse modifiers listed in Table A-1, hold down the listed key combination while you perform a mouse operation.

TABLE A-1
MOUSE MODIFIERS

KEYBOARD COMBINATION	COMMAND
Alt+Double-click	Opens Properties dialog box for the item
Ctrl+Click	Select multiple items in a list
Ctrl+Click-and-drag	Hold this down while you click-and-drag a file to copy instead of move it
Ctrl+Shift+Click-and-drag	Hold this down while you click-and-drag a file to the Windows desktop to create a desktop shortcut to the item
Shift+Click	Select multiple adjacent items in a list

TABLE A-2

NAVIGATION

KEYBOARD COMBINATION	COMMAND
Alt+Enter	Opens Properties dialog box for the item
Alt+Space bar	Opens window menu in upper-left corner of program windows
Alt+Tab	Switch between open programs
Alt+F4	Close current window
Alt+F6	Switch between windows in the current program
Ctrl+Alt+Delete	Opens Windows Task Manager, where you can force an unresponsive program to quit
Ctrl+Esc	Opens Start menu
Ctrl+Tab	Moves between tabs in a multi-tab dialog box
Shift+Delete	Deletes item permanently, without sending it to the Recycle Bin
Shift+F10	Opens context menu for selected item, as if you right-clicked on it
Shift+Tab	Moves focus to previous command in dialog boxes or on the Windows desktop
Tab	Moves focus to next command in dialog boxes or on the Windows desktop

Most modern keyboards include a Windows key with the Microsoft Windows logo. Table A-3 lists special commands that can be used in conjunction with the Windows key.

TABLE A-3

WINDOWS KEY COMMANDS

KEYBOARD COMBINATION	COMMAND
Windows	Opens Start menu
Windows+Break	Opens System Properties dialog box
Windows+Tab	Moves focus between Start menu, Quick Launch bar, taskbar, and system tray
Windows+D	Show desktop
Windows+E	Opens Windows Explorer
Windows+F	Opens Search window

KEYBOARD COMBINATION	COMMAND
Windows+M	Minimizes all windows
Windows+R	Opens Run dialog box
Shift+Windows+M	Restores all windows
Windows+F1	Windows Help and Support

TABLE A-4
COMMON PROGRAM COMMANDS

KEYBOARD COMBINATION	COMMAND
F1	Help
F7	Check spelling
F12	Save As
Ctrl+A	Select All
Ctrl+B	Makes text bold
Ctrl+C	Copy
Ctrl+F	Find
Ctrl+I	Makes text italic
Ctrl+N	New file
Ctrl+O	Open a file
Ctrl+P	Print
Ctrl+S	Save
Ctrl+U	Underlines text
Ctrl+V	Paste
Ctrl+X	Cut
Ctrl+Y	Redo
Ctrl+Z	Undo
Ctrl+Home	Go to top of document
Ctrl+End	Go to end of document

TABLE A-5

ACCESSIBILITY

KEYBOARD COMBINATION	COMMAND
Left Alt+Left Shift+Num Lock	Toggles MouseKeys on and off; use keypad numbers to move mouse pointer when MouseKeys are enabled
Left Alt+Left Shift+Print Screen	Toggles display between normal and high contrast settings
Press Shift five times	Toggles StickyKeys on and off
Hold right Shift key for eight seconds	Toggles FilterKeys on and off
Hold Num Lock key for five seconds	Toggles ToggleKeys on and off

TABLE A-6

INTERNET EXPLORER, WINDOWS EXPLORER

KEYBOARD COMBINATION	COMMAND
F1	Help
F2	Rename selected file or folder
F3	Opens Search pane
F4	Opens Address bar menu
F5	Refresh
F6	Places cursor focus in Address bar (Internet Explorer)
F6	Moves cursor focus between panes (Windows Explorer)
F10	Reveals hotkeys for menus (see note)
F11	Toggle between full-screen and standard view
Esc	Stop current operation
Left arrow	Collapses folder tree when browsing folder list
Right arrow	Expands folder tree when browsing folder list
Alt+Enter	Opens Properties dialog box for the item
Alt+Home	Go to Home page
Alt+Left arrow	Back
Alt+Right arrow	Forward

KEYBOARD COMBINATION	COMMAND
Ctrl+A	Select All
Ctrl+C	Copy
Ctrl+E	Opens Search pane
Ctrl+H	Opens History pane
Ctrl+I	Opens Favorites pane
Ctrl+N	New window
Ctrl+V	Paste
Ctrl+X	Cut
Ctrl+Z	Undo

Note: Many programs provide hotkeys that help you use keyboard commands. To see how hotkeys work, choose **Start ➤ All Programs ➤ Accessories ➤ Notepad** to open Notepad. Now press the **Alt** key. When you press the Alt key, the first letter of each menu name along the top of the window is underlined. The underlined letter is the hotkey for that menu. For example, the hotkey for the File menu is F. To use that hotkey and open the File menu, press Alt+F. Whenever you see a menu or command that has a hotkey, simply press Alt and the underlined letter to use that hotkey.

APPENDIX B
WEB SITES MENTIONED IN THIS BOOK

The Internet can be an invaluable resource that can help you make the most of Windows XP. Countless Web sites are ready to provide even more useful information than what is found in *50 Fast Windows XP Techniques*, and I have mentioned some of them in this book. Table B-1 provides a quick reference to some of the utilities that I mention in this book, and Table B-2 lists Web sites for resources on virus protection, privacy, and Internet security. Table B-3 lists some Web sites covering multimedia and communications products, including remote controls that can be used with your home media server. Table B-4 lists a couple of Web sites where you can find a wide variety of software downloads for almost any computer use you can imagine.

TABLE B-1
UTILITIES

WEB ADDRESS	COMPANY	SOFTWARE
www.microsoft.com/windowsxp/pro/downloads/powertoys.asp	Microsoft	TweakUI, PowerToys
www.ntius.com/	NewTech Infosystems	Backup NOW!
www.tgtsoft.com/	TGT Soft	Style XP

TABLE B-2
ANTIVIRUS, PRIVACY, AND SECURITY PROGRAMS

WEB ADDRESS	COMPANY	SOFTWARE
www.lavasoft.de/	Lavasoft	Ad-aware
www.mcafee.com/	McAfee Security	McAfee Virusscan, Antispyware, and more
www.norton.com/	Symantec Worldwide	Norton AntiVirus, firewalls, and other security solutions
www.pandasoftware.com/	Panda Software	Panda AntiVirus, Platinum Internet Security, etc.
www.popupcop.com/	EdenSoft	PopUpCop
www.sys-shield.com	SysShield	AbsoluteShield IE Popup Blocker, AbsoluteShield Track Eraser, AbsoluteShield File Shredder
www.zonelabs.com/	Zone Labs	ZoneAlarm firewall

TABLE B-3

MULTIMEDIA AND COMMUNICATION

WEB ADDRESS	COMPANY	PRODUCT
www.ati.com/products/remotewonder/	ATI Technologies	RemoteWonder
www.griffintechnology.com/griffinmobile/	Griffin Technology	Total Remote
www.harmonyremote.com/	Intrigue Technologies	Harmony Remote
www.microsoft.com/windows/messenger/	Microsoft	Windows Messenger
www.microsoft.com/Windows/Plus/	Microsoft	Microsoft Plus!
messenger.msn.com/	MSN	MSN Messenger
www.netop.com/	Danware	NetOp Remote Control

TABLE B-4

MISCELLANEOUS DOWNLOAD SITES

WEB ADDRESS	COMPANY
www.microsoft.com/downloads/	Microsoft downloads
www.microsoft.com/windowsxp/downloads/	Microsoft Windows XP-specific downloads
www.tucows.com/	Tucows

INDEX

Continued

Continued

ABOUT THE AUTHOR

Keith Underdahl is a digital media specialist residing in Albany, Oregon. Keith serves as a program manager and customer support manager for Ages Software. Among other things, he develops and documents Windows programs, and provides technical support on those programs to users of Windows XP and other operating systems. Mr. Underdahl is an experienced author and has written numerous books, including *Teach Yourself Microsoft Word 2000*, *Microsoft Windows Movie Maker For Dummies*, *Macworld Final Cut Pro 2 Bible* (co-author), *Adobe Premiere Pro For Dummies*, and *Digital Video For Dummies*, 3rd Edition.

COLOPHON

This book was produced electronically in Indianapolis, Indiana. Microsoft Word 2000 was used for word processing; design and layout were produced using QuarkXPress 4.11 and Adobe Photoshop 5.5 on Power Macintosh computers. The typeface families used are: Chicago Laser, Minion, Myriad, Myriad Multiple Master, Prestige Elite, Symbol, Trajan, and Zapf Dingbats.

Acquisitions Editor: Tom Heine
Project Editor: Sarah Hellert
Technical Editor: Lee Musick
Copy Editor: Kim Heusel
Editorial Manager: Robyn Siesky
Editorial Assistant: Adrienne D. Porter
Production Coordinator: Maridee V. Ennis
Cover Art: Abbie Enneking
Layout: Beth Brooks, Sean Decker, Jennifer Heleine, LeAndra Hosier
Proofreading: Vickie Broyles
Quality Control: John Greenough, Susan Moritz, Angel Perez, Charles Spencer
Indexing: Sherry Massey
Vice President and Executive Group Publisher: Richard Swadley
Vice President and Publisher: Barry Pruett
Composition Director: Debbie Stailey

Think fast

Hone your skills with *50 Fast* guides to almost everything from digital photography to operating systems.

0-7645-2500-X

0-7645-4174-9

0-7645-5823-4

Also available:

WILEY
Now you know.
wiley.com